Learning to Effect

SRHE and Open University Press Imprint
General Editor: Heather Eggins

Michael Allen: *The Goals of Universities*
Sir Christopher Ball and Heather Eggins: *Higher Education into the 1990s*
Ronald Barnett: *The Idea of Higher Education*
Ronald Barnett: *Improving Higher Education*
Ronald Barnett: *Learning to Effect*
Tony Becher: *Academic Tribes and Territories*
Robert Berdahl et al.: *Quality and Access in Higher Education*
Hazel Bines and David Watson: *Developing Professional Education*
William Birch: *The Challenge to Higher Education*
David Boud et al.: *Teaching in Laboratories*
John Earwaker: *Helping and Supporting Students*
Heather Eggins: *Restructuring Higher Education*
Colin Evans: *Language People*
Gavin J. Fairbairn and Christopher Winch: *Reading, Writing and Reasoning: A Guide for Students*
Oliver Fulton: *Access and Institutional Change*
Derek Gardiner: *The Anatomy of Supervision*
Gunnar Handal and Per Lauvås: *Promoting Reflective Teaching*
Vivien Hodgson et al.: *Beyond Distance Teaching, Towards Open Learning*
Jill Johnes and Jim Taylor: *Performance Indicators in Higher Education*
Margaret Kinnell: *The Learning Experiences of Overseas Students*
Peter Linklater: *Education and the World of Work*
Ian McNay: *Visions of Post-compulsory Education*
Graeme Moodie: *Standards and Criteria in Higher Education*
John Pratt and Suzanne Silverman: *Responding to Constraint*
Kjell Raaheim et al.: *Helping Students to Learn*
John Radford and David Rose: *A Liberal Science*
Marjorie Reeves: *The Crisis in Higher Education*
John T.E. Richardson et al.: *Student Learning*
Derek Robbins: *The Rise of Independent Study*
Tom Schuller: *The Future of Higher Education*
Geoffrey Squires: *First Degree*
Ted Tapper and Brian Salter: *Oxford, Cambridge and the Changing Idea of the University*
Gordon Taylor et al.: *Literacy by Degrees*
Kim Thomas: *Gender and Subject in Higher Education*
Malcolm Tight: *Academic Freedom and Responsibility*
Malcolm Tight: *Higher Education: A Part-time Perspective*
David Warner and Charles Leonard: *The Income Generation Handbook*
Susan Warner Weil and Ian McGill: *Making Sense of Experiential Learning*
David Watson: *Managing the Modular Course*
Thomas G. Whiston and Roger L. Geiger: *Research and Higher Education*
Gareth Williams: *Changing Patterns of Finance in Higher Education*
Alan Woodley et al.: *Choosing to Learn*
Peter W.G. Wright: *Industry and Higher Education*
John Wyatt: *Commitment to Higher Education*

Learning to Effect

Edited by
Ronald Barnett

The Society for Research into Higher Education
& Open University Press

To the memory of
Robert Murray

Published by SRHE and
Open University Press
Celtic Court
22 Ballmoor
Buckingham
MK18 1XW

and
1900 Frost Road, Suite 101
Bristol, PA 19007, USA

First published 1992
Reprinted 1995

A catalogue record for this book is available from the British Library

ISBN 0 335 15759 9 (hb) ISBN 0 335 19499 0 (pb)

Library of Congress Cataloging-in-Publication Data
Learning to effect / edited by Ronald Barnett.
     p.   cm.
   Includes bibliographical references and index.
   ISBN 0-335-15759-9 (hbk)   0 335-19499 0 (pbk)
   1. Education, Higher – United States – Curricula.   2. Curriculum
planning – United States.   I. Barnett, Ronald, 1947–   .
LB2361.5.L43   1992
378.1'99'0973—dc20   92–17385 CIP

Typeset by Graphicraft Typesetters Ltd, Hong Kong
Printed and bound in Great Britain by
Biddles Ltd, Guildford and King's Lynn

Contents

Contributors

Graham Badley is Head of the Centre for Educational Development at Anglia Polytechnic University.

Dr Ronald Barnett is Senior Lecturer in the Centre for Higher Education Studies at the Institute of Education, University of London.

Dr Gaie Davidson directs a national project on credit accumulation and transfer based at the University of Kent, and funded by the Universities' Council on Adult and Continuing Education.

Professor Roger Ellis is Professor of Psychology and Dean of the Faculty of Social and Health Sciences at the University of Ulster.

Professor Michael Eraut is Professor of Education at the Institute of Continuing and Professional Education in the University of Sussex.

Norman Evans is Director of the Learning from Experience Trust.

Dr Malcolm Frazer is Chief Executive of the Council for National Academic Awards and is Chief Executive of the Higher Education Quality Council. He previously taught chemistry for nearly 30 years at the Polytechnic of North London and the University of East Anglia.

Graham Gibbs is the Head of the Oxford Centre for Staff Development at Oxford Polytechnic.

Dr Sinclair Goodlad is Senior Lecturer in the Presentation of Technical Information at the Imperial College of Science, Technology and Medicine, University of London.

John Hughes is BP Fellow for Student Peer Tutoring at the Imperial College of Science, Technology and Medicine, University of London.

Dr Elisabeth Lillie is a Senior Lecturer in French at the University of Ulster, and is currently in charge of a postgraduate conversion programme for Language graduates in Applied Languages for Business.

A.J. Tribe is Head of the Division of Mathematics and Science Education, Hertfordshire University.

Diana Tribe is Head of the Centre for Legal Studies, Hertfordshire University and Associate Research Fellow at the Institute of Advanced Legal Studies, University of London.

Dr Susan Weil is Head of Higher Education Development for the Office for Public Management, and formally Associate Director of the Higher Education for Capability Initiative.

Dr Peter W.G. Wright is Higher Education Adviser to the Employment Department, where he works primarily on the Enterprise in Higher Education programme.

Introduction

1

What Effects? What Outcomes?

Ronald Barnett

Overview

This book is intended to examine contemporary issues of curriculum change in higher education. In brief, the issues addressed are those of (a) curriculum purpose, (b) curriculum delivery and (c) curriculum impact on the wider society. Inevitably, in tackling such large issues, other significant matters come into view. Just some of the matters which are raised in more than one chapter are these:

1. *The relationship between the curriculum and the world of work*: Goodlad and Hughes; Ellis; Tribe and Tribe; Evans; Wright; Lillie; Weil.
2. *The relationship between theory and practice in the curriculum*: Goodlad and Hughes; Ellis; Eraut.
3. *The nature of knowledge in the contemporary curriculum*: Eraut; Goodlad and Hughes; Ellis; Evans.
4. *Experiential learning*: Evans; Eraut; Wright; Tribe and Tribe; Goodlad and Hughes.
5. *Skills and training*: Tribe and Tribe; Eraut; Wright; Weil.
6. *Competence and outcomes*: Ellis; Tribe and Tribe; Eraut; Lillie; Davidson; Wright; Weil.
7. *Assessment* (given curriculum changes of the kind implied in 1–6): Ellis; Tribe and Tribe; Frazer; Evans; Davidson; Wright; Weil.
8. *The quality of learning*: Gibbs; Evans; Wright; Ellis.
9. *Students having control over their learning*: Weil; Wright; Davidson; Tribe and Tribe.
10. *Teaching quality*: Gibbs; Frazer; Badley; Wright; Weil.
11. *Staff development* (both for curriculum change and for enhanced learning quality): Wright; Weil; Evans; Badley; Frazer.
12. *Identification of institutional goals* (in the context of 1–10): Badley; Wright; Weil.

13. *Institutional change* (given 12): Wright; Weil; Badley; Goodlad and Hughes; Frazer; Davidson.
14. *Institutional leadership* (for 13): Badley; Evans; Weil; Davidson.

By way of summarizing that admittedly lengthy list, this book can be read as an examination of three contemporary issues of institutional and curriculum *change*:

1. the ways in which the higher education curriculum is changing in response to the messages coming at it from the wider society, especially from the world of work;
2. how a higher quality of curriculum delivery might be achieved in pursuit of (1);
3. how institutional change might be effected in order to bring about both (1) and (2).

In the rest of this chapter, I will attempt to offer an analytical framework by which we might understand the changes – at curricular, institutional and national levels – currently under way and which are the subjects of this book, and within which the other contributions can be placed.

Learning: a public matter

Learning is a human process which has an effect *in* those undertaking it. Learning requires neither teaching (someone else to assist the learning) (see Chapter 4) nor an institution to provide a framework of resources. Learning does not even require an intention to learn on the part of the learner; it is possible to learn things, without intending to do so, as when one eavesdrops on a conversation or chances on a television programme. Effects of some kind, however, there have to be.

It makes sense, therefore, to enquire into learning effectiveness across education in general. However, such an enquiry has special sense in the context of higher education. Across most of the educational system – at least, across compulsory education and across technical and vocational education of the 16–19 age group – teachers' room for professional choice is limited. Syllabi, teaching methods, assessment methods and processes, and even the curriculum itself tend to be defined and controlled by external agencies of the state. In higher education, however, all those areas of professional activity are much more under the control and direction of the faculty. It follows that the possible effect on learners is relatively open and, therefore, worthy of examination.

Formal openness of learning outcomes does not necessarily lead to real openness. Until recently, higher education was not notable for its examination of learning. Driven, quite legitimately, by a dominant interest in knowledge, issues of learning occupied a marginal place in the debates of the academic community. Over time, and largely under the prompting of external agencies, that position has changed. Through the work (in the UK) of the Council for National Academic Awards in the polytechnics and colleges sector, the Enterprise in Higher Education initiative of the Department of Employment (Chapter 13), the Higher Education for Capability initiative of the Royal Society of Arts (Chapter 12), the annual Partnership Teaching Awards prizes offered by industry and commerce,[1] and most recently the Committee of Vice-Chancellors and Principals (CVCP, 1991), the character and quality of teaching in higher education have come onto the public agenda of the academic community.

Perhaps the key point to be derived from this shift in the discourse and motivations of the academic community is that it has compelled an assessment of the aims of the teaching process. No longer can it be taken for granted that students' learning is a direct function of their teachers' research activities or interests. That is to say, learning conceived as the transmission (by the teacher) and the assimilation (by the student) of the cognitive contents of the teacher's mind can no longer carry any *legitimacy*. The carving out, the protection, and the advocacy of the *Academic Tribes and Territories* (Becher, 1989) cannot offer us an adequate account of academics' activities as teachers.

But this 'Copernican revolution' (see Chapter 5) in conceptualizing learning in higher education is only the start of a question-raising process. For what kind of learning are we to promote in higher education? What kind of learning, if any, is particular to a genuinely *higher* education? What kinds of effect is learning in higher education to have?

In the generality of things

It may be tempting to generate answers to these three questions which are general in character and which perhaps hold across subject domains. Institutions of higher education, however, are loosely coupled organizations, with comparatively little vertical integration and even less horizontal integration between their basic units (Clark, 1983). The dominant allegiances within the basic units – the departments – are to disciplines, not as inert bodies of knowledge but as dynamic networks sustaining self-identities, professional formation and development, and cognitive perspectives. Curricula and teaching strategies are likely, accordingly, to be coloured in the first place by the individual's discipline or field of enquiry rather than by a receptiveness to any organizational strategy.

However, from time to time, that disciplinary loyalty is broken. At the institutional level, individual leaders have promoted a common initiative running across all departments. Well-known examples include that of the new universities in the UK in the 1960s, which introduced new formations of curricula dependent on broad fields of enquiry, so creating a new map of learning (Briggs, 1964); and, in the USA, efforts at Chicago and Harvard to develop general educational programmes for all their students (see respectively Hutchins, 1936; Boyer and Levine, 1981).

More recently, as we have already noted, curriculum design and delivery have been influenced by initiatives orchestrated at the national level. Perhaps the most important of these is the Enterprise in Higher Education initiative, since the sheer size of the programme in monetary terms (several hundreds of millions of pounds) has prompted real changes in institutions as they have sought firstly to win a contract and then to implement it (NFER, 1991). However, a national initiative requires active support and leadership from an institution's senior management if it is to have a real impact on the internal patterns of professional life, if academics' loyalties to their disciplines – in their teaching – are to be modified by a recognition of new considerations bearing on curriculum design, delivery and evaluation (see Chapter 13).

The examples just cited point to two forms of attempt to soften disciplinary influences. The first is that of the educationalists who believe that there is such an enterprise as higher learning, rather than a conglomeration of many species of higher learning. It is not, perhaps, coincidental that books by past presidents of both Chicago (Hutchins in 1936) and Harvard (Bok in 1986) contain the term 'higher learning' in their titles. Correspondingly, the efforts to develop new curricula in the 1960s-founded UK universities were led by educationalists such as Briggs, Sloman and James. In other words, in both sets of examples, we see the cross-subject innovation being attempted from *within* the academic community.

By contrast, the more recent cross-curricular innovations – in the UK, at least – are being prompted by influences from *outside* the academic community. Not only in the Enterprise in Higher Education initiative but also in the Royal Society of Arts' Higher Education for Capability initiative, and in the publications of the Council for Industry and Higher Education, we see examples of such external promptings aimed at higher education. Other less overt examples are also available. The credit accumulation and transfer movement was first given national prominence by the Council for National Academic Awards but has been given Government support, if only verbally (Chapter 11) and is one of the elements of the CNAA's work which is remaining after that organization's closure.

This shift in cross-curricular initiatives from those internal to the academic community to those external to it has its impact on the terms of the debate. Whereas the former sets of initiatives, including those in the USA to a lesser extent, were based on an aspiration to develop intellectual cross-fertilization, the more modern developments have their point of origin in the hope of effecting greater linkages between students' academic work and the wider society, particularly the capacities required from graduates in the labour market. Supplanting the broad academic themes, issues or fields marked out by the educators (such as Briggs and Hutchins) have been terms such as 'enterprise' and 'personal transferable skills' and so forth. That new terminology, accordingly, can be read as a metaphor, a search for a new curriculum code (cf. Bernstein, 1971). There is, as yet, little clarity about how to graft or, indeed, if the basis exists for grafting onto traditional higher education curricula such extramural agendas or whether we should not again attempt to redraw completely the map of knowledge.

Operationalism: a new unifying principle?

The controversy that has been generated by the idea of competence, as adumbrated by the NCVQ, suggests that here, in that idea, lies just such an attempt (NCVQ, 1991). In itself, the term 'competence' is probably benign. The fears of its detractors perhaps are based in a concern that its actual exposition in this case, being based on industry-led standards of performance (Burke, 1989, chapters 3 and 5; Black and Wolf, 1990), amounts to an attempt to import into one human activity (education) the interests and conceptions of another (industry).

I do not wish to enter that debate here. The point is that now we find, as with other initiatives reflected in terminology such as 'enterprise' and 'capability', attempts to identify principles of curriculum reform which are both cross-subject and are oriented to the capacities of graduates to be successful in the wider world. If there is a unifying idea behind these ideas, it is not that of economic survival but of personal effectiveness beyond the educational arena. There is, here, arguably, a form of operationalism. An effective curriculum has become one which enables individuals to identify and put into effect strategic actions. The underlying image is that of individuals acting in an instrumental way on their environment. Alternative conceptions of individuals, such as interacting with others mutually to enhance understanding, or to critique one's surroundings, or to engage in an aesthetic intervention on it, are less in evidence (cf. Habermas' critical theory).[2]

The higher education curriculum has always, in different ways, been oriented towards society. What is new about contemporary developments is the way in which the curriculum (at least in the UK) is now being colonized by the state, with unifying agendas being urged onto the academic community. Questions, therefore, arise about the relationship which such extra-mural interests are to have to the conventional agendas of the disciplinary community. It may be that the academic community itself, seized of the need to survive in a climate of diminishing relative resources, will itself accommodate relatively painlessly to the new agendas. That is a sociological matter and can be bypassed here. The key issue for curriculum design is whether the new elements are to be integrated with a discipline-based programme or whether, in the new agendas, there is sufficient substance to provide organizing principles for new kinds of curricula in higher education.

Whatever happened to liberal education?

If the idea of liberal education is taken to imply a form of learning organized without regard to the apparent requirements of the wider society, then the idea of liberal education is dead. Practically speaking, higher education has become part of the modern society. In that sense, societal considerations in delivering a curriculum are almost inescapable. Certainly, there will be pockets of resistance and exclusivity, where such extramural influences are evaded or not seriously felt. But in the generality of the case, higher education has become part of the knowledge apparatus of the modern society and is willy-nilly answerable to and influenced by that wider field.

This is not a matter of regret. Or, at least, regret is an unhelpful response. The question is: by what principles is learning to be organized? Can a range of different interests and influences be met in the construction of the curriculum? Are there general principles that might inform learning in higher education, or are the forms that learning takes simply to be the pragmatic outcome of local skirmishes, as disciplinary sub-cultures, the market forces of student choice, professional and industrial requirements, and managerial structures work themselves out at the course level?

Learning, then, is no longer the sole province of the academic community. Both its form and content are subject to the influences of the wider world (including student preferences). 'Competence', 'capability', 'enterprise', 'transferable skills', 'experiential learning', and 'problem-based learning': these terms (as this volume demonstrates) are part of the new vocabulary of higher education in the UK. If, for no other reason than that questions are now being raised about it, learning in higher education has become problematic. Social groupings, other than the academic community, feel they have a legitimate interest in the higher education curriculum. It can no longer constitute a secret garden. The curriculum can no longer remain an exchange between the individual lecturer and a group of students, the character of which is often unknown either to the other members of the course team or to the head of department.

The public interest

Three factors are immediately apparent behind this new prominence of curriculum debate. Taken together, they begin to substantiate the point that the higher education curriculum has become a matter of *public* interest.

Firstly, modern society has become a 'learning society'. The phrase is ambiguous, however, and carries a range of possible interpretations. It could mean:

- That society values – and rewards – learning.
- That the members of society will have to renew their learning throughout their lifetimes for their own *individual economic well-being*.
- That *personal growth* and renewal is integrally bound up with learning through the individual's lifespan.
- That significant learning takes place *widely* across society, and not just in formally designated institutions.
- That *responsibility* for learning is distributed throughout society: citizens have a social and moral responsibility to continue to educate themselves.
- That people are seen to be the most important economic resource and that, amidst social and technological change, *continuing investment in people* has to be made for economic competitiveness.

- That important *social problems come under rational scrutiny* and are, thereby, subject to what we can learn in order to deal with them in an informed way.
- That *society can learn about itself*, progressively advancing its decision-making to ever more refined rational processes.

The elements of this list work on at least three different levels of development: of individual development; of economic development; and of social development. Such a categorization opens the question of whether there might not be tensions between development at those different levels.

Whatever the meaning, however, learning matters. But part of the force of the phrase is in its inner logic. A learning society is one in which all citizens are obliged to go on learning throughout their lives. Two implications follow. Firstly, learning opportunities are dispersed throughout society. No longer can the formal institutions of learning claim a monopoly of provision. Secondly, discrete items of information are soon redundant. They have a limited life. On both counts, hard questions arise over the substance of what is to be learnt in higher education. 'Learning to learn', 'transferable skills', 'problem-solving skills', skills in handling 'information technology' and learning from experience take their place in the vocabulary of higher education. Whether these terms have real cash value as ideas informing curriculum design is, though, a further matter deserving investigation.

Secondly, the quality of student learning has become a matter of public interest. Partly, the interest is linked to the emergence of a mass higher education system, in which there arises an apparent tension between the goals of access and quality (Berdahl *et al.*, 1991). Partly, the interest arises from the international research on student learning over the past 20 years which is now informing the practices of lecturers responsible for course delivery (Marton *et al.*, 1984) (see Chapter 10). Partly, too, the issue arises as a result of the market being given more prominence in determining the shape and character of higher education. Further, the matter is of importance since the state's funding bodies have flagged the quality of courses as a consideration in resource allocation.

Thirdly, the issue of 'professionalism' has begun to get a hearing in relation to the role of academics as teachers. *Qua* teachers – as distinct from their role as researchers and scholars – what are the demands on academics? In their interactions with students, what are the expectations to which they feel themselves to be subject? What are they trying to do, and what considerations might they reasonably be expected to entertain in order successfully to bring off those intentions? How do they understand their responsibilities in promoting the student's learning, if indeed they see things in that way? To what extent is there, or ought there to be, an academic ethic underpinning those teacher–student transactions?

There are signs that a debate along these lines is beginning to take off (CVCP, 1991).[3] But the fact that such a debate is only now coming into view is indicative of there having been no explicit consensus across the academic community as to the character of the academic profession so far as the teaching function is concerned. This is not just a comment on the binary system of higher education as it has existed. The so-called public sector of polytechnics and colleges failed collectively to raise explicitly such an issue, even though it had received a 'teaching' mission from the state in the 1960s. Nor did the Council for National Academic Awards focus specifically on the matter in any of its publications.

These issues – the arrival of the learning society; the emergence of mass higher education and of an increasingly heterogeneous student clientele exerting its market influences; and the nature of professionalism among the academic community – are not exhaustive. Two obvious others are the need for greater teaching efficiency and effectiveness, as the total costs of the system rise; and the growing determinedness of graduate employers to voice their perceived curricular aims (CIHE, 1987, 1988). All these points taken together are a collective testimony to the claim that higher learning is now felt to be more than a matter for academics.

The state and higher education

Identifying these issues, important as they are, does not in itself begin to supply an adequate answer to the question: why this new-found interest in the higher education? The cited issues are hardly more than an exemplification of the interest; they do not seriously begin to account for the interest now being shown by the state in the inner life of higher education. That is to say, the arrival of the learning society and of mass higher education are a contributory but not a sufficient cause of the wider interest in the curriculum. The Enterprise in Higher Education initiative, to take the most obvious example, cannot be explained in those terms.

The example points to a changing relationship between the state and higher education. An adequate answer to the preceding question accordingly requires the beginnings of an analysis at a structural level which enables us to understand the forces at work. The work of Jurgen Habermas, especially his book, *Legitimation Crisis* (Habermas, 1976), may be helpful here. Habermas argues that the modern state is faced with a series of structural problems of systems steerage, each one arising to displace the one before it. The problems arise in different spheres of society, as one set of societal crises is in turn displaced by another. First, the state finds the task of solving the periodic economic crises of late capitalism intractable. The failure to solve the crisis leads to a motivational crisis in society (economic expectations which had been generated are now thwarted), and to the state backing off from its economic mission but turning instead to ways of handling the motivational crisis. This new mission obliges it to take an interest in the life-world of individuals, so as to resolve the new legitimation crisis.

We can see parallel signs in the UK, surely, of how the state has developed its agenda in relation to higher education. In broad-brush terms, an interest in the 1950s and 1960s in manpower planning (through higher education) was supplanted by budget-capping (1970s), and by an insistence on commercial models of management and of performance review (1980s), and (late 1980s onwards) by an intervention in the character of the education on offer itself. In other words, the state's *modus operandi* has developed from a distant interest in economic value to concerns over the efficient management of the system through to the character of the life-world of the actors concerned. Each move on the part of the state has brought a deeper involvement in the inner life of academic institutions, such that the state is beginning to intervene actively in the character *both* of the student experience and of the teacher–student transactions.

A story such as this at least starts to go below the surface debates and concerns of the moment to explain at a structural level of analysis why those debates and concerns have a public resonance. The growing contemporary interest in the higher education curriculum *is* new in that it is being prompted and fanned by forces external to the academic community.

An analysis of this kind says nothing about the worth of the moves being enjoined on the academic community. What it does is to alert us to the social dynamics at work. It also suggests that evaluations of the curriculum changes should incorporate questions such as:

- What interests are being served by these changes?
- What interests are being downplayed or marginalized?
- If there is a state agenda in operation, to what extent is it long term?
- Given the ecological and economic issues facing the planet, and the possible role of higher education in addressing them, to what extent is the state's agenda global or merely nationalistic in character?

The changing curriculum

Admittedly, student learning has always been subject to re-evaluation. Except for rare periods (such as the eighteenth century), higher learning has been in a dynamic state. Arguably, however, the contemporary pressures for curricular change, and for modifying the character of student learning, are more complex than before (Squires, 1990). Student learning has become almost everyone's business – that of the taxpayer, the state (with an eye on world trade), students (in a developing higher education market), employers, and newly emerging professions seeking to gain legitimacy by securing a graduate entry stream – alongside the academic community.

Elsewhere (Barnett, 1992), I have depicted the changes to which the curriculum is subject in the way depicted in Figure 1.1. In one of its axes, the diagram draws a distinction between two kinds of interest bearing on the curriculum: those internal to the academic community and those external to it. The diagram also points to a further distinction between curricular aims which have a specific intention and those which have more general or diffuse

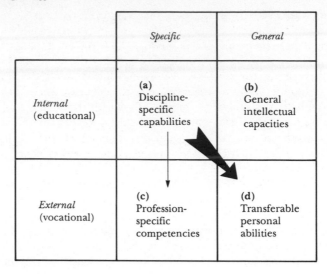

Figure 1.1 Changing structure of curriculum objectives: a schema

curricular intentions. Placing these two distinctions against each other gives us the quadrants shown.

We can hypothesize that in contemporary society, curricula of higher learning are likely not to be restricted to any one quadrant, but are liable – amoeba-like – to spread out in one or more directions as curriculum designers respond to the influences bearing on them. We can, I believe, go further than such a general statement. I would contend that, given the balance of influences at work in the recent past and contemporaneously, the following hypothesis presents itself as fruitful. It is that, until recently (in the UK, at least), the dominant influence on the curriculum was the academic community. Curricula, generally, were therefore situated mainly in box (a). Certainly, a number of curricula were also framed to fulfil the specific requirements of professional bodies, and were also located in box (c) as well. Currently, however, we are seeing various influences at work which are tending to propel curricula in general in the directions both of box (c) and of box (d).

So far as the movement in the direction of specific objectives derived from the world of work are concerned (box (c)), we are witnessing professional bodies being more explicit about the 'competences' they are looking to in their field (Chapter 6), we are seeing professional practice becoming a more significant part of the curriculum (Chapter 5), we are seeing more professions looking to higher education to offer an entry route and professionals themselves are being granted more direct influence in the design of curricula and the assessment of students. Some of these developments are prompted by or gain tacit support from the work of the National Council for Vocational

Qualifications (Jessup, 1991; NCVQ, 1991) in its establishment of industry-led standards of work-based 'competence' for assessment. Although the NCVQ has so far focused on the provision of education at the 16–19 levels, it has more recently been engaging in conversations with professional bodies, and is likely soon to have a direct impact on the design of curricula in higher education, if only on that growing proportion of programmes which are oriented towards specific sectors of the labour market. (Its orientation towards specifying learning outcomes is likely to be picked up across programmes in general.)

So far as the movement in the direction of more general objectives rooted in the wider world is concerned (box (d)), this is less certain but some indicators can be picked out. Firstly, the Council for Industry and Higher Education has been sketching out desiderata of graduates coming onto the labour market in terms of the general capacities that it would hope to see developed in all graduates (CIHE, op. cit.). Secondly, many institutions of higher education are picking up the terminology of personal transferable skills (NAB, 1986), and are beginning to implement programmes of curricular development in which identified 'transferable skills' (such as communication skills and information technology skills) are embedded institution-wide. Thirdly, the two national programmes mentioned earlier – the Enterprise in Higher Education initiative and the Higher Education for Capability initiative – have also sparked off institution-wide activities as part of a programme of strategic development, again aimed at imparting identified aims to all programmes (Chapters 12 and 13).

General *academic* capacities (which would fall into box (b)) are not, it would appear, being given such definite backing. This is the territory inhabited by the general educational principles to which the Council for National Academic Awards gave its allegiance over 25 years, even if their precise specification was modified from time to time (CNAA, 1992). The list included such capacities as

> the students' intellectual and imaginative powers; their understanding and judgement; their problem-solving skills; . . . their ability to see relationships within what they have learned . . .; each programme of study should stimulate . . . an enquiring, analytical and creative approach and encourage independent judgement and critical self-awareness.

Those kinds of general intellectual capacities are also to be seen in the list produced by the NAB/UGC joint statement (UGC, 1984). However, a willingness to identify such general capacities, *internal* to the academic community (box (b)), is not evident at the current time. What is now called forth are skills and capacities which are intended to promote the effectiveness of the students (as graduates) in the wider world. That is, the skills now being favoured are those situated in box (d).

What effects?

There are two qualifications to make to the analysis just offered. Firstly, even if there are currents at work which are tending to propel curricula in certain directions, the likelihood is (as I have suggested) that any single curriculum is not located in any one quadrant, but will spread across them and possibly occupy some part of all four quadrants. Secondly, even if the basic framework is felt to be inadequate (where, for example, might we put 'experiential learning'?), the general point remains. Higher education curricula in the modern society are subject to manifold influences and pressures and are in some state of dynamic change: 'dynamic' because the balance of pressures is itself changing, at both the national and the local level, as national and institutional policies are modified. Course teams are increasingly being persuaded or are persuading themselves to make almost continuous changes, as their perceptions of the dominant influences alter.

There remains, however, an even more fundamental point, which is apparently obvious, but which may be worth making. It is that whatever effects a curriculum has – whether intended or unintended – effects there are. What is apparent is that the range of possible effects on students is increasing and is open for decision. Unless, at the strategic level, we become reflective practitioners, our curricular decisions may be influenced by unrecognized forces at work, or may lead to effects on students with uncertain value, or both.

The following questions, therefore, arise over the effects of curriculum change in higher education:

1. What effects on students are sought as a result of curricula changes? What is their justification?
2. What societal effects are anticipated through the shaping of the curriculum?
3. To what extent are teachers successful in having the effects on students that they intend?
4. Is students' learning as effective as it might be?

Successively, these are questions for (1 and 2) all those who are attempting to influence the curriculum, whether inside or outside the academic community; (3) those delivering the curriculum and their institutional managers; and (4) students and teachers together.

The plan of this book

This book treats issues of higher learning at four levels: *institutional, professional, course* and *national*. The assumption is that we can raise intelligible questions – essentially, the four questions identified earlier – about student learning and the curriculum at each of these analytic levels.

The authors have, understandably enough, treated the questions in ways that are appropriate to their own concerns. Dimensions, therefore, of teaching effectiveness or learning effectiveness or graduate effectiveness receive varying levels of attention in each chapter. Also, between them, the authors offer the perspectives of those engaged in research, teaching, development, and policy formation. Collectively, the chapters provide, as a result, an interweaving of issues, levels, and perspectives on contemporary aspects of learning in higher education. However, I believe that the central issue running through the volume remains clear: how, at the different levels of the system, might learning be made more effective? Putting the key question that way, of course, raises a further issue: what is meant by effective learning?

The institutional perspective (Chapters 2–4): Given that the operating units have a high degree of professional autonomy (Becher and Kogan, 1992), the question arises as to whether we can intelligibly talk of an institutional level of responsibility for effecting curricular development and, if so, in what ways. The collective answer of the three chapters here is that we can, but the answer requires qualification.

Institutional leadership is a necessary component of cross-institutional curriculum development (Chapter 2) but the implicit message of the three chapters is that it will be most effective when it builds on, explicitly, a sensitivity to the faculty as having its own mission and a sense of the character of the academic enterprise as seen by the faculty. Part of the leadership task may lie in widening those perceived purposes, and in working with the faculty to develop a common discourse in which those new perceptions can be articulated (see also Chapters 12 and 13); but the professionals' own views of their teaching function has to form the starting point for those conversations.

The professional perspective (Chapters 5–7): This raises issues of curriculum development over courses having a professional orientation (perhaps now the majority of higher education programmes).

There are two dominant issues. Firstly, what is to be the balance between theory and practice (or between boxes (a) and (c) of Fig. 1.1)? As Eraut (Chapter 7) and Ellis (Chapter 5) show, put like that, this is too naive a question. For complex issues arise over what we take practice and knowledge to be in the professional domain. Secondly, what is to be the balance between profession-specific capabilities and those which have a more generic use value in the world of work (or between boxes (c) and (d)) (Chapter 6)?

The course perspective (Chapters 8–10): As addressed here, these chapters are intended to shed light on ways of making the student experience more effective. They tackle three distinctive approaches: introducing into the curriculum elements aimed at enhancing students' employability on graduation, irrespective of the subject studied (Lillie, Chapter 8), incorporating a degree of experiential learning into the curriculum so as to involve the students more directly in their own learning (Evans, Chapter 9), and adopting teaching approaches which are explicity designed to improve the quality of learning (Gibbs, Chapter 10). Deploying again the diagram, Lillie's study shows how the humanities curriculum is spreading from box (a) to box (d). Gibbs' account has a different message: it is possible to improve learning effectiveness without shifting the fundamental character of the curriculum (that is, by focusing on the quality of delivery and less by moving the balance from one box to another). Evans' story, on the other hand, poses questions for my earlier analysis: how is experiential learning to be understood? Is it a matter of widening our conception of valid academic knowledge (that is, widening our conception of the contents of box (a))? Is it a matter of drawing in forms of understanding acquired in particular experiences in the world of work (box (c))? Or is it more a means of incorporating evidence of general relevant capacities and functioning, whether characteristic of intellectual life in general (box (b)) *or* of the wider world (box (d))?

The national perspective (Chapters 11–13): This explores case studies of attempts to institute changes in the curricula of UK higher education on a national level: establishing a national credit accumulation and transfer scheme (Chapter 11) and the implementation and evolution of the Enterprise in Higher Education initiative (Chapter 13) and of the Capability in Higher Education initiative (Chapter 12). There is perhaps a double message from those chapters. Firstly, however precisely conceived at their inception, the rationale and character of national initiatives will be modified over time, as they are taken up at the local level. Secondly (and it is a corollary of the first point, and takes us back to the first section on the institutional perspective), if national initiatives are to take off, if they are to attract real enthusiasm among professionals responsible for curriculum delivery, institutional leadership is essential, but will have to be exercised in such a way that professionals are given space in which to develop their own voice and perspectives.

If there is a concluding observation, it is this. In UK higher education, we have entered a conversation about the appropriate character of higher learning for the approaching century. There are many legitimate voices and perspectives in that debate; and there is no necessary end-point at which they can all be resolved with equal weight. The different voices and perspectives express contrasting starting points and values over the proper ends of higher learning (cf. Rorty, 1989). The four boxes in Fig. 1.1 are testimony to the point. Accordingly, there will be different *legitimate* ways of accommodating those different points of view. We should, at least, be prepared to go on with our conversations, exploring the possibilities of interpretation and accommodation, before those conversations are brought prematurely to an end.

Notes

1. In the 1991 round, the Partnership Teaching Awards were comprised of 27 prizes for different subjects and curricula aims in higher education. Details available from

the Partnership Office, c/o RSA House, 8 John Adam Street, London, WC2N
6EZ.
2. For recent accessible introductions to the work of Jurgen Habermas, scc Roderick
(1986) and Rasmussen (1990).
3. Also, the appearance of issue 1 of *The New Academic*, Autumn 1991, a magazine of
'teaching and learning in Higher Education', published by the Standing Conference for Educational Development.

References

Barnett, R. (1992) *Improving Higher Education: total quality care.* Buckingham, Open
University Press.
Becher, T. (1989) *Academic Tribes and Territories.* Milton Keynes, Open University
Press.
Becher, T. and Kogan, M. (1992) *Process and Structure in Higher Education,* 2nd edn.
London, Routledge.
Berdahl, R., Moodie, G. and Spitzberg, I.J. (eds) (1991) *Quality and Access in Higher
Education.* Milton Keynes, Open University Press.
Bernstein, B. (1971) 'On the classification and framing of educational knowledge' in
M.D.F. Young (ed.) *Knowledge and Control.* London, Collier-Macmillan.
Black, H. and Wolf, A. (eds) (1990) *Knowledge and Competence: current issues in education
and training.* Sheffield, COIC.
Bok, D. (1986) *Higher Learning.* London, Harvard University Press.
Boyer, E. and Levine, A. (1981) *A Quest for Common Learning.* Washington, Carnegie
Foundation.
Briggs, A. (1964) 'Drawing a new map of learning' in D. Daiches (ed.) *The Idea of a
New University.* London, Deutsch.
Burke, J.W. (ed.) (1989) *Competency Based Education and Training.* London, Falmer.
CIHE (1987) *Towards a Partnership: higher education – government – industry,* London,
CIHE.
CIHE (1988) *Towards a Partnership: the company response.* London, CIHE.
Clark, B. (1983) *The Higher Education System: academic organization in cross-national
perspective.* London, University of California Press.
CNAA (1992) *The Management of Academic Quality in Institutions of Higher Education:
a guide to best practice.* London, CNAA.
CVCP (1991) *Teaching Standards and Excellence in Higher Education: developing a culture for
quality.* Sheffield, CVCP USDTU.
Habermas, J. (1976) *Legitimation Crisis.* London, Heinemann.
Hutchins, R. (1936) *The Higher Learning in America.* New Haven, Harvard University
Press.
Jessup, G. (1991) *Outcomes: NVQs and the emerging model of education and training.*
London, Falmer.
Marton, F. *et al.* (1984) *The Experience of Learning.* Edinburgh, Scottish Academic
Press.
National Advisory Body (1986) *Transferable Personal Skills in Employment: the contribution
of higher education.* London, NAB.
NCVQ (1991) *Guide to NVQs.* London, NCVQ.
NFER (1991) *Enterprise in Higher Education: 2nd year national evaluation.* Final Report.
Slough, NFER.

Rasmussen, D.M. (1990) *Reading Habermas*. Oxford, Blackwell.

Roderick, R. (1986) *Habermas and the Foundations of Critical Theory*. Basingstoke, Macmillan.

Rorty, R. (1989) *Contingency, Irony and Solidarity*. Cambridge, Cambridge University Press.

Squires, G. (1990) *First Degree*. Milton Keynes, Open University Press.

UGC (1984) *A Strategy for Higher Education into the 1990s*. London, UGC.

Part 1

The Institutional Perspective

2

Institutional Values and Teaching Quality

Graham Badley

Introduction

When the Warnock Committee was established by the Polytechnics and Colleges Funding Council, its overall task was to establish flexible criteria of teaching quality based on an examination of (mainly UK) good practice and then to advise on possible strategies which would serve to raise the quality of teaching (*THES*, 21 April 1989, p. 9). However, when the Warnock Report was published, it was criticized as 'an opportunity missed' because it failed to provide even 'workaday definitions' of good or quality teaching (*THES*, 26 October 1990). The THES was, perhaps, being both naive and unfair: naive because quality is, as philosophers would say, an 'essentially contested concept'; and unfair because the Warnock Committee did at least identify three 'underlying principles' of good teaching and 'five necessary conditions' which 'must be fulfilled within institutions and without which good teaching cannot exist' (PCFC, 1990, paras 2.8). Warnock's three underlying principles of good teaching do not at first sight appear all that remarkable in themselves:

1. That 'teaching' must be interpreted broadly as the whole management and promotion of learning by a variety of methods, including interaction between teacher and student, and the accessibility to the students of a wide range of learning resources (paras 2.2 and 2.3); that 'teaching' is not simply lecturing or conducting seminars but is more generally defined as a purposive activity requiring 'the initiation and management of student learning by a teacher' (para 2.3); good teaching and learning also depend on 'the importance of the institutional climate within which learning takes place . . . a climate within which high standards in scholarship, professional activity and, in some cases, related research can flourish' (para 2.4).
2. That teaching must be responsive to students' needs especially at a time when institutions are expected to teach more students, to accommodate those with different backgrounds and expectations and to adapt their

methods 'so that all students participate in a worthwhile learning experience, with a satisfactory outcome' (para 2.6).
3. That the conditions necessary for good teaching must be taken seriously, their satisfaction given priority at every level of institutional activity (para 2.2).

The first two of these principles are relatively commonplace. What would be remarkable however would be the wholehearted implementation of the third principle for it would lead to a total institutional commitment to improving the quality of teaching as a matter of priority. The third principle requires, according to Warnock, five necessary conditions for its fulfilment (see para. 2.8):

1. That there should exist clarity of aims and objectives related specifically to teaching, and confidence that they are worthwhile and appropriate to students' needs.
2. That there should be a policy regarding curriculum organization and delivery, including a readiness to consider different methods of promoting learning.
3. That there should be a policy for the professional development of teaching including staff appointment, induction, appraisal and development.
4. That there should be means by which the views of students and employers can be used in judgement of the curriculum, its delivery and outcomes.
5. That there should be an identifiable framework within which an institution can evaluate its own success in meeting its objectives and adjust its practice accordingly.

Warnock calls these conditions 'necessary' as if they had some sort of logical force. Whether or not a philosophical analysis of 'good teaching' would disclose such conditions must however remain a matter for contentious debate. That these five conditions are desirable depends also of course on the view of higher education that is taken.

Nevertheless Warnock's third principle – that the conditions necessary for good teaching must be taken seriously, their satisfaction given priority at every level of institutional activity – if adopted nationally would require each institution of higher education to implement (ibid., para 3.3)

a coherent policy which will benefit the staff and the students and is shared throughout its departments and courses. This policy should be applied equally to the common resources (such as library and student support services) which together make up the environment of the whole institution.

In effect, the Warnock Committee recognized that the 'total quality' concept is in some ways applicable to higher education but they rightly warn that 'the concepts of industry are no more than metaphors' and that as such they should be used with caution (ibid., see paras 5.1–5.8). The Committee also asserted that the institutional adoption of their five necessary conditions would ensure that teaching would become effective and efficient but it would not ensure excellence (ibid., para 5.12):

> for excellence in teaching, something else is needed, which goes to the heart of the institutional ethos, the way it conducts itself throughout its activities and the value which it places upon the quality of its own teaching.

The Committee recommended that PCFC should require a statement of the enhancement of teaching quality from each institution seeking an allocation of funds for additional student places:

- the institution should specify initiatives designed to enhance or sustain its teaching quality (para 5.16); and
- an institution's commitment to the enhancement of its teaching quality is best demonstrated by a commitment of resources and time to specific teaching developments (para 5.10).

What follows in this chapter is, in effect, a case study outlining the initiatives undertaken by one major institution of higher education (albeit in an American context) which demonstrates its total commitment to an institutional ethos which seeks the enhancement of teaching quality and makes for excellence in the student experience.

Miami-Dade Community College

Miami-Dade Community College was founded in 1960 and has become America's largest multi-campus community college with over 41 000 credit students (*College Times*, 28 March 1989) and over 2800 full-time staff. It is a publicly-supported two-year community college which fulfils a number of important functions including that of providing college transfer courses (which, in effect, allow students to complete the first two years of a degree course in the college before transferring to a university for the final two years) and a comprehensive range of adult and continuing education programmes for the whole community. Indeed, Miami-Dade exemplifies the new mission adopted in the American community college movement, the mission to renew the community itself:

> Perhaps more than any other institution, the community college also can inspire partnerships based upon shared values and common goals. The building of community, in its broadest and best sense, encompasses a concern for the whole, for integration and collaboration, for openness and integrity, for inclusiveness and self-renewal.
>
> (AACJC, 1988, p. 7)

Miami-Dade embodied this notion of community building in its earlier statements of institutional goals. For example, specific goals included:

- To recruit actively students from all segments of the community and to minimize barriers to admission.
- To provide appropriate college resources to assist the community in identifying, analysing and solving problems.
- To provide opportunities to each member of the community regardless of sex, race, religion, age, national origin, handicap or financial resources.

(Miami-Dade, 1983–85, p. 7)

Miami-Dade has effectively underlined its responsiveness to the educational needs of the community and has assumed a leadership role in actively educating the community and improving its environment. It proudly adopts an 'open admissions policy', one goal of which is 'to assist in the democratization of the community by providing all its citizens with access to higher education' (Lukenbill and McCabe, 1978, p. 16).

Nevertheless, Miami-Dade is adamant that the community college mission is not simply to provide access but 'to provide for successful learning by the community members' (ibid.). It is this local concern with successful learning which connects Miami-Dade with the new American and international focus on improving teaching:

> At the center of building community there is teaching. Teaching is the heartbeat of the educational enterprise and, when it is successful, energy is pumped into the community, continuously renewing and revitalizing the institution. Therefore, excellence in teaching is the means by which the vitality of the college is extended and a network of intellectual enrichment and cultural understanding is built. Good teaching requires active learning in the classroom. It calls for a climate in which students are encouraged to collaborate rather than compete. Thus, building community through dedicated teaching is the vision and inspiration of this report.

(AACJC, 1988, pp. 7–8)

The rest of this chapter outlines the way in which Miami-Dade has pursued its concern with teaching excellence, its 'enthusiastic emphasis on teaching quality' (Roueche and Baker, 1985, p. 25) through a major project which, according to its President, is the most significant the college has ever undertaken (Miami-Dade, 1986–87).

The Miami-Dade Teaching/Learning Project

During the 1970s, Miami-Dade Community College reviewed its general education programme (somewhat similar to Liberal Studies or General Studies courses in UK further and higher education) largely because of widespread staff and student dissatisfaction with it. One report objected to

> required aspects of present courses, the relevance of such courses to current social and personal problems, overly-large class size, inadequate

auditoria, instructional techniques, and the need for more humanism in general education and in education in general.

(Lukenbill and McCabe, 1978, p. 18)

Such objections were obviously neither locally exclusive to Miami-Dade nor nationally restricted to American institutions of higher education. The Miami-Dade review brought about a number of changes which enabled staff to monitor and direct student progress more effectively through the use of, amongst other things, compulsory entrance testing, placement and counselling. However the college also recognized that more attention needed to be given to the teaching and learning process itself and this led the college President, Dr Robert H. McCabe, to invite 120 of his senior staff to a conference hotel in June 1986 to examine a paper on raising the priority of teaching and learning at Miami-Dade. In effect, this created the Miami-Dade Teaching/Learning Project. In October 1986, a full-time Project Director (Mardee Jenrette) was appointed and a full-day 'conversation about teaching and learning' was held among 30 staff, college managers and external consultants (including, for example, K. Patricia Cross, then of Harvard University). The conversation produced a list of preliminary issues as well as recommendations and guidelines for a Teaching/Learning Project Steering Committee. The first edition of a project newsletter was also written and distributed during October 1986.

During December 1986 and January 1987, the college President sponsored a series of campus meetings to encourage staff to participate in the project, to exchange ideas and to suggest further issues to explore. January 1987 also saw the publication of the first draft of the project's assumptions, goals and components as well as the establishment of four sub-committees to examine institutional values, faculty excellence, new faculty and the teaching/learning environment. The project assumptions were listed in order to establish a context for the overall project:

- Diversity is a key to teaching and learning at Miami-Dade and is to be valued.
- Shared values concerning teaching and learning at Miami-Dade can be identified.
- Behaviours that contribute to effective teaching and learning can be identified.
- The quality of educational programs and the teaching and learning environment can be enhanced by collaborative efforts of all College personnel.
- There is a continuing need for all College personnel to acquire knowledge and skills.

(Miami-Dade, 1986–87)

The goals of the project were stated as

- To improve the quality of teaching and learning at Miami-Dade Community College (M-DCC).

- To make teaching at M-DCC a professionally rewarding career.
- To make teaching and learning the focal point of college activities and decision-making processes.

(Miami-Dade, 1986–87)

The most impressive aspect of these two lists is not that teaching quality is seen to be a major priority for such a large college but that the college has agreed to put teaching and learning at the focal point of its decision-making processes. This signals a valuing of teaching and learning as the central activities of college life thereby making explicit what is often in other institutions either a hidden or a neglected assumption. It also shows that teaching and learning are highly valued by the college's leaders (and especially by its President) since it was they who were instrumental in the project's inception.

Institutional values

The purpose of the sub-committee working on values was

to identify and reach consensus on shared values concerning teaching and learning at M-DCC.

(Miami-Dade, 1987–88)

By December 1987, seven values had been adopted by the President's Council and the college Board of Trustees. These values, operationally defined as 'those beliefs which guide the institution in the development of its mission, goals, philosophy and operational procedures' (Miami-Dade, 1986–87), were identified through an extensive survey of staff, students and the community. Thus Miami-Dade Community College explicitly values

- Learning.
- Change to meet educational needs and to improve learning.
- Access while maintaining quality.
- Diversity in order to broaden understanding and learning.
- Individuals.
- A systematic approach to decision-making.
- Its partnership with the community.

(Miami-Dade, undated)

It is interesting to note here that the document emphasizes learning rather than teaching with the implication, perhaps, that the improvement of learning itself is a higher value than the improvement of teaching. Nevertheless, the values document does list 53 supporting statements which include specific references to teaching whereby the college:

- Creates an environment conducive to teaching and learning.
- Provides the resources necessary for teaching and learning.
- Respects and accepts different teaching styles.

- Encourages a positive attitude toward teaching and learning.
- Surveys students' perceptions about courses, programmes, and the teaching/learning process.

(ibid.)

Other specific assertions which might be of particular interest to teachers outside the USA include statements that the college:

- Encourages the free interchange of ideas and beliefs.
- Provides a variety of scholarships and financial aid programs.
- Publishes explicit performance expectations for faculty, staff and administrators.
- Publishes explicit performance expectations for students.
- Rewards achievement.
- Provides accessible campus and outreach centres.

(ibid.)

This values document is regarded as 'the foundation of all that will follow' (Miami-Dade, 1987–88) and forms part of the recruitment, selection and orientation (induction) programmes for new teaching staff; it is used as a yardstick for resource allocation; it has become a basis for the evaluation of college administration and services; it is included in college publications and, most important of all, it is reflected in the Faculty Excellence document (ibid.).

Faculty Excellence

The intention 'to describe and reach consensus on a core of fundamental characteristics of faculty excellence as related to effective teaching and learning' (Miami-Dade, 1987–88) was realized in the adoption of a Faculty Excellence document in October 1988. The document describes the qualities and characteristics of excellent teaching and non-teaching faculty in terms of four main categories: motivation, interpersonal skills, knowledge base and application of knowledge base. Each category will be summarized.

Motivation
Excellent faculty members at Miami-Dade Community College, whether classroom teachers, librarians, counsellors, or serving in any other faculty capacity:

Are enthusiastic about their work.
Set challenging individual and collective performance goals for themselves.
Set challenging performance goals for students.
Are committed to education as a profession.
Project a positive attitude about students' ability to learn.
Display behaviour consistent with professional ethics.
Regard students as individuals operating in a broader perspective beyond the classroom.

Interpersonal skills
Excellent faculty members at Miami-Dade Community College, whether classroom teachers, librarians, counsellors, or serving in any other capacity:

Treat all individuals with respect.
Respect diverse talents.
Work collaboratively with colleagues.
Are available to students.
Listen attentively to what students say.
Are responsive to student needs.
Are fair in their evaluations of student progress.
Present ideas clearly.
Create a climate that is conducive to learning.

Knowledge base
Excellent faculty members at Miami-Dade Community College, whether classroom teachers, librarians, counsellors, or serving in any other capacity:

Are knowledgeable about their work areas and disciplines.
Are knowledgeable about how students learn.
Integrate current subject matter into their work.
Provide perspectives that include a respect for diverse views.
Do their work in a well-prepared and well-organized manner.

Application of knowledge base
Excellent faculty members at Miami-Dade Community College, whether classroom teachers, librarians, counsellors, or serving in any other capacity:

Provide students with alternative ways of learning.
Stimulate intellectual curiosity.
Encourage independent thinking.
Encourage students to be analytical listeners.
Provide cooperative learning opportunities for students.
Give constructive feedback promptly to students.
Give consideration to feedback from students and others.
Provide clear and substantial evidence that students have learned.

The categories and summary statements were the end result of a process which involved the sub-committee in:

- Reviewing research on learning principles, effective teaching, learning styles, and learning assessment.
- Devising a survey instrument to measure ratings of faculty attitudes and behaviours which enhance student learning.
- Field-testing and revising drafts of the survey.
- Administering the survey to all Miami-Dade full-time faculty members, all M-DCC full-time administrators and a random sample of M-DCC students.

- Analysing the results, drafting a report and then discussing the draft report at a Teaching/Learning Project retreat.

(see Miami-Dade, April 1988a)

The sub-committee concluded that faculty, administrators and students showed a high degree of support for all four descriptors which together form a composite definition of faculty excellence at Miami-Dade.

(ibid., pp. 2–3)

In sum, excellent teachers at Miami-Dade are meant to be:

- Motivated and motivating.
- Skilled interpersonally.
- Knowledgeable about their subjects.
- Knowledgeable about teaching and learning.

It would be an interesting exercise to examine how these items would be received in other institutions in other countries. My own view is that they are a valuable summary of teaching quality in higher education and that they are similar to other summaries such as, for example, the simple equation of superior teaching with:

Competence in subject matter
+ communication skills
+ commitment to facilitating student learning
+ concern for individual students.

(Moses, 1985, p. 312)

The chief value of the Miami-Dade document on Faculty Excellence is, though, not that it could or should be adopted by other colleges or polytechnics or universities elsewhere but that it is a definition of Miami-Dade's own beliefs and values about teaching quality which the college has arrived at through its own efforts and discussions. The document is literally the college's own and summarizes its own explicit beliefs, enthusiasms, commitments and positive attitudes. The process of arriving at the final document as well as the document itself demonstrate, in advance of the Warnock Report, a commitment to a broad interpretation of teaching, to a view of teaching as being responsive to student needs and, overall, to a serious acceptance that the conditions for encouraging good teaching must also be provided.

New faculty

The purpose of the New Faculty sub-committee was to make recommendations on those processes that

affect the recruitment, selection, and integration of new faculty into the College.

(Miami-Dade, 1987–88)

Miami-Dade Community College is faced, like many other colleges, with the challenge of recruiting new faculty with the knowledge, skills and attitudes to match its own mission and goals. It needs, therefore, effective, efficient and goal oriented recruitment policies and practices. Having surveyed faculty and staff, the sub-committee concluded that current practices varied by campus, by department and by position. It therefore set about attempting to standardize its recruitment practices.

One interesting feature of the sub-committee's work was a faculty orientation (induction) programme in 1988 for all new full-time faculty regardless of experience or previous association with the college. It recommended a separate budget for the programme and the establishment of 'The New Faculty Orientation Committee', composed of staff development directors from each campus and a representative from the college's Human Resources Department, to plan, conduct, evaluate and modify the programme. Apart from being informed about the college, new faculty need time to adjust to their new roles and

> to feel welcome, to develop collegial relationships and a sense of belonging, and to identify with the college and its faculty.
>
> (Miami-Dade, January 1989a)

The new 1988 programme stated four main goals:

- To acquaint new faculty with information on Miami-Dade that will aid them in undertaking their responsibilities.
- To enable new faculty to identify with Miami-Dade and feel a sense of belonging.
- To pass on the Miami-Dade value system to new faculty.
- To prepare new faculty to assume the professional responsibilities of their new roles.

> (Miami-Dade *Orientation Program Brochure 1988*)

These goals were to be achieved through a five-day pre-service orientation programme which included information about the college, campus and department, the teaching/learning environment and departmental expectations of faculty; monthly campus meetings to allow for discussion and the introduction of new information about college services and the teaching/learning process; day-to-day support through a mentor system; additional staff development activities; and a faculty handbook.

The sub-committee had surveyed previous new faculty and had based their new orientation programme on such findings as:

- Professional satisfaction was often provided by their interactions and experiences with students.
- Almost half of the new faculty wanted to learn more about teaching and learning strategies.

- The most frequent source of stress was class load (class size and number of preparations) with over half saying that the teaching load was 'overwhelming', 'excessive', 'astonishing' or 'heavy'.

(Miami-Dade, January 1989a, pp. 3–4)

The sub-committee recommended that:

new teachers should have a maximum of about six hours of teaching per week during their first term in order to aid the orientation process. (All things being equal, new teachers would be expected to teach up to 15 hours per week in their second term.)

The Faculty Mentor Program may also be briefly described. Each new teacher would be provided with his/her own mentor. First, mentors are expected to:

- Review course objectives and departmental information on courses.
- Review teaching strategies for specific units.
- Invite new faculty members to sit in on student advisement sessions (tutorials).
- Provide orientation to surroundings (on and off campus based on responsibilities).
- Provide 'Helpful Hints' to the new teacher to help make daily activities go smoothly.
- Help new faculty anticipate problem areas.
- Have lunch with new faculty member.
- Be a comprehensive resource on curriculum planning, presentations, class management, student motivation, and student evaluation.
- Accompany new faculty member to Faculty Senate meeting.
- Schedule meeting with new faculty member on weekly basis (1 hour).
- Contact faculty in department to encourage them to invite new faculty member to sit in on their classes.
- Complete training on classroom observation and be available to sit in on new faculty member's classes and give feedback to faculty member (focus on content and teaching style and strategies).
- Personally introduce the new faculty member to all other department members and to key resource/service personnel on campus.
- Provide advice, direction and encouragement.
- Attend a reception for new faculty and introduce new faculty member to those attending.
- Look for all opportunities to make the new faculty member feel welcome.

Desirable qualities for mentors were listed as:

Willingness to be a mentor.
Nominated.
Experience in the college.
Current knowledge in subject area.
Personal warmth.

Empathy.
Excellence in working with students.
Good communication.
Flexible.
Resourceful.
Good sense of humour.
Ability to listen.
Available.

Mentors complete a training programme which focuses on the helping relationship, clarifying the specific relationships between the mentor and the new faculty member and the mentor and the chairperson. Some mentors are also trained in classroom observation. Mentors are also paid a flat fee of $800 to recognize and reward their work.

The Faculty Mentor Program is regularly evaluated through feedback elicited from new faculty, chairpersons and the mentors themselves. Evaluations have been very positive.

The teaching and learning environment

Miami-Dade has long since realized that high-quality teaching can hardly be provided in a low-quality environment. The Teaching/Learning Environment Sub-committee was created in order mainly 'to improve the quality of service and to create some connections between faculty and support areas in order to improve teaching and learning' (Miami-Dade, April 1988b). The sub-committee identified 30 support services within M-DCC and interviewed their heads in order 'to define each service as it relates to teaching/learning and to identify successes and problems' (ibid.). These interviews revealed a desire to increase communication between the support services and rest of the college, to improve the quality of services and 'to bring services into greater congruence with the teaching/learning mission' (ibid.). Faculty were also surveyed in order to define their perceptions of and relations to the various support services.

The final report of the sub-committee stressed M-DCC's function as a teaching institution but noted that 'it is often the perception of teaching faculty that conditions in the classroom are not consistent with this teaching/learning priority' (ibid.). Faculty complaints about equipment and about clerical, audio-visual or caretaking support showed the need to achieve congruency between what the college says it values and what it demonstrates it values in its support services. It recommended therefore that 'The President should guarantee that supporting teaching/learning is the first priority in the budget decisions at all levels' (ibid.). The sub-committee also recommended that every service area should establish, in collaboration with faculty, a set of goals related to teaching/learning as well as a procedure to evaluate their achievement. A college-wide retreat of selected faculty and heads of support services helped in this process of collaboration and brought about more effective communications between services and campuses. Plans for service area staff training were also submitted by each vice-president: 'training should be mandatory so that everyone understands the priority of the College, the predominance of the teaching/learning mission, and how that emphasis effects all of our behaviours on our jobs' (ibid.).

What is most remarkable about this aspect of the project is that faculty and support service staff have been brought together to collaborate in a college-wide attempt to examine and improve the overall teaching/learning milieu. It is as if the college itself has become one immense quality circle in order to focus its faculty and staff on its main function – the provision of quality teaching and learning for its students. The project director has pointed out that 'classrooms also make a statement about teaching and learning' (Jenrette, 1989) and as such must come into the same kind of user-evaluation process that, for example, good hotels operate to get feedback on the services they provide. This could also involve service staff being assigned to, and made responsible for, particular rooms so that a quality environment could be more effectively monitored and achieved, for the overall benefit of students and teachers particularly. It would be true to say, however, that a proper system of user evaluation for classrooms has yet to be established.

Other developments in the teaching/learning project

Three new sub-committees were added during 1987/88 which increased the number of Miami-Dade personnel directly involved in the project to over 50. The Classroom Feedback sub-committee was created in order 'to make recommendations on classroom feedback as a technique to improve teaching and learning' (Miami-Dade, 1987–88). The college collaborated with the University of Miami to develop for its own teachers a postgraduate course on classroom feedback entitled 'Workshop on Education Analysis and Appraisal of Learning Processes in Higher Education', a course which was piloted in 1988–89. A newsletter was also produced highlighting feedback techniques in use by M-DCC faculty. The major goal of the course is to develop higher education faculty who are reflective and self-assessing teachers with 70 per cent of the course content devoted to an analysis of the learning process and formative assessment (University of Miami, 1988). (The required course text is K.P. Cross and T.A. Angelo (1988) *Classroom Assessment Techniques: A Handbook for Faculty*, Ann Arbor, Michigan: NCRIPTAL). A project newsletter distributed to all college staff made clear that the sub-committee was most interested in classroom feedback as a means of sharing constructive information between students and faculty about the improvement of teaching and learning (Miami-Dade, January 1989b).

The sub-committee also recommended, amongst other things, that each campus should have a resource centre to assist faculty with classroom research or feedback, that staff development days should be set aside to enable faculty to broaden their knowledge about the use of classroom feedback and that the postgraduate course should be developed in a modular format to provide learning opportunities for individuals to take particular course segments. All of these recommendations were accepted and have been implemented.

The Learning to Learn sub-committee was established to explore student performance and to make recommendations on the support faculty might need to improve teaching and learning. Examples of the factors to be explored include student learning styles and cultural background. Again, M-DCC collaborated with the University of Miami to develop a postgraduate course for its own teachers entitled 'Effective Teaching and Learning in Higher Education' which was piloted in 1989.

The Faculty Advancement sub-committee undertook to explore current M-DCC practices and to make recommendations relating to faculty evaluation and the institutional reward system. The system for performance review is intended to

- Define performance criteria (of staff as teachers, librarians, counsellors, etc.) as per the M-DCC Faculty Excellence document.
- Assist professional growth rather than quantify levels of performance or make ratings.
- Establish an appeals procedure.
- Focus on the main professional responsibilities of faculty.
- Involve faculty control in establishing procedures for performance review.
- Require extensive training for department chairs in the process of performance review.

(Miami-Dade, March 1989, p. 7)

A similar proposal for continuing contract (that is for teachers who wish to secure tenure) will require faculty to develop and maintain a performance portfolio and will provide training for all faculty in the preparation of performance portfolios. By way of comparison, the President of Harvard University announced in 1991 that he was planning to introduce teaching portfolios to document the teaching skills of Harvard's teaching faculty (*Chronicle of Higher Education*, 8 May 1991, p. A15). Also, at Miami-Dade, a new proposed system for promotion was to be based on 'consistent quality of performance as outlined in the Faculty Excellence Document'.

Another programme which has aroused considerable interest in the American higher education world is the M-DCC 'endowed chair program', the purpose of which is to reward faculty excellence. To be eligible, a faculty member must complete six years of full-time faculty status at M-DCC and provide documentary evidence of excellent performance as a faculty member for the immediately preceding three consecutive years, the criteria being based on the Faculty Excellence document. Usually, the chairs will be awarded for three years but the award could be extended. Each chair holder will receive an annual award of $5000 plus $2500 for expenses to be used at the faculty member's discretion. The $10 million required for endowing 100

Teaching Chairs is being raised by the Endowed Teaching Chair Campaign co-chaired by two M-DCC Foundation Board members who have each personally agreed to endow a chair and to attract additional chairs from the local community:

> 100 holders of endowed chairs will serve as a continuing reminder and reaffirmation to colleagues within the institution and to the larger community as well that academic excellence begins with excellence in teaching, promotes the improvement of student quality, and enhances the opportunity to succeed for the students and thus for the institution.
>
> (AACJC, April/May 1989, p. 63)

Conclusion

The Miami-Dade Teaching/Learning Project is an excellent case of a re-educative change strategy (see Chin and Benne, 1976) in which the clients themselves (M-DCC teaching faculty) are being helped and encouraged to grow as professional teachers in order to improve their abilities to provide better learning for their students. The Teaching/ Learning Project has sought to involve the whole college – its trustees, administrators, faculty, staff and students – in a series of explorations and innovations designed to improve the quality of teaching and learning at Miami-Dade. It has sought their commitment through sub-committees, lunches, conversations, retreats, surveys, workshops, courses, the production of reports and videotapes, conference presentations, consultancies and visits. It has attempted to seek change by examining its own values with regard to teaching and learning and by establishing a consensus on faculty excellence. It has taken an action learning or action research approach to change through its collaboration with the University of Miami and with other external consultants. The college has shown a remarkable willingness to resource the change process through its appointment of a project director, through its staffing of the subcommittees and through its use of external consultants and external facilities. It has also benefited from the overall leadership of its president who has shown from the outset a determination to see that the project makes a real impact on the college: If we're not ready, we won't do it. We're going to take as long as it takes to do this well.

(Miami-Dade, 1987–88)

Indeed, without the strong leadership provided by the college president and his Board of Trustees, the project could hardly have had the impact it has already had both locally and nationally nor could there have been any real hope of endowing 100 teaching chairs.

Overall, the Miami-Dade Teaching/Learning Project serves as an important example of institutional change which is remarkable in a higher education context in that it has focused on the improvement of teaching and learning. It has made teaching explicitly important through its mission statements, values statement, statement on excellence, its newsletters and its various workshops and programmes. It has proposed and implemented new systems for the selection, orientation, appraisal, training and promotion of staff, all based on the notion of teaching excellence. That some of these issues remain controversial and contested is hardly surprising. But there is no sense of an authoritarian power-coercive thrust (see Chin and Benne, 1976) to this series of changes nor to the strategies employed. In fact, many of the documents emphasize democratic faculty control over the procedures to be adopted and they require senior staff such as departmental chairs to be evaluated by faculty and to be trained in the various processes involved.

If the Miami-Dade Teaching/Learning Project succeeds in its three main aims of improving teaching/learning quality, making teaching more professionally rewarding and making teaching and learning the focal point of college decision-making, then it will undoubtedly enhance the college's already high national and international reputation. It will also, by actively involving its local community in the project, further demonstrate a commitment to community building and community service which is such a significant feature of American higher education. What Miami-Dade seeks to achieve is what all American higher education seeks – 'the more people who can be persuaded to enrol in a college or university, the better' (Trow, 1989, p. 5).

But Miami-Dade, through its Teaching/Learning Project, also seeks what it has often called 'access with excellence': excellence in both teaching and learning. And through this project in particular Miami-Dade has demonstrated that it meets most, if not all, of Peters and Waterman's 'excellent attributes for any organization' by, for example,

- Having a bias for action – by improving teaching/learning through a major, well resourced project.
- Staying close to the customer – by listening to students, support staff, faculty, administrators, trustees, and the community at large.
- Being autonomous and entrepreneurial – by owning its project, by taking risks, and by seeking funds.
- Seeking productivity through people – by showing respect for its faculty as professional teachers and for all staff as the source of a quality college environment.
- Being value driven – by re-examining its central beliefs and values as a teaching institution.

(see Peters and Waterman, 1982)

However, having described the project as an outstanding example of institutional commitment to teaching and learning I must also enter a note of caution. The project has, inevitably, benefited from the Hawthorne effect – the stimulation of continuous change brought about by the adoption of new aims, new values, new structures and new processes. A visitor to the college soon becomes aware of the buoyancy of its staff and their enthusiastic sense of involvement in an important set of tasks. But the project has yet to be formally evaluated: it has yet to demonstrate clearly and thoroughly that it has succeeded in achieving its three main aims of improving the quality of teaching and learning, of making teaching more professionally rewarding and of making teaching and learning the focal point of college decision-making. Also, despite (or even because of) the Teaching/Learning Project, Miami-Dade will continue to be judged against other criteria such as: the proportion of its students who transfer to universities; whether or not the college provides an effective education for minority and disadvantaged students; and whether or not the college meets the broad range of educational and training needs of its local community.

Overall, though, even if Miami-Dade were to be judged in the Warnock Report's terms, it would nevertheless be regarded as successful: it has actually specified and implemented numerous initiatives designed to enhance and sustain its teaching quality; and it has clearly demonstrated its commitment to excellence in teaching and learning through a well-resourced and long-term major project.

References

AACJC (1988) *Building Communities: A Vision for a New Century.* A report of the Commission on the Future of Community Colleges. Washington, DC, American Association of Community and Junior Colleges.

AACJC (1989) 'The Teaching/Learning Project at Miami-Dade Community College' and 'The Presidential Blue Ribbon Committee for the Endowed Teaching Chair Program'. *Community, Technical, and Junior College Journal*, April/May, 59(5), 62–4.

Chin, R. and Benne, K.D. (1976) 'General strategies for effecting changes in human systems' in W.C. Bennis *et al.* (eds) *The Planning of Change.* London, Holt, Rinehart & Winston, pp. 22–45.

College Times (1989) 'Los Angeles, Miami-Dade, Orange Coast, Top 1988 Enrollment'. *The Community, Technical, and Junior College Times*, March, p. 1.

Jenrette, M. (1989) Interview with G.F. Badley at Miami-Dade Community College, New World Campus, Miami, Florida, 17 March 1989.

Lukenbill, J.D. and McCabe, R.H. (1978) *General Education in a Changing Society.* Dubuque, Iowa, Kendall/Hunt Publishing Company.

Miami-Dade (1983–85) *Catalog 1983–85*, Volume XXI.

Miami-Dade (1986–87) 'The Teaching/Learning Project' Summary Report (year one).

Miami-Dade (1987–88) 'The Teaching/Learning Project' Summary Report (year one).

Miami-Dade (undated) *Teaching/Learning Values At Miami-Dade Community College.*

Miami-Dade (1988a) *Report of the Faculty Excellence Subcommittee (Draft 3)*, 18 April 1988.

Miami-Dade (1988b) *Teaching/Learning Project Bulletin*, April 2(a).

Miami-Dade (1988) *Faculty Excellence at Miami-Dade Community College*, October.

Miami-Dade (1988) *Orientation Program Brochure 1988.*

Miami-Dade (1989a) *New Faculty Subcommittee Recommendations*, January.

Miami-Dade (1989b) *Teaching/Learning Project Bulletin*, January 3(6).

Miami-Dade (1989) *Faculty Advancement Subcommittee Draft Proposals*, 6 March.

Moses, I. (1985) 'High quality teaching in a university: identification and description'. *Studies in Higher Education*, 10(3), 301–13.

PCFC (1990) *Teaching Quality: Report of the Committee of Enquiry Appointed by the Council* (The Warnock Report). The Polytechnics and Colleges Funding Council.

Peters, T.J. and Waterman, R.H. (1982) *In Search of Excellence*. London, Harper and Row.

Roueche, J.E. and Baker, G.A. (1985) 'The success connection creating a culture of excellence'. *AACJC Journal*, August/September pp. 20–6.

Trow, M. (1989) 'American higher education past, present and future'. *Studies in Higher Education*, 14(1).

University of Miami (1988) University of Miami, *Workshop in Education Analysis and Appraisal of Learning Processes in Higher Education*: Draft 2, School of Education, University of Miami, 19 April 1988.

3

Reflection through Action: Peer Tutoring as Service Learning*

Sinclair Goodlad and John Hughes

Introduction

Service learning, or study service (Goodlad, 1982), the process through which students combine their personal learning with work which is of direct and tangible benefit to other people, offers higher education institutions the opportunity to combine their traditional task of stimulating academic reflection with activity which meets the current political imperative of immediately visible usefulness. The thesis of this chapter is that the inherent instability of service learning will only be overcome if the fundamental components of effective curricula – attention to theory, practice, society, individual – are held together by concentration of students' attention onto specific problems. One of the key tasks of facilitators of service learning is to identify problems as the focus of students' study which lie at the heart of existing academic disciplines. This chapter argues that only in this way will effective, reciprocal alliances become possible between universities and community action agencies, and concentrates on peer tutoring to suggest how some of these objects may be achieved. In this context we consider the following: the scheme of peer tutoring and its location within a matrix of concerns which constitute effective curriculum design; the distinction between the functioning of *institutions* and the role of *individuals*; some of the questions arising from the activity which can aid academic reflection.

Peer tutoring: the 'Pimlico Connection'

Tutoring (the activity by which one person instructs another) in one form and another has been practised at many levels of education for centuries

* The basic thesis of this paper was developed for a keynote address given by Sinclair Goodlad (under the title 'Uniting Service and Learning: new pedagogies for students') at the Sixth Annual International Conference of the Partnership for Service-Learning, Phoenix, Arizona, February 1989.

(Gordon and Gordon, 1990). By contrast, *peer* tutoring, the system of instruction in which learners help each other and learn by teaching, was most comprehensively developed by Andrew Bell and Joseph Lancaster in the late eighteenth century. (Tutors and those tutored are 'peers' in that they are all still studying in formal education.) In recent years, it has been developed in the United States as a form of enrichment for the programme of study of both tutors and tutees. For example, Cahalan and Farris (1990) report that college-sponsored programmes involving college students tutoring elementary and secondary students were found in 29 per cent of all two- and four-year colleges and universities. Of 3212 institutions, 921 ran at least one programme. Nationally, in 1987–88, an estimated 1700 programmes involved some 71 000 college students serving 240 000 elementary and secondary students. (Whitman (1988) offers a conveniently compact review of some schemes, mostly in the USA, within higher education.)

In Israel, the PERACH project, initiated in 1974, deploys university and college students as tutors to needy children all over Israel. At present, more than 12 000 tutors are active annually (Fresko and Carmeli, 1990).

In the United Kingdom, schemes involving students as tutors in schools are now run by the following further and higher education institutions:

Birmingham University	Loughborough University
Brighton Polytechnic	Newcastle-upon-Tyne University
Cambridge University	North London Polytechnic
Central London Polytechnic	Nottingham Polytechnic
City Polytechnic	Oxford University
City University	Paisley College
City & East London College	Polytechnic of Wales
East London Polytechnic	Queen Mary & Westfield College,
Hackney College	London
Hammersmith & West London	Reading University
College	Salford University
Hatfield Polytechnic	Sheffield University
Imperial College, London	South Bank Polytechnic
King's College, London	Strathclyde University
Kingston College of Further	Tower Hamlets College
Education	University College London
Kingston Polytechnic	University of East Anglia
Leicester University	Warwick University
London School of Economics	Wirral Metropolitan College

We expect the number of institutions involved to rise to over 50 by October 1992.

Some of these schemes are being supported by British Petroleum (BP) through its *Aiming for a College Education* programme (see British Petroleum, 1991; Hughes, 1991a).

How do such schemes contribute to the education of those who take part? In the peer tutoring scheme known as 'The Pimlico Connection' (upon which many of the BP-sponsored schemes are modelled), students from Imperial College, London, help to teach science, mathematics, and technology in local schools. Between 1975, when the scheme began, and the end of the last academic year (1991) some 966 tutors have given over 22 000 hours of instruction to over 11 800 pupils.

Research carried out on 633 tutors, 5629 pupils, and 186 teachers between 1979–89 and 1990–91 indicates that all parties to the arrangement benefit. For example:

- 63 per cent of pupils find lessons easier to follow.
- 70 per cent of teachers find lessons more enjoyable with tutors present.
- 95 per cent of student tutors get useful practice in communicating scientific ideas.

Similar results have been obtained from other schemes in the UK (Beardon, 1990). 'The Pimlico Connection' is described in extensive detail elsewhere (Goodlad and Hirst, 1989; chapter 5), so we will sketch here only the salient features of the scheme.

Each Wednesday afternoon (a time free from normal laboratory and lecture classes), some 100 student volunteers from Imperial College go to neighbouring schools (both primary schools and secondary schools) to help with the lessons. They do not take entire classes by themselves – that is to say, they are not teachers. Rather, they act as tutors, helping the teachers who remain in charge of the planning and operation of the syllabus and who are legally, morally and educationally responsible for the class at all times.

A typical class could be a Science class (say Year 9 in the National Curriculum) in a large inner-city comprehensive school. Right from the beginning of the project, teachers asked for help with these and other classes for the following reasons:

1. Many pupils have little interest in Science, seeing it as a dry, specialized subject with little apparent relevance to their daily lives. In large classes (up to 30 pupils per class), it is not possible for the teachers to give enough individual attention to pupils to break down the resistance that they show or to give them the detailed help that they need.
2. The rate of truancy from Science and other subjects can be very high. The sympathetic help of another young person can help to provide that extra stimulus to the pupil to reduce selective truancy.
3. Science in the National Curriculum relies heavily on learning by experiment. However, in areas of high social deprivation in inner-city schools in classes with pupils who might have considerable learning difficulties, it becomes difficult for pupils to perform experiments successfully or make deductions from them. Because supervision of large groups is difficult, before the arrival of the tutors, some classes had been given only very limited access to experimental apparatus – which they tended to break or mishandle.

4. At the end of the third year (Year 9), pupils might opt for single or double certificate Science as part of the National Curriculum in Year 10. This choice will be important in post-16 career possibilities as single Science GCSE is often insufficient for many academically-based courses. Teachers hope that, through their personal enthusiasm for the subject, the student tutors may perhaps persuade pupils to continue studying Science.
5. Many pupils lack enthusiasm to learn; they do not see post-16 education and training as relevant to them. The assistance of, and positive role-model provided by, a student tutor can help to liberate them from this line of thinking and thus help them to gain the qualifications for entry to further and higher education.

In each year of the tutoring, students have worked with pupils of all ages and abilities from primary to A Level – but always in a mode which is a compromise between structured tutoring (in which the content is programmed or laid out in detailed steps) and unstructured tutoring (in which tutors are given a wide degree of choice in the materials they administer). Activities are often based upon work sheets or published material to guide pupils through the experiments. These sheets provide a useful intermediate mode between totally unstructured tutoring (where the lack of experience of tutors can be a weakness) and totally structured tutoring (which can be somewhat inflexible and which can diminish the value of having university students as tutors).

In some classes, teachers like the students to act as monitors, moving freely around the classroom trouble-shooting as necessary. In other classes, teachers assign tutors to work with individuals or small groups, where the students engage the pupils in discussion about the experiments they are performing, answering questions, and posing supplementary questions to guide pupils through the subject matter. Supervision of experiments is particularly useful when, as with the distillation of tar, apparatus or techniques are potentially hazardous, and where one teacher without help would be very hard pressed to see that all the pupils behaved properly.

Students are recruited from all academic departments of Imperial College. They receive a half-day training session at the beginning of the university academic year. The object of this training (apart from helping students to get to know each other) is to focus the minds of the students on the task ahead of them – progressively moving from a qualitative evocation through film or video-tape of the experience of being at school (which for some of them may be a few years distant), through a role-play simulation of the learning-experience of being a tutee, to specific advice on being a tutor. Students are given a detailed list of tutoring techniques (reproduced as appendix A of Goodlad and Hirst, 1989, and further expanded in Hughes, 1991b).

In each year of the scheme, tutoring has been limited to 15 weeks – that is the Autumn Term, and the first half of the Spring Term. This limitation on time has been designed to ensure no interruption to the service to the schools. From the second half of the Spring Term onwards, final-year students tend to be involved with job-interviews on Wednesday afternoons, and all students

Table 3.1 Pupils' opinions (years 1979–89 and 1990–91)

	Percentages of pupils responding		
Parameter	*More*	*Less*	*About the same as usual*
Interest of lessons	55	4	40
Ease of following lessons	63	4	31
Enjoyment of lessons	54	5	38
Amount of learning in lessons	54	5	38

$n = 5629$ (response rate $5629/8309 = 68\%$)

become increasingly preoccupied with examinations. The scheme has been limited to 15 weeks so that schools can rely on the presence of tutors, without the potential irritation of the scheme disintegrating by pressure on students to be elsewhere.

Evaluation

In their open-ended responses to questionnaires, pupils have been very appreciative of the scheme. Also, there has been astonishing similarity from year to year in pupils' responses to closed-ended questionnaires. Table 3.1 gives findings for the years 1979–89 and 1990–91 for which we have detailed data.

Student tutors likewise report a variety of types of benefit from the scheme as Table 3.2 illustrates. Many features of this table merit comment; however, we will note only five:

1. First, as with most forms of service learning (the process through which students combine personal learning with work which is of direct and tangible benefit to other people), 92 per cent of students benefit by feeling that they are doing something useful with what they have already learned.
2. Secondly, and perhaps most important for the learning which students achieve from their service learning, some 95 per cent benefit by getting practice in the simple communication of scientific ideas (greatly 55 per cent; somewhat 40 per cent).
3. Thirdly, again an important element of their education, some 87 per cent benefit by gaining insight into how other people perceive their subjects (greatly 35 per cent; somewhat 52 per cent).
4. Fourthly, some 82 per cent benefit by getting to know something about people with different social backgrounds to their own (greatly 39 per cent; somewhat 43 per cent).
5. Fifthly, although tutoring can be demanding, it is noteworthy that 62 per cent find that it does not interfere with their studies.

Table 3.2   Percentages of students indicating that they thought they had benefited from being a tutor in the ways listed (years 1979–89 and 1990–91)

Parameter	Greatly	Somewhat	Not at all	Not sure
By reinforcing your knowledge of some aspect of your subject?	3	38	56	3
By getting practice in the simple communication of scientific ideas?	55	40	2	2
By gaining insight into how other people perceive your subject?	35	52	10	3
By increasing your self-confidence?	17	59	18	6
By getting to know something about people with a different social background to your own?	39	43	14	4
By feeling that you were doing something useful with what you had already learned?	49	43	6	4
Did the tutoring interfere with your college studies?	1	29	62	7

$n = 633$ (response rate 633/918 = 69%)

Table 3.3   Percentages of teacher opinions (years 1979–89)

With tutors lessons were:	Easier to handle	More difficult to handle	About the same as usual
	63	6	26
Teaching was:	More enjoyable	Less enjoyable	About the same as usual
	70	2	23
Pupils seemed to learn:	More than usual	Less than usual	About as much as usual
	69	3	25

Teacher responses: $n = 186$ (response rate 186/301 = 62%)

Just to complete the picture, a brief word on the opinions of school teachers about the peer tutoring is shown in Table 3.3.

It is all very well for student tutors to have interesting and valuable experiences: crucial is the fact that pupils seem to benefit from it. However, equally important from an operational point of view is the overall satisfaction of teachers with the arrangement. If a service learning arrangement is not congenial to them, it will not survive for long. In this regard, it is noteworthy

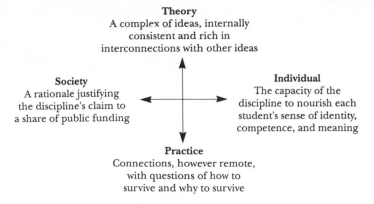

Theory
A complex of ideas, internally
consistent and rich in
interconnections with other ideas

Society
A rationale justifying
the discipline's claim to
a share of public funding

Individual
The capacity of the
discipline to nourish each
student's sense of identity,
competence, and meaning

Practice
Connections, however remote,
with questions of how to
survive and why to survive

Figure 3.1　Elements of curriculum design

that the majority of teachers found lessons easier to handle and more enjoyable, and felt that their pupils were learning more than usual.

The place of tutoring within curriculum design

The model for curriculum design in service learning which we commend here seeks to maintain a balance between a number of concerns which constitute sound education. Because the model is developed at length elsewhere (Goodlad, 1988), we recapitulate the elements of it only briefly here. For heuristic purposes, the model separates out elements which in practice are interwoven in complex ways. For example, all practice implies theory, and all theories have implications for practice. Likewise, individuals are perceived through the social roles they inhabit, and society is an accumulation of social institutions through which individuals relate to each other. The point of the model is to propose a *balance* of concerns as the object of curriculum design. The elements are shown in Figure 3.1.

Current political pressures on higher education institutions demand that issues representing the interests of society, individual, and practice should find a place in the curriculum. Service learning in general, and tutoring in particular, seem well equipped to meet these demands by addressing readily identifiable social problems in practical ways. What may be less obvious is that they can also nourish the fundamental business of universities, that is the articulation and elaboration of the theory on which academic disciplines are based, which in turn leads to new forms of perception and concern. To ensure the success of a service learning programme, the attention to logistics is paramount (Goodlad and Hirst, 1989; chapter 7); but to ground service learning in *theory* is, in our judgement, the really fundamental issue which will ultimately determine its success or failure in the long term.

One of the principal justifications of service learning is that it is work in which students combine study leading to the award of an academic qualification with some form of direct practical service to the community. Students do not compete with paid professionals; rather, they do *work which would not otherwise be done*. If service learning is effective in this regard, it has a legitimate claim to public funding.

Most students who take part in service learning are volunteers. Presumably, they would not present themselves if the capacity of the activity to nourish each individual's sense of identity, competence, and meaning was not at least potentially present. One of the aims of designers of service learning placements is to ensure that the work done does indeed succeed in this regard. However, and recognizing the positive reactions of the Imperial College students to their tutoring, we will not dwell on this aspect of curriculum design.

Again, most service learning is intimately connected with practice (making and doing) – and tutoring in particular is directly concerned with questions of how to survive and why to survive, being as often as not a method of conveying the basic life-skills of literacy and numeracy to tutees.

The question which service learning facilitators must, however, address if they are to persuade colleagues in academic disciplines to take service learning seriously, is how the service learning meshes with the *theory* which it is the proper business of universities to explore.

This matter is one of such importance that we recall Walter Moberly's observation that a university is a 'thought organization' not a 'will organization' and its aim is understanding rather than action.

> It is a society for the pursuit of knowledge and not for the promotion of this cause or the prevention of that abuse.
>
> (Moberly, 1949, p. 39)

If one takes the view, as we do, that the effectiveness of institutions derives from a certain specialization of function, one would wish to hold to the perception that universities should indeed, as Moberly recommends, concentrate their *institutional* attention on highly specific matters. That is to say, *qua institutions*, they (or rather the departments within them) should rightly be concerned with understanding the underlying patterns and causes of things. As *institutions*, they are not, and should not be, involved in the business of sorting out muddles on the ground, except incidentally when, by deepening understanding of fundamental physical or social processes, they offer insights which lead to action. Minogue (1973, p. 99) offers as an example study of the behaviour of cells where the solution of an academic problem *may* lead to the solution of a practical one, namely by providing a cure for cancer.

However, it is fundamental to our understanding of what constitutes sound learning, and a reason justifying service learning as a method of study, that *individuals* cannot, and for the sake of their mental and spiritual sanity should not, distance themselves from the world of action. To achieve a balanced education, individuals need to move in and out of theory organizations and

Table 3.4 Differences in institutional emphases and intent

Theory (of academic agency)	Practice	Action agency
Nutrition	Cooking	Restaurant
Engineering	Construction	Factory
Theology	Worship	Church
Literary Criticism	Books/Plays	Publishing/Theatre
Musicology	Performance	Conservatoire
Political Science	Politics	Government
Geography	Planning	Town Planning Department
History	Recording/Interpretation	Museum
Philosophy	Concept Clarification	Administration

action agencies. Table 3.4 indicates the appropriate division of labour with the university being, in each case, the place where theory is promoted. This list emphasizes the important differences of *institutional* emphasis and intent between academic agencies and action agencies although in practice (as in a medical school in a hospital) the boundaries are often blurred. The 'theory agencies' are university departments, and in the parlance of Becher and Kogan (1980), the 'basic units' through which the enterprise of higher education is organized. To achieve a balanced education, *individual students* need to move between these types of agencies. What is crucial is that one should not expect the *agencies themselves* to lose their clarity of purpose.

One of the tasks of a service learning facilitator is to help students, and the academic tutors, to see the range of possible issues for theoretical meditation arising directly from service learning opportunities, and to help students to manage the transitions from one to another.

Learning opportunities from peer tutoring

To illustrate the fertility of placements in service learning for generating theoretical questions, let us revert once more to peer tutoring. Some, but not all, of the students who take part in the 'Pimlico Connection' attend a course on the 'Communication of Scientific Ideas' (taught by Sinclair Goodlad) as a Humanities option (usually accounting for 10 per cent of the academic credit in the year in which a student takes it) within a degree programme. In place of one of the coursework essays, they are allowed to write an analytical report on some aspect of their tutoring. Frequently, in tutorials and seminars, students ask: 'Well, I can report what I did; but what analytic ideas should I pursue?' Our technique is to use what we call the 'Gestalt Fix' on them, namely, to ask them to think about the tutoring they have done and then to say the first words or phrases which come into their heads. (The notion here is that the figure/ground perception that the question elicits will indicate the *current* configuration in which the students' ideas are located. This will give a frame into and onto which other ideas can be woven.) Typically the words the students utter are: 'noise'; 'enthusiasm'; 'chaos'; 'satisfaction'; 'bad discipline'; 'friendly'; 'mixed ability'; 'teachers under siege'; 'frustration'; and so forth. Our response to such suggestions is: 'Fine, you have the beginnings of an essay!'

The key task of academic disciplines is to bring order into the chaos of individual perceptions. By identifying through the 'Gestalt Fix' their principal *concerns* students are offered the opportunity for academic engagement.

Take a typical tutoring scene from the 'Pimlico Connection': eager student (motivated, enthusiastic with a high level of success in the education system) trying to interest wriggling pupil (inner-city child who does not see the relevance of education and whose family has no history of post-16 involvement) in some aspect of Science. The situation bristles with potent questions. The basic question – of why Science does not seem to appeal to large numbers of pupils in inner-city schools – offers points of purchase for many disciplines. We will not attempt a complete cut and shuffle of disciplines, but rather highlight a few of the questions which might arise for the students and to which the disciplines (italicized in parentheses) offer fruitful approaches:

1. What aspect of Science is being studied? Facts? Principles? Processes? From all the infinite variety of observations made by scientists, and all the procedures for making them, and theories to account for them, why have these particular ones been chosen for special attention by pupils on this day, in this school, in this place? How do these questions of Science relate either to the fundamental structures of the discipline (that scientists might wish to pass on to others) or to the world picture which students and pupils use in practice to make sense of things? (*Science, Philosophy, Sociology*)
2. Do these studies, and should they, relate in any way to the chosen careers either of tutors or tutees? (*Economics, Sociology*)
3. Why is it that the offspring of professional workers are so much more successful in the UK educational system than the offspring of other social classes? Why, for example, is not the typical scheme that of a Black tutor and a White child? (*History, Sociology, Psychology, Social Psychology*)
4. Where have these people come from? What are the differential life chances of people from different backgrounds in making economic success in UK society? Should education be adapted specifically for the interests and needs of recent arrivals, who may speak languages other than English? Should there be a uniformity of cultural approach or some form of multicultural approach? (*History, Anthropology, Sociology, Literature, Economics*)
5. What other influences are at work on the pupils? Granted, as research shows, school children spent some 26 hours a week watching television compared to some 24 hours a week actually in study at school, what is the impact on their thinking of the world shown by television? If, as is often the case, they seem to have greater interest in the content of television

than in the content of their studies, could/should the content of television programmes be brought into the teaching as subject material? If not, how can teachers compete with the glamour and glitter of the rival media? Who, in any case, should determine what is studied? (*Political Science, Sociology, Psychology, Social Psychology, Economics*)

6. Where has the curriculum come from? Who controls what is done in schools and why, and with what authority? Who pays for what is done? Who determines how long pupils should stay in school? What areas of public life should be left to the marketplace and what areas should be the subject of detailed state or local political intervention? What place should the National Curriculum have in our society? (*Political Science, Anthropology, History, Sociology, Economics*)

7. If pupils seem to perform differently in their scientific studies, why is this? Are there differences in intelligence which can be separated out from differences in application, dedication, and experience? How do educational measurements differ from measurements in other spheres? (*Science, Political Science, Anthropology, History, Philosophy, Psychology, Social Psychology, Sociology*)

Locating service-learning experience within academic frameworks

The questions above pertaining to a single situation in tutoring offer fuel for a number of academic disciplines. The value of student peer tutoring as an element in teacher training is, of course, self-evident. Intending teachers need to think about such matters in depth before entering their professional careers. However, many of the issues raised by the tutoring encounter penetrate to the heart of many academic disciplines, such as history, sociology, social geography, anthropology, psychology, economics, political science, etc. and, indeed, science itself (and its numerous sub-disciplines).

Prima facie, peer tutoring may seem attractive only in the area of professional development; for instance in promoting the core skills of the CBI (CBI, 1989) and BTEC's common skills (BTEC, 1991). But the professional skills encapsulate many questions which are fundamental not only to professional education but also to other types of education.

The original object of 'The Pimlico Connection' was to provide an opportunity for students of science and engineering to get realistic practice in the communication of technical information. Skill in communication is not just a frill; it is at the very core of professional practice. Whatever else professionals do, a key part of their work is that of making clear to people less well informed than the professionals the areas of their choice in technical matters. For example, doctors explain to patients that this or that mode of treatment (or none at all) is possible; the patients then have to choose what they wish to do – with or without the help and intervention of the doctor. Again, lawyers explain to their clients the ways in which the law affects the client's situation;

but the client ultimately gives instructions to the lawyer. Likewise, architects ascertain their clients' general wishes and explain the technical options (usually with drawings and/or models); the client then decides what is to be done. The fact that professionals usually go on to execute the wishes of their clients should not obscure the fact that the primary task of professionals is that of indicating to clients the grounds of the choices available to them (see chapter 1 of Goodlad, 1984).

In all professions, it is necessary for the professional person to communicate ideas and information simply and effectively to other people. In some professional schools (in Engineering, for example), specific instruction in communication skills is included, through report-writing exercises and so forth. Such work is often tedious for the students concerned and the reports they write are boring for the faculty to read. Communication strictly defined, means 'sharing'. One cannot communicate unless one has something one wishes to share. Most students know how dispiriting it can be to write reports for their professors when they know that the professor knows everything that they, the students, could possibly write. Communication exercises are, however, transformed when they are done for real. That is why experiential learning in general (i.e. learning from experiences outside the classroom), and service learning in particular, is so attractive to students, for they work with actual clients and have the interest and responsibility of writing reports/making statements which someone positively wants to read or listen to. Similarly, intending professionals can get tremendous stimulus from trying to explain technical ideas to other people in peer-tutoring schemes. Many of the Imperial College students who have taken part in the 'Pimlico Connection' have had no intention of becoming teachers; but they nevertheless have greatly valued and enjoyed the experience of explaining things to other people.

At the basic level of developing communication skills, the experience of communicating relatively low-level technical knowledge can be more challenging than explaining complex information to people who already have a highly-developed framework of ideas in which to 'locate' it. To explain ideas to non-specialists requires the communicator: to *build* a framework of ideas into which new material can be placed; to respond to the needs of a specific audience; to decide the specific purpose of communication; to organize ideas in some sort of structure; to choose the order of presentation; to know the precise use of simple words; and so on. All these communication skills can readily be practised in peer tutoring. What is often overlooked is that with minimal prompting, students can be invited to think about the *framework of ideas itself* – in short, to confront the theoretical foundations of their academic disciplines by testing, through their essay writing, the capacity of the disciplines to illuminate the situations that the students have met.

The new pedagogies for students which service learning (of which peer tutoring is but one example) require are basically ones which *work upwards and outwards from specific problems to the co-ordinating concepts of disciplines*, rather than pedagogies which start with setting out the concepts and then allow students to find examples. An analogy is that of teaching map-reading. One approach is to drop students in the countryside and let them figure out where they are, and thereby determine how useful or otherwise the map is. A contrasting approach is to have a lecture course on maps (the history of map-making, the design and printing of maps, theory and practice of notation, and so forth) and then, when the students have passed some examinations in cartography, to let them loose. The art of curriculum planning in service learning is to know how much of which technique to use when. To drop students into (possibly hostile) unfamiliar terrain with no map at all is simply irresponsible; to talk them through every detail of the map before they can have a look round is likely to bore them and to miss opportunities for learning. Some interweaving of thought and action is called for.

Although tutoring, like all service learning, must treat the needs of clients as primary, our judgement is that the *academic orientation* of service learning activities for facilitators and students must be from detail towards the co-ordinating ideas of academic disciplines.

In *Educating the Reflective Practitioner*, Donald Schön (1987, p. 3) identified a crisis of confidence in professional knowledge:

> In the varied topography of professional practice, there is a high, hard ground overlooking a swamp. On the high ground, manageable problems lend themselves to solution through the application of research-based theory and technique. In the swampy lowland, messy, confusing problems defy technical solution. The irony of this situation is that the problems of the high ground tend to be relatively unimportant to individuals or society at large, however great their technical interest may be, while in the swamp lie the problems of greatest human concern. The practitioner must choose. Shall he remain on the high ground where he can solve relatively unimportant problems according to prevailing standards of rigor, or shall he descend to the swamp of important problems and nonrigorous inquiry?

In much higher education, abstraction is equated with virtue; the high, hard ground of theory is seen as the proper concern of universities. 'Marsh' problems are shunned. The reasons are well known: in short, 'international visibility' is difficult to achieve from the marsh. For better or worse, most academics are rewarded for the outward and visible signs of their activity, not for the inward and spiritual qualities that give rise to them. The principal tangible currency is publication, and the safest form of currency-minting is that done within very strict confines where principles of exclusion and concentration lead to clarity of vision, and where the process of assay (peer review) can work effectively.

There is nothing intrinsically wrong with this process. It leads to great competitiveness in universities and, at best, the emphasis on refinement of concept leads to very fruitful intellectual insights, and many practical benefits from even the most seemingly esoteric pursuits (for example, solid-state physics). The institutional pressure on academics to publish is not, however, very conducive to involvement with service learning.

Two particular, and by now well-tried, modes of study are very effective for drawing out the disciplinary threads from service learning placement-experiences: problem-based learning and project work.

Problem-based learning has achieved its most spectacular successes in medical education (see, for example, Barrows and Tamblyn, 1980; Neufeld and Chong, 1984), although examples are now to be found in an increasing number of disciplines (see, for example, Boud, 1985). It is noteworthy that medical degree courses based on problem-based learning have been most successfully developed in *new* medical schools such as MacMaster in Canada, Maastricht in Holland, and Newcastle New South Wales in Australia. That is to say, a new *institution* has had to be invented to contain the new idea (although the General Medical Council of the United Kingdom is currently proposing that all UK medical schools implement within 10 years a core-plus-options curriculum designed around problem-based learning). There are, of course, notable efforts to establish problem-based options in conventional degree courses (see Cawley, 1989); but it is an uphill struggle. Rather than attempting to break the concrete in which existing practices are set, most innovators in problem-based education simply abandon the old, outworn structures and build new ones.

Again, project work has now become an accepted part of many forms of degree course (Goodlad, 1975); but project work that goes beyond the bounds of a single discipline is still somewhat rare. Socio-technical project work in engineering education, which was the subject of a significant initiative of the Nuffield Foundation in the 1970s (see Goodlad, 1977), has never really taken off. The socio-technical projects were of great interest to students; but faculty felt ill at ease straying from the well-worn tracks of their disciplines. Although the intention was that students should study problems in which technical questions (concerning the design of physical systems and devices) had to be disentangled from social, political, ethical and such-like issues, faculty soon started to propose projects which shunned 'marsh' issues in favour of identifiable 'technical' questions, that is those to which some sort of numerical answer could be given.

The implications of the above observations are these: new pedagogies which, like service learning, seek to unite thought and action, must, if they are to survive, recognize institutional realities. That is to say, unless we are to simply abandon the idea of universities as specialized institutions making their own uniquely important contribution to society, new pedagogies must emphasize *theory* – presenting occasions for students to reflect upon their social action with a view to discerning underlying themes, regularities, patterns, concepts, and organizing principles. Service learning facilitators, including organizers of tutoring projects, need to help students to discern in the bewildering details of their placements *the connectedness of things*. Faculty and students need to develop skill in demonstrating to colleagues how study of even the grittiest administrative detail can lead to some perception by the students of intellectual order.

Concluding observations

While actionless thought is corrupting, thoughtless action is positively dangerous. Service learning in general, and tutoring in particular, force attention back onto the fundamental aims and purposes of universities and the enduring core of most forms of higher education. If we encourage learning without regard to the context of ideas that alone give significance to that learning, we run the risk of patronizing (and under-selling) students. Service learning, as one mode of 'learning to effect', highlights the danger of our contemporary obsession with usefulness. We may be in danger of confusing means with ends, and leaving universities as ponderous candidates for 'Jim'll Fix It' badges (or perhaps Queen's Award to Industry logos) to the neglect of their longer-term concerns with intellectual pattern, order, system and meaning. In short, our developing pedagogies should retain a concern with disciplines (rather than fields) and with the fruitfulness of modes of analysis rather than an exclusive concern with the problems that those modes of analysis illuminate.

References

Barrows, H. and Tamblyn, R. (1980). *Problem-based Learning: an approach to medical education.* New York, Springer.
Beardon, T. (1990) 'Cambridge STIMULUS' in S. Goodlad and B. Hirst (eds) *Explorations in Peer Tutoring*, Chapter 5. Oxford, Basil Blackwell.
Becher, T. and Kogan, M. (1980) *Process and Structure in Higher Education.* London, Heinemann.
Boud, D. (ed.) (1985) *Problem-based Learning in Education for the Professions.* Sydney, Higher Education Research and Development Society of Australasia.
British Petroleum (1991) *Aiming for a College Education.* London, British Petroleum.
BTEC (1991) *Common Skills: General Guidelines.* London, Business and Technician Education Council.
Cahalan, M. and Farris, E. (1990) *College Sponsored Tutoring and Mentoring Programs for Disadvantaged Elementary and Secondary Students.* Higher Education Surveys Report, Survey Number 12, May. Sponsored by the National Science Foundation, the National Endowment for the Humanities, and the US Department of Education. Washington, DC, Higher Education Surveys.
Cawley, P. (1989) 'The introduction of a problem-based option into a conventional engineering degree course'. *Studies in Higher Education*, 14(1), 83–96.
CBI (1989) *Towards a Skills Revolution.* London, Confederation of British Industry.
Fresko, B. and Carmeli, A. (1990) 'PERACH: a nation-wide student tutorial programme' in S. Goodlad and B. Hirst (eds) *Explorations in Peer Tutoring*, Chapter 4. Oxford, Basil Blackwell.
Goodlad, S. (ed.) (1975) *Project Methods in Higher Education.* Guildford, Society for Research into Higher Education.

Goodlad, S. (1977) *Socio-technical Projects in Engineering Education.* University of Stirling, General Education in Engineering Project.

Goodlad, S. (ed.) (1982) *Study Service: an examination of community service as a method of study in higher education.* Windsor, NFER-Nelson.

Goodlad, S. (ed.) (1984) *Education for the Professions: Quis Custodiet?* Guildford, Society for Research into Higher Education and NFER-Nelson.

Goodlad, S. (1988) 'Four forms of heresy in higher education: aspects of academic freedom in education for the professions' in M. Tight (ed.) *Academic Freedom and Responsibility.* Guildford, Society for Research into Higher Education and the Open University.

Goodlad, S. and Hirst, B. (1989) *Peer Tutoring: an introduction to learning by teaching.* London, Kogan Page.

Goodlad, S. and Hirst, B. (eds) (1990) *Explorations in Peer Tutoring.* Oxford, Basil Blackwell.

Gordon, E.E. and Gordon, E.H. (1990) *Centuries of Tutoring: a history of alternative education in America and Western Europe.* Lanham, Maryland: Universities Press of America Inc.

Hughes, J.C. (1991a) *Tutoring: students as tutors in schools.* London, BP Educational Service.

Hughes, J.C. (ed.) (1991b) *Tutoring: resource pack.* London, BP Educational Service.

Minogue, K.R. (1973) *The Concept of a University.* London, Weidenfeld and Nicolson.

Moberly, W. (1949) *The Crisis in the University.* London, SCM Press.

Neufeld, V. and Chong, J. (1984) 'Problem-based learning in medicine' in S. Goodlad (ed.) *Education for the Professions: Quis Custodiet?* Guildford, Society for Research into Higher Education and NFER-Nelson.

Schön, D. (1987) *Educating the Reflective Practitioner.* London, Jossey-Bass.

Whitman, N.A. (1988) *Peer Tutoring: to teach is to learn twice,* ASHE-ERIC Higher Education Report No. 4. Washington, DC, Association for the Study of Higher Education.

4

Promoting Learning

Malcolm Frazer

Introduction

Some languages have the same word for 'teaching' and 'learning'. More sophisticated languages use two words, because teaching and learning are quite different. Not only is it ungrammatical for a teacher to say: 'I'll learn you'; it is also impossible! Only an individual can learn, although a teacher might facilitate the process. There is an analogy with selling and buying. Nothing is sold until it is bought, and nothing is taught until it is learnt. Selling is to buying as teaching is to learning. The teacher's role is to promote learning.

This chapter is about how teachers can promote learning and how institutions can help teachers to promote learning. It is in the interests of everyone – society and government, who provide the resources for higher education; students and employers, who are the clients of higher education; and the institutions and teachers, who are the providers of higher education – that the learning achieved by each student is of the highest possible quality.

Quality learning requires quality teachers. Throughout this chapter, 'teacher' will be used in preference to the title 'lecturer' normally used in higher education. Teaching is a noble profession going back to the Greek philosophers and should not be lowered by confusing it with lecturing, which is only one of many of the available methods of promoting learning. Furthermore, lecturing is not always very effective in promoting learning. Perhaps the most cost-effective action for improving the quality of learning in higher education would be to ban the title 'lecturer'. Academic staff ('teachers', 'senior teachers', etc.) would then no longer assume that the main teaching method they were expected to use was the lecture.

Anecdote 1*

A colleague looked up from marking final examination scripts and said: 'I can't understand it, no one knows anything about this topic, and yet I gave them a lecture on it. I told them.'

Comment: Telling isn't teaching. In fact there was no teaching because there had been no learning.

This introduction has distinguished learning from teaching without defining either. In the next two sections are attempts to define the characteristics of quality learning and quality teaching in higher education.

What is learning in higher education?

One of many attempts to define the characteristics of quality learning in higher education is displayed in Table 4.1 (Frazer, 1992). Learning is not just about absorbing (remembering and understanding) knowledge; much more it is about developing positive attitudes and useful skills. Learning has occurred if someone knows more, or can do more, than before. But that is not enough. Effective learning induces curiosity, self-confidence and self-awareness with respect to knowledge and how that knowledge is acquired and applied. Successful learning helps to develop skills so that the knowledge an individual possesses can be used to good effect.

What characterizes a quality teacher?

One attempt to list the characteristics of a teacher in higher education who will be successful in promoting learning is shown in Table 4.2 (Frazer, 1992). The five attributes are in decreasing order of importance with the first being paramount. Characteristic (1) makes it essential for teachers in higher education to have time and resources to be engaged in research or some other form of professional or scholarly activity. The effort and time to be devoted to such activity will vary from subject to subject and individual to individual but should never be zero. Research activity is part of preparing for teaching. However, deciding on the balance of effort and time an individual teacher should devote to research activity and teaching activity (described in the next paragraphs) is not easy. Overemphasis on research, with an attitude to teaching that precludes adequate preparation and is excused with the false notion that students will learn by osmosis from simply being in contact with

---

* All the anecdotes are true and based on the author's experience.

Table 4.1   Some characteristics of quality learning

1. Love and respect for scholarship.
2. Love and respect for the subject and a desire to see the subject used to help society.
3. Desire to know more about the subject.
4. Knowledge of and competence in the subject consistent with the course level.
5. Knowing how to learn.
6. Knowing the limits of the knowledge and skills so far acquired.
7. Realisation that learning is a life long process.
8. Problem solving or opportunity taking (i.e. problem recognition, definition and formulation of solutions, or approaches to solutions).
9. Knowing how to find out (i.e. how to use libraries and other databases).
10. Ability to formulate an argument.
11. Integrating knowledge from different fields.
12. Communication skills (writing and reading; speaking and listening).
13. Skills of critical analysis.

Table 4.2   Characteristics of a quality teacher by rank order

Rank	Characteristic
1.	Up-to-date professional knowledge, skills and competence in the subject. This is the *sine qua non* for every teacher.
2.	Affective characteristics such as: love of the subject, a desire to share that love with others, a willingness to go on learning, a desire to help others learn and develop, and a willingness to self-evaluate performance as a teacher and to seek feedback from students and criticism from others, and finally a willingness to work in a team.
3.	An understanding how people learn, and of any special learning difficulties associated with specific knowledge and skills to be taught and with the particular students, a realisation that the most important task in promoting learning is to motivate the students.
4.	Personal characteristics such as: a sense of humour, patience, confidence, capacity for hard work.
5.	Competence with teaching techniques including audiovisual and other methods; competence with assessment methods.

someone at the frontiers of knowledge, is as detrimental to promoting quality learning as totally ignoring research/professional/scholarly activity. There should be more conscious reflection by individual teachers, based on guidance and possibly counselling from the institutions, on the balance of effort and time to devote to research and teaching. Unfortunately, the widespread belief (usually well founded, even in institutions which do not place generating knowledge high in their missions) that promotion depends on success in research does not help to produce a proper balance.

Teaching activity is much more than the time in contact with students. For every hour in direct contact with students a teacher will need a minimum of two hours for preparation and sometimes ten hours or more. The two-hour minimum applies however familiar the teacher may be with what is to be *learnt*.

Anecdote 2

A colleague said: 'Good! I don't need to prepare this. I know the topic so well I can easily talk about it for an hour.'

Comment: Talking rarely promotes learning of any quality. Familiarity can be a barrier to assisting others to learn. Short cuts are taken. What is so obvious to the teacher, may not be to the students. The colleague should have devoted time to:

(i) reflecting on likely student difficulties with the topic (perhaps based on recalling what it was like when first learning the topic – misconceptions and struggles to overcome them); and

(ii) how the topic could be used to help the set of students with their particular abilities and aspirations to develop higher order skills and attitudes (e.g. as listed in Table 4.1).

In addition to preparation and direct contact with students there are many other activities a teacher must engage in to be successful in promoting learning. These include:

1. Devising and planning the course leading to a description of its context, the aims and objectives, and the content and the teaching and assessment methods (all this is usually done as part of a team).
2. Counselling students before (selection) and during the course.
3. Ensuring that the resources and the environment for learning are available.
4. Assessing students, not only formally as part of the examination/assessment arrangements, but also informally and continuously in order to diagnose individual students' problems with learning.
5. Monitoring and evaluating the teaching and learning.
6. Reflecting on what changes are necessary in order to make improvements so that the whole cycle can begin again with (7) replanning.

Promoting learning is a cyclic process, starting with planning and ending with reflection leading to changes and replanning. This is shown in Figure 4.1. Scrutiny of this diagram should emphasize that teaching involves much more than stage 3 ('contact time').

In summary, learning of quality does not happen simply as a result of contact between teacher and student. In addition, there are all the other

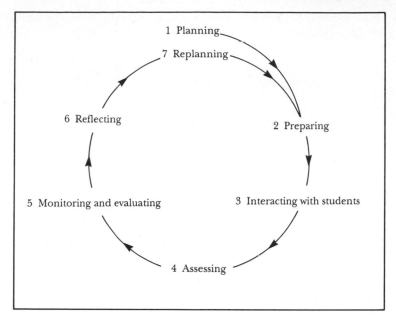

Figure 4.1 The cycle of stages for promoting learning

activities displayed in Fig. 4.1 and also there is the need to have up-to-date knowledge and professional competence as a result of involvement in research or related activities. Traditionally, universities have had three functions: (1) to generate, (2) to safeguard, and (3) to transmit knowledge. Not all institutions in higher education now place functions (1) and (2) high in their missions, but nevertheless their teachers must be active in research if teaching, function (3), is to be effective. This section has ignored some other duties of most teachers in higher education including administrative work and responsibilities for aftercare with their students such as counselling on future employment and writing references.

How can learning be promoted?

Human beings have an enormous capacity to learn. This is most striking in the first five years or so of life. During that period, there is a great curiosity and a need to learn in order to survive, to be mobile and to be able to communicate. To assist with this rapid rate of learning, there is a 'teacher' (at least for children living in a stable family), who is a highly motivated, loving, caring parent working with a low teacher:student ratio (probably 1:1). When formal education begins it is different. Inevitably, the school teacher has to constrain the individual curiosity for reasons of safety, the demands of the curriculum and the needs of the whole group. Sometime during school life, the child first experiences the great demotivator:

Someone else is deciding what I'm expected to learn

Despite this, much learning continues at school, partly because research has revealed much about how children learn and how teachers use the results of this research. We know much less about how adolescents and adults learn. More research is needed, but it is already clear that at every age learning is most likely when an individual has identified a personal need to possess some particular knowledge or skill. This need may result from: (1) a threat (e.g. unsatisfactory employment without a qualification), (2) an opportunity (new skill to be deployed at work or leisure), or (3) a desire to satisfy curiosity. In other words, motivation is a key prerequisite for learning. For every age group, but especially for higher education, the teacher's main role is to stimulate his or her students with a need to learn, and then to help them identify and define what they should know and/or be able to do in order to satisfy that need. In the next section, are some examples of how the capacity to learn can be exploited.

Anecdote 3

As a student I attended a set of lectures which by popular consent were admirable. The subject coverage was comprehensive and the performance would have been rated highly (articulate, immaculate in blackboard skills, well paced and with touches of humour). I obtained the best set of notes I ever had. In the end of term examination I recalled enough of the notes to pass but I learnt very little.

Comment: The lecturer decided what he thought the students should learn, he told them and told them well; but he never challenged them, never made them think for themselves or want to know for themselves. The lectures were so complete and clear, that there was no motivation to learn.

Some examples of promoting learning

Promoting learning through problem solving

Problem solving (opportunity taking) is an important skill to be developed in its own right (see Table 4.1), but it can also be a powerful stimulus for creating a need to know. The natural curiosity and competitiveness of human beings can be aroused through the challenge of a problem. A carefully selected problem which will require students to build on what they already know, but which will involve them in finding out more, is a powerful stimulus to learning. The teacher needs to make careful, professional judgements when selecting the problems. Failure would be demotivating and so the solution must be within the reach of the majority of students, but must not be so obvious that there is no challenge. Breaking the problem down into steps and releasing 'clues' or additional knowledge until every student has completed each step is one way of keeping up the challenge but preventing demotivation by failure. Problems do not have to be in the form of questions; they can be in the form of statements that challenge orthodox beliefs. Problems do not have to be of the type where there is a unique answer known to the teacher but not to the student, but can be open ended with several possible solutions or even no solution.

Anecdote 4

Early in a first year course in chemistry I presented students with a real life story about insurance claims for houses in the United States which had been rewired and then burnt down. Motivation resulted from it being a true story with human interest but where knowledge of chemistry would be needed. The majority of students took up the challenge. The students were told the story and asked to come back in two weeks with a 'solution', 'several solutions', 'courses of actions leading to solutions', etc. As the teacher I had two responsibilities: to watch the students carefully in order to identify those who had not been motivated by the original story and to provide further stimulation for them; and secondly, to ensure by early liaison with the library that there was adequate material which would allow the students to progress towards a solution.

Comment: The students learnt much, not only about the properties of metals and alloys but also about the skills of using information sources in the library, about skills of reasoning and, most importantly, they gained confidence in their own ability to use the knowledge they had acquired.

Promoting learning through peer groups

It is possible for students to learn more from each other than from their teacher. There are several reasons. Students see their teachers also as assessors and so are reluctant to display their ignorance by making mistakes or asking elementary questions in front of the teacher. A student having difficulty with a concept can be helped by someone who has just overcome the difficulty and therefore is sympathetic and understanding of the causes of the blockage or misconception. There is a competitive element within a peer group which can motivate learning. Peer groups can work at their own pace. In this form of promoting learning, the role of the teacher is to organize the groups, provide tasks for them and only intervene with support if requested. Groups of three, four or five are optimum. Ways of ensuring that every member of a group participates include requiring individuals to prepare their ideas, solutions to problems and so on, before joining the group and not allowing the group to appoint its own chair or spokesperson.

Anecdote 5

A colleague said: 'That must be an important test you are giving those students. I have never seen them work so hard.' It was a second year group of about 60 students. In fact, I had just given them five minutes to prepare their thoughts before splitting into groups of four for a 20-minute discussion. That discussion period was equally intense because the students knew that at the end I would call some at random to present the conclusions of their group. There would be no self-appointed spokesperson to shield the weaker students.

Comment: More was learnt in sessions like these than by a didactic
        presentation.

Promoting learning through advance organizers

The idea that learning is promoted if the learner is prepared for learning by recalling and structuring what he/she already knows was first put forward by Ausubel (Ausubel and Robinson, 1972). Unsuccessful learners come to a lecture or some other activity with the attitude: 'Here I am, like a sponge, ready to absorb knowledge and skills – tell me, make me do – and I will learn.' This attitude to learning will not work. A teacher should help the learner to prepare not only by motivating ('What do I need to know or be able to do?') but also by forming a secure basis for learning ('What do I know or am able to do already in this area?'). People learn by building on what they already know.

Anecdote 6

Before presenting a new topic in chemistry (let us call it X), I would start by giving the students five minutes to write down four items of knowledge which they thought they already knew about topic X or which were closely related to topic X. They were then asked to write down what they would most like to know about topic X (also four items, if possible).

After five minutes, the students would be asked to form groups of four. This can be done in very large lecture theatres by simply asking the odd numbered rows to turn and face the even numbered rows. From each individual's four ideas the groups were asked to distil out the most important four ideas from the group.

Comment: Devoting the first 15 minutes of a one-hour session to preparing the students' minds in this way is invaluable. It also helped me to have some idea of what they knew already and what they wanted to know.

Promoting learning through assessment

Self-assessment is particularly important. It is always possible to cheat the examiners but never possible to cheat oneself. Teachers should provide plenty of opportunities for the students to assess themselves. Fixed response tests, problems with unique solutions and essay topics should be provided regularly with keys to the tests, answers to the problems and model essays provided subsequently. If forced to make a presentation to a large group ('lecture'), it is often helpful to start, or break in the middle or end with a short test. A test at the beginning is a simple way of producing an advance organizer.

Anecdote 7

I would provide each student attending a lecture with a cube having each face differently coloured. From time to time, a carefully selected multiple-choice question was presented from an overhead projector and the students were asked to hold up the coloured face corresponding to the correct response.

Comment: The students were challenged, and I was able to obtain instant feedback on progress by estimating the number of cubes with the colour corresponding to the correct response.

Teachers need feedback, but learners need it even more. All student assignments should be returned promptly (the students need to remember what the assignment was) with detailed comments. Writing these comments is time consuming but is as much part of teaching as preparing or delivering a lecture. Students may have worked for several hours on an assignment; they deserve more than comments such as: 'beta minus', 'a fairly competent attempt', 'terrible – you are wasting my time'. In order to promote learning, comments should be constructive, should correct all mistakes and misconceptions with references to guide the students, but above all should be encouraging.

Promoting learning through developing learning skills

Learning should be a conscious process. Teachers should encourage their students to think about how they are learning, what works best for them, what their difficulties are and how they might transfer success in one area of learning to success in another. Many departments now provide learning resources rooms which are stocked with aids to learning and with individual learning programmes which allow students to proceed at their own pace. A feature of such resources should be the opportunity to talk to tutors about individual approaches to learning.

How can institutions help to promote learning?

What can institutions do to assist their teachers and thereby enhance their students' learning? Perhaps the greatest contribution would come if institutions developed a culture which converted them from 'teaching institutions' to 'learning institutions'. Many institutions are now taking over the ideas which have been developed in industry of total quality management (that is, involving everyone in actions to improve every aspect of the enterprise). Total quality management in an institution of higher education involves the management, the teachers, the support staff, the students, the advisers from outside (including external examiners) and the employers of graduates. This would help to develop an ethos in which teacher and student were working together with the common cause of promoting and improving learning. Institutions should become self-critical communities dedicated to learning and scholarship. They can encourage this by several means, deploying each one in the most effective way. They are:

1. Assisting staff with self-assessment and their own critical analysis of their achievement of goals.
2. Appraisal of teaching effectiveness leading to decisions about salaries and promotion.
3. The use of peer review and external involvement.

In the polytechnics and colleges sector in the UK, the Council for National Academic Awards has done much to promote this approach (Silver, 1990).

Teachers need support and can gain much from being involved in networks within and between institutions. Subject based networks are particularly important. There should be ready access for all teachers to sources of intelligence on best practice on curriculum development, teaching (general and subject related), student assessment and course evaluation. In-house and national programmes of staff development in each of these areas should be encouraged and supported by each institution.

Finally, and in line with the emphasis throughout this chapter on learning rather than teaching, institutions need to bring to centre stage their resources for learning. Foremost is the library, but there are also computer centres and

learning resource centres making use of, and developing, the latest on information technology. Institutions should promote and encourage better links
between these resources and teachers. Increasingly using new information
based technologies, students will learn on their own, at their own pace, and
in their own way. This changes, but no way diminishes, the important role
of the teacher. Teachers will find themselves spending less time on presenting, and more time on preparing materials for learning, guiding, motivating and assessing their students in order to deal with their essential task
of promoting effective learning.

References

Ausubel, D.P. and Robinson, F.G. (1972) *School learning: an introduction to educational
    psychology*. London, Holt, Rinehart & Winston.
Frazer, M.J. (1992) *Quality Assurance in Higher Education*. London, Falmer Press.
Silver, H. (1990) *A Higher Education: The Council for National Academic Awards and British
    higher education 1964–89*. London, Falmer Press.

Part 2

The Professional Perspective

5

An Action-Focus Curriculum for the Interpersonal Professions

Roger Ellis

Introduction

This chapter is about the initial training of a group of professions I have described as interpersonal (Ellis, 1980). Their primary method is face-to-face interaction with clients, patients, pupils or students. They include health care in its various forms, social work and teaching. In broad terms, the chapter is about the curriculum and the so-called integration of theory and practice. To get some grip on this elusive issue, various models are proposed and one, which focuses on professional action, is advocated as ideal. The approach is related to current concerns with competence and quality. Nursing and social work, recently subject to dramatic curriculum change, are considered as representative examples.

Over the last 20 years, there has been a steady increase, in both universities and polytechnics, in the number of degree courses which include a licence to practise. They include degrees in nursing and social work and also more novel developments such as physiotherapy, occupational therapy, speech therapy, radiography and chiropody. Assumptions in this chapter are that these courses have much in common, that there are mutually beneficial lessons to be learned and that in many ways they address issues which are increasingly the problems of higher education as a whole. While there have been curriculum developments and comparable problems and approaches in each of these professions, nursing and social work have been subject to the most far-reaching structural influences through *Project 2000* and the new *Diploma in Social Work*, respectively. Central to these developments has been the perennial but ever challenging issue of the integration of theory and practice.

The chapter hinges on a theoretical model for the curriculum which I have called *the action-focus curriculum*. Before setting out this model, I want to look in some detail at what is implied by theory and practice in the context of professional training; at what might be involved in their integration; and at several models which represent different approaches to integration. In respect of what I will argue is the most effective model, I will set out ways in which it would be operationalized thus providing a checklist against which curricula may be evaluated. With this checklist established, I will then evaluate the effects of *Project 2000* and the new *Diploma in Social Work* on the training curricula for nursing and social work. In particular, I will compare and contrast the approaches involved and the extent to which they might encourage or inhibit the focus on action which I am advocating.

Theory and practice

The action-focus model was first introduced as part of a guidebook to social skill training (Ellis and Whittington, 1981). The model addresses the so-called 'integration of theory and practice'. Like many slogans, this one may be inspiring to live by but it can be less than helpful to live with. What exactly does it mean? At its most rudimentary level, it means that the work that students do in college should make sense when they are out working in practice. Thus the essays, written examinations, role-plays and other activities which occupy students during their course should be seen as relevant to their work out on placement. At a more sophisticated level, it may refer to the integration of various kinds of knowledge. There are those derived from relevant academic disciplines, those that come from the body of knowledge which the profession has and those that arise before, during and after professional practice. Integration may be simply theoretical in that one fact or theory relates to another across disciplines or subjects but is usually expected to be, in part at least, practical: thought and speculation should affect action and vice versa.

Practice is relatively easy to define. It is the range of observable activities carried out by the professional or the apprentice-professional in providing a service for patients and clients. Theory, however, may refer to a number of different things. It may be the content of academic disciplines deemed relevant to professional practice. Thus, nursing students are expected to master material from physiology, psychology and sociology, all of which are considered to have concepts and findings relevant to professional practice. Another interpretation of theory is that it is the developing body of ideas and evidence which are the property of the profession itself. Nursing, for example, would lay claim to sufficient specialized or even unique material to justify for itself the title of academic discipline. Other professions are more obviously parasitic on established academic disciplines for their theory.

At a more basic level, if practice is behaviour, then theory is the complex of unobservable, more or less conscious, thoughts and internal processes which each professional may lay claim to or be assumed to have. In this sense, we are all theorizers whatever our level of education or understanding. It is a reasonable assumption that all human beings not only behave and may be observed doing so but also that they consciously reflect on their behaviour; that is they theorize about what they might do, what they are doing, and what they have done. Following this line of argument, every professional might be assumed to have, at the very least, a body of personal theory about the events they perceive and their own behaviour. If this theory is to be made explicit it would be in the form of a series of *propositions* about behaviour and the circumstances in which it occurs. These propositions might refer to individual events but will also include generalizations about categories of events and their interrelations.

An important characteristic of a profession would be sets of common propositions shared by members of that profession. Thus personal theory would shade into professional theory. All professionals will also have encountered systematic bodies of propositions known as academic disciplines. Theory therefore might be conceived as existing at three levels: personal; professional; and academic. Integration then might be concerned with the ways in which these levels interact. For example, how might personal theory about reality and causality be influenced by propositions at theoretical and empirical levels from psychology? How might theories from sociology influence the models of reality which characterize professional theory?

Integration, as already stated, is concerned primarily with the interaction between reflection and action. How then might the various theoretical notions which a professional may articulate, whether derived from a recognized discipline or simply their own beliefs or reflections, relate to their actions? Does the theory which a trainee faithfully reproduces in an examination paper have any bearing on the way in which they identify problems in practice, act to solve them and evaluate the success of these actions?

A useful distinction is between *knowing how* and *knowing that* (Ryle, 1949). The starting point for this distinction is the notion that behaviour, at whatever level of complexity, must be initiated and organized by some kind of representation in the central nervous system. However, it is one thing to have some internal pattern which allows us to consistently unfold a complex sequence of behaviour. It is another to be able to reflect on that pattern and translate it into a set of propositions. Thus, a professional golfer knows how to reproduce, as situations require, a range of appropriate quality swings. He knows how. It is a quite different operation for him to be able to set out in propositional form what is necessary to achieve these swings. This propositional knowledge would be 'knowing that'. It should be apparent that these are different, if related, forms of knowledge and that having one by no means guarantees the other. For example, at the level of 'knowing that', I can describe the series of operations necessary to type a letter using an electric typewriter; my skills in knowing how and doing the job are however severely limited. On the other hand, there are many competent typists who know how to achieve high speed and accuracy but who would find it difficult to explain in detail exactly what is going on. A further complication is that too much propositional knowledge – 'knowing that' – may get in the way of effective performance – 'knowing how'. This distinction applies in any area where complex psychomotor skills exist. Doing is one thing, describing doing in a systematic way is another. The same distinction applies in the area of social skills which is the province of the interpersonal professions.

Another important distinction is between *descriptive* and *prescriptive* knowledge. Descriptive knowledge is a set of propositions concerning what is believed to be the case in any particular area of phenomena. Thus, psychologists work to produce descriptive knowledge, at least at a probabilistic level, regarding human behaviour and its environment. This is not the same however as describing what *should* be the case. Such knowledge is prescriptive and based on assumptions of the desirable and worthwhile. As David Hume (1748) pointed out, the so-called naturalistic fallacy consists in stepping from description to prescription as if there were a logical connection. There is not: we are never justified logically in proceeding from *is* statements to *ought* statements. To give an extreme example, if it is the case that children learn more quickly if beaten with barbed wire, should we therefore beat the children in this way in order to accelerate their learning? Clearly, this step cannot be taken without raising moral issues which are separate from the *is* statement. This may seem a recondite line to explore but it is crucial to our understanding of difficulties which arise when academic disciplines are integrated with professional practice. At one level, academic disciplines are dedicated to descriptive statements about reality. Professional practice, on the other hand, must be in part about prescription in that professionals must know what they ought to do. It is when a profession looks to an academic discipline for prescription that it is frustrated. The step from description to prescription is not straightforward.

The descriptive/prescriptive distinction does not imply all that needs to be said about academic disciplines. However, disciplines are not inert bodies of established knowledge. Rather, they are an approach to evidence and a way of finding out and testing propositions. Thus conceived, their integration with practice takes on a different complexion. Academic disciplines are not simply bodies of propositional/descriptive knowledge. They have their own prescriptions about the legitimacy of evidence and the approach to be adopted to knowledge. When a psychologist says we should concentrate on behaviour as evidence this is a prescriptive (ought) statement rather than a descriptive (is) one. If we accept this argument, we might be led to make different demands of academic disciplines in professional courses. Rather than asking how a piece of knowledge might inform action, a question becomes, for example: how might the approach of a psychologist to finding out and testing knowledge influence the actions of a professional?

With these reflections as background, we can categorize different approaches to the integration of knowledge from academic disciplines with professional theorizing and action. Elsewhere, I have proposed four curriculum models whereby an attempt is made to relate an academic discipline to professional practice. I called these four models of the curriculum (Ellis and Whittington, 1979):

1. Personal education.
2. Semantic conjunction.
3. Emergent.
4. Action focus.

The personal education model

Those who subscribe to the personal education model argue that any academic discipline in its authentic form is a valuable experience for students on a professional training course. Persons so educated will be able to face the problems of the classroom, clinic or agency in a creative, flexible and rational fashion having been disciplined in their approach to knowledge, through problem-solving, analysis and expression of a disciplined body of knowledge. Encountering two such disciplines would be even better since comparisons would be encouraged and so would increase the likelihood of generalizable concepts. This approach occurs in its purest form when professional training is conceived as a proper postgraduate activity available to good graduates in any discipline. A current example of the same kind of thinking is represented by the idea of higher-order transferable skills. Here, it is argued that disciplined thinking inculcates higher-order skills which will generalize to any other body of knowledge or area of activity. A variation on this idea is the notion of enterprise competencies first introduced as a corrective to higher education but subsequently found to be the very things which higher education is best at, and hence the province of academe itself. Like the man who found himself to have spoken prose all his life, higher education has been inculcating enterprise skills for years (cf. Chapter 13).

The personal education approach essentially avoids the problems which we have been discussing. There is no need for teachers to agonize over which parts of their disciplines are most relevant to the trainee nor do they need to ask in detail what the practical implications are of what is taught. However, even the most fervent advocates of the personal education model would probably concede that there should be some criteria of relevance for the particular topics which are chosen for the course. There is unlikely to be time for a fully fledged introduction to any academic discipline so there have to be some grounds for selection. This moves towards the semantic conjunction model.

The semantic conjunction model

Within this model, an attempt is made to select topics within an academic discipline because they appear to be about those things which do or should interest the professional in question. There is here an apparent similarity in the respective vocabularies of groups of professionals and of related academic disciplines. Thus, for example, occupational therapists are concerned with the way stroke patients learn or relearn skills: since the study of learning is also an important part of the discipline of psychology occupational therapists should have a course in the psychology of learning. This approach is superficially persuasive: a course in developmental psychology is given to health visitors because they work with mothers and the newborn; group dynamics are taught to social workers because they must interact with clients; doctors are taught about conformity since patients must comply with their advice. Much worthy and conscientious planning and teaching has followed and, indeed, does follow this model, but all too often it fails.

There is a marked discrepancy between scientific enquiry surrounding a topic and the practical decisions and actions which professionals take and undertake in the area described by that topic. Prospective physiotherapists interested in the way patients learn an exercise regime are unlikely to find much illumination in the legitimate scientific investigation of the startle response of the woodlouse. The investigation of perceptions of fullness as a ratio, despite its crucial significance in differentiating between the theories of Piaget and Bruner, is not immediately helpful to the health visitor in undertaking an assessment of an infant. Thus, the drives towards understanding on the one hand and action on the other, while related in principle, are often widely divergent in practice.

Even when the timescale and focus of scientific investigation and professional action are similar, there is still a disjunction between the descriptive objectivity of the academic and the need for prescriptive advice felt by the professional. It is not unknown for an academic enquiry into a topic on which policy makers are required to take decisions to conclude with a greater sense of uncertainty than that with which it commenced.

So there are problems with this approach despite its face validity. The apparent connection between professionals and academics using the same word may be misleading. There is a difference between the imperatives of academic objectivity and the exigencies of professional activity in both timescale and degrees of certainty permitted and required. There is the difference between 'knowing how' and 'knowing that'. Finally there is the step from description to prescription.

My impression of the professional curriculum is that it still operates predominantly within this model. No degree course in the UK is structured entirely on practical skill acquisition. There are always substantial elements derived from disciplines deemed relevant. Yet the problems of effective integration remain.

The emergent model

As a kind of sidestep from these theoretical and practical problems, it has become fashionable to base the curriculum on problems raised by the students: thus the syllabus emerges from the preoccupations of students regarding their professional work. The curriculum is, therefore, an emergent rather than pre-planned one. This approach is particularly prevalent in professional development courses where the students can be expected to have problems enough in their concurrent professional practice. In courses of initial training it might be unreasonable to expect the inexperienced to know enough of practice to recognize any difficulties. The approach has the pedagogical virtue of starting with issues which are real to students. However, eventually the member of staff has to introduce material from a recognized body of knowledge and the problems of integration remain. The technique should be recognized as a pedagogical device to lure a student into the syllabus: it is not a syllabus in itself nor is it anything more than a partial solution to the integration of theory and practice. To begin with, it is far too arbitrary and *ad hoc* to allow for systematic planning by teachers in relation to the approach and material of their specialism.

The action-focus model

In this approach, as the name implies, the student's action as a professional is made the central focus of the curriculum. This action is conceived as having three stages: planning, implementation and evaluation. Implementation is the central part of a professional's work; it is the behaviour of the professional, it is the things he or she does for, with, or to patients or clients. Planning is the process of deciding what will be done; evaluation the determination of whether the action has achieved the desired objectives. Now, each of these stages has elements of observable behaviour and of unobservable reflection. The reflection may be virtually concurrent with the behaviour or constitute a prolonged preparation for it or indeed occur after it. Reflection is, of course, unobservable in itself except in the trivial sense that we may say that somebody is quiet, apparently preoccupied and hence, quite possibly, reflecting. Evidence of reflection is required and this could take the form of a set of statements – propositions concerning the behaviour and events in question. In the interests of simplicity, and for the purpose of this initial analysis, it is assumed that action is primarily behavioural and observable whereas planning and evaluation are concerned with propositions about what might be and what has been. The problems of integrating theory and practice may now be considered as the requirement to integrate propositions from established bodies of knowledge with those involved in planning and evaluation.

Earlier, reference was made to the difficulties of moving from the descriptive to the prescriptive. It was established that the academic disciplines were fundamentally descriptive in nature whereas the grounds for professional action had to be prescriptive and point to particular courses of action. Thus, for example, a social anthropologist might be interested in describing the patterns of behaviour and assumed values which characterize a treatment group whereas a professional would have to decide the best way to behave in such a group in order to achieve desirable ends. Thus, the professional must decide what ought to be done and description alone will not produce an answer. Rather, the professional must deduce, on the basis of key values, the course of action and intended outcome which is acceptable. If it were demonstrated fairly conclusively that perceptual isolation subdued unruly adolescents, a residential social worker might still proscribe the treatment on moral grounds. The evidence of the efficacy of the treatment would not in itself lead to the ethical issues involved and hence would not translate into imperatives for action or non-action. However, reflection on the nature of academic disciplines reveals that while their subject matter is descriptive of events and their relationships, their approach to knowledge is highly pre-scriptive. Scientific method for example is prescriptive regarding standards of evidence, methods of data gathering and inference from data.

The secret of integration, therefore, is to relate these prescriptions regarding knowledge to the reflective activities of the professional. To give a specific example: psychology would be integrated with planning and evaluation by encouraging the students to think as psychologists in identifying problems in their work, plan-ning activities to address those problems and evaluating whether actions had been successful. This assumes, of course, that the face validity of psychology for particular professions carries over into this more profound application of psychology's essential methods. For the occupational therapist referred to above, the argument is: you are interested in learning, psychologists are interested in learning, therefore you should try to study and understand learn-ing in the way that a psychologist would in order to inform the decisions you take and the actions you perform as a professional.

The action-focus curriculum, therefore, is one where the actor as planner, intervener and evaluator is informed by both the approach and substance of appropriate academic disciplines. It thus combines the face validity of the semantic conjunction approach with the salience of the emergent curriculum but in a planned and structured way. The semantic conjunction approach, it will be recalled, identified an apparent connection between professional prac-tice and academic enquiry through the initial similarity of language used. However, this impression of relevance often failed to survive a more detailed study of the actual substance of the discipline. The emergent curriculum was based on problems raised by students and thus was, by its nature, highly relevant to them but did not allow for a systematic treatment of relevant theory or findings.

Obviously, the action referred to must finally be that which occurs in pro-fessional practice. All professional courses include sustained periods of super-vised work experience as an apprentice-professional. But we are talking here about the integration of theory and practice in the curriculum. To achieve this through an action focus requires some middle ground of a practical nature between the college course and the relatively uncontrolled environ-ment of real agencies and hospitals. For that reason, I introduced the action-focus curriculum in relation to Social Skill Training which may still be the best example of the approach within a college curriculum. Social Skill Train-ing (or micro-teaching or micro-counselling as it may be called) is an approach to the acquisition and development of interactional skills based on a structured-practice–feedback–practice cycle. Closed-circuit television is usually employed to provide audio-visual feedback on performance. Its potency in the action-focus curriculum is that the interactional skills being practised make the ideal focus for planning and evaluation and for the inte-gration of approaches and substantive knowledge from social psychology and indeed other disciplines which are concerned with face-to-face interaction such as linguistics, sociology and social anthropology. This information has a direct bearing on how students conceive and perceive effective social interaction. It influences how they observe sequences of interaction and what they see happening. It determines how they plan their own behaviour, how they observe and analyse the behaviour which they see in the audio-visual record and how they modify behaviour. The sequences of behaviour and the role-plays in which they occur are, of course, carefully chosen to be relevant to professional practice. Other students or, in some cases, even drama students, act out the parts of clients or patients. Sometimes real clients, pupils or patients are involved, with, of course, due attention to the ethical issues involved.

This approach has proved to be a highly effective way to link the acquisition of practical competencies with the capacity to reflect on practice using perspectives from academic disciplines. It further uses both the approach and the substance of relevant academic material to determine key features of planning, action and evaluation.

In principle, the same approach could inform all the areas of practice which are relevant to a profession and could cover technical as well as social skills. The approach has been around for some time. How does it relate to current preoccupations?

Professional competence

A major current interest is the competence of vocations. There is a widespread concern with what constitutes effective skills for specified jobs, how these skills might be reliably assessed and how they might best be acquired in a cost-effective manner. This approach is a kind of Copernican shift in education and training. Whereas previously the training course came first, followed by a concern with how students might be assessed to judge if they had met the course's objectives, the starting point is now assessment. There can be an infinite number of ways that students might prepare for assessment with the course one way only.

The National Council for Vocational Qualifications is a body concerned with the assessment of competence for specific jobs, vocations and professions. It is not a conventional validating body for courses. The approach of the Council is to begin with statements of competence, that is, a set of skills, attitudes and knowledge which have been demonstrated to be effective to achieve particular purposes in specific occupations. Then comes the evidence that an individual has this competence. Then comes reliable and valid means of assessing this evidence. The Council accredits agencies who claim to be able to answer these questions and carry out reliable and valid assessment for a particular job or set of jobs. The whole approach is action-oriented and rooted in the realities of performance on the job. Preparation for this assessment may well be at the candidate's place of work with employment-based inputs as appropriate. Theoretical material, if justified, may well be acquired through distance learning or by other means independent of academic institutions. Thus, action conceived as work-based competencies has become the focus of a new kind of curriculum and it is for colleges to demonstrate that they have something to offer in preparing and perhaps assessing students for practice. The attraction of this scheme to employers is that it gives them much closer control over the training of employees and enables them to match competencies to the requirements of their job. This is seen as preferable to the relatively uncontrolled, and expensive, education provided by colleges which are relatively autonomous in the setting of objectives. This view, in a particularly crude form, was adopted by Kenneth Clarke in his 1991 Southport speech which advocated that teacher training should take place primarily in the schools.

However, a concentration on competence begs a number of questions. In a review of competence with regard to four professions (Ellis, 1989), I found both conceptual and empirical confusion and an absence of any systematic body of knowledge in nursing, teaching, medicine and speech therapy. These were chosen as representative of the interpersonal professions and I have no reason to believe that knowledge here is any further advanced in social work or the professions allied to medicine. There is then a big gap at the centre of the picture. Whether the aim is an action-focus curriculum or a competency-based assessment and training, the substantial knowledge of professional competence is at best patchy and primarily implicit. That is, people behave as if they knew what competence was but have failed to articulate this knowledge in any comprehensive and systematic way.

In reviewing the literature on competence in teaching, Cameron-Jones (1989) quoted a useful distinction made by Medley. *Competence*, he argued, referred to the totality of skills, knowledge and attitudes deemed sufficient for a profession or a professional. A *competency* (plural competencies) would be a single skill or attitude or piece of knowledge which would be a part of this repertoire. *Performance* was a tightly defined competency or set of competencies which could be reliably and publicly observed. *Effect*, the bottom line, would be that which was achieved by performance, the cure of a patient.

Taking these definitions for the professions in question (and, I suspect, many that are not), we lack a body of knowledge which sets out competence in behavioural terms and can relate these behaviours to desirable results. In the absence of this knowledge, it is difficult to see how students can be assessed as competent or how competent action can be made the focus of a curriculum. Nevertheless, professionals do work effectively, and students are selected, trained and assessed. So we have to assume that there is a body of implicit knowledge informing these practices and judgements. The urgent need is for this implicit knowledge to be explicated. I have set out (Ellis, 1989) a number of approaches which can be adopted to take this explication further. These include: behavioural observation and analysis; reconstitutive ethnography; task analysis; critical incident analysis; and the Delphi method to elicit expert judgements.

Quality assurance

Another matter of current interest is quality assurance. As a method of managing, cost-effective delivery is based on four basic principles.

1. There is an emphasis on the consumer as an arbiter of quality.
2. There is the need to specify standards both for the product or service in question and for the means of production for this entity.
3. There is a requirement regularly to monitor or audit reality to check whether standards are being met.
4. There has to be a commitment and capability to put right any deficiencies which are detected at the monitoring stage.

This admirable approach can be applied to the delivery of a health or social service and to the delivery of courses and teaching. However, the specification of standards for the essentially psycho-social events which constitute teaching, or health care or personal social services poses problems. The major element in the services concerned is the so-called competence of the professional concerned and the problems surrounding this have already been outlined. In the absence of detailed knowledge about competence, professional qualifications, assessment, selection and now quality assurance face difficulties. I have developed this argument at length (Ellis, 1989) but also set out a number of methods, as outlined above, which might be used to explicate professional competence and fill this major gap.

Indicators of an action-focus curriculum

Undoubtedly, our ignorance regarding competence has slowed down the adoption of an action-focus curriculum. However, it is possible to specify indicators against which we can assess the degree to which a curriculum is moving in that (presumably) desirable direction.

1. Assessment of practice and contribution to Honours degrees
If action is the focus of the curriculum then the assessment of action should be at the centre of the course. Since courses of professional training typically require students to spend the equivalent of a year in supervised practice in hospitals and other agencies, the assessment will be of their performance on that placement (or placements if they are intercalated throughout the course). Surprisingly, even Honours degree courses named after the profession concerned and leading to a licence to practise are prone to award the degree and to classify Honours on the basis of academic work alone. Satisfactory completion of placement is a kind of gate which the student has to pass through in order to allow the classification of the award on the basis of academic work. No more striking example can be found of the separation of theory and practice. If the practice is insufficiently differentiated to allow for classification in assessment then it is difficult to see how the academic

material and approach could be integrated with it systematically and in detail as required by the action focus model.

Objections to assessing practice fall into two camps. First, there are those who can see that it is desirable, in principle, but would argue that existing assessment schedules and the variability of placements preclude detailed assessment of the kind required. A simple 'pass/fail' is the best we can achieve reliably and validly. Others object to the idea in principle, arguing that it is inappropriate to classify students in this way since the predictive validity of such assessment is unproven and its short-term vocational and political effects undesirable. We never know whether a doctor or airline pilot is a First Class or Third Class Honours; we are simply assured that they are safe to practise: a 'pass/fail' judgement. There are undoubtedly ways round the practical objections. However, the objections may point, in principle, to practices which are antipathetic to Honours degrees with professional titles. Medicine's solution to this is to award Honours degrees to doctors or doctors aspirant who take a sidestep into Anatomy or Physiology or even Medical Sciences, a clear example of the semantic conjunction approach to integration. Aspirant doctors who follow this curriculum complete further studies in Anatomy or Physiology to Honours degree level before returning to their clinical studies. Thus, the model is of pre-clinical academic studies followed by clinical practice. Those who show particular academic talent at the pre-clinical stage complete further academic studies before proceeding. They thus gain two qualifications against the standard one and are especially well-equipped to pursue research.

For those who wish to classify practical performance, two principal methods have been followed. One is to reduce professional competence overall to a series of competencies or areas of competence, each of which is awarded a grade or mark. These are then summed in some way to give an overall mark or grade which can feed into the formula for Honours classification. While this has the advantages of an analytical approach, it is based on uncertain theoretical and empirical ground. In all professional areas, there is an urgent need for systematic and sustained research to identify the features of effective professional practice. Meanwhile, any assessment schedules must be seen as provisional. This approach may be described as reductionist in that performance is reduced to component skills or behaviours and summative in that scores on these basic elements are added to give an overall result. The approach has the statistical weaknesses that such rating and summing systems do have inherent regression effects. Faced with the need to rate a student on a particular attribute or area of performance there are two main tendencies. One is to play safe by choosing the middle category; the other is to consider all geese as swans and award everyone the highest grade. When these grades are summed there are the usual regression effects leading to clustering of results either about the average in the first case or skewed towards the top in the second.

An alternative approach is to use an assessment scheme which operates as it is intended to finish. Thus, if the end result required is to classify practical performance in the established Honours bands of First, Upper Second, Lower Second and Third, and if a typical distribution is anticipated for these classifications, then these should be used to categorize performance at every stage of the course. On degree courses which lead to a professional quali-fication, there has to be a negotiation between college staff and agency staff who supervise students on placement to determine the grade, mark or classification. A common problem is the disposition of practice supervisors to bunch students in the higher grades. The negotiation between assessors should be, firstly to recognize the typical distribution of students into bands and, secondly, to produce descriptions of the typical performance of a student who would be located in each band. For example, if placement supervisors understand that First Class Honours are typically awarded to the best 10 per cent, then they are asked to describe the kind of performance of which they think that proportion of trainees – and they would be the best – are capable. Similar descriptions can then be produced for the other bands in relation to their anticipated frequency of occurrence. This system has the advantage of starting from the reasonable assumption that there are individual differences in performances (as there are for all known human activities); that assessors can recognize these differences; and that Honours classifications should recog-nize these assessed differences and in proportions which broadly mirror conventions of distribution. This approach is, of course, wholly compatible with the identification of areas of competence and performance which are the elements and criteria which underpin the Honours classification.

Some time has been spent on this issue. Not only is it a major problem in the new professional Honours degrees which have been the main structural development in education and training for the health and social service professions but also the approach to it is a clear indicator of the location of the course in the curriculum models under review. A 'pass/fail' approach to placement is usually associated with a clear dichotomy between academic and professional studies. This in its turn places clear limits on the integration of theory and practice. Assessment of practice for Honours, on the other hand, seems to influence the structure of the whole curriculum. With this central focus on the classification of performance on placement, topics for college-based study are selected for their relevance to, and utility for, per-formance on placement. In particular, they should have a direct bearing on the decisions which practitioners have to make: how they conceive prob-lems and how they conceive of, and evaluate, solutions.

2. College-based practice

Since supervised practice is relatively uncontrolled in its nature and subject to variability of situation, opportunity and supervision, another indicator of the action-focus approach is the extent to which controlled and supervised practice, often of a simulated nature, is a feature of the college curriculum. Such controlled and graded experience, with the opportunities afforded for detailed feedback and further practice, provides the ideal of pegs on which to hang a theoretical input. This input in its turn must be seen to influence the way in which students perceive, plan for, act in and evaluate simulated or controlled practice. Thus, for example, trainee health visitors would prepare for the home visits which are a crucial part of their work by practising the initial encounter with the client when they first enter their homes. Students prove adept at simulating the behaviour of those visited and this itself can give them insights into the feelings such persons may have. The trainee is prepared for the simulation through sensitization to key skills and practice is given in discriminating, for example, between open and closed questions. The trainee then practises questioning in the simulation and has an opportunity to view personal performance prior to practising again to improve or refine it. This constitutes the classic discrimination-practice–feedback-practice cycle of Social Skill Training which is considered in detail in Ellis and Whittington (1983). Examples of the background material which is taught in relation to component skills can be found in Hargie *et al.* (1981) and includes coverage of non-verbal communication, reinforcement, questioning, reflecting, set induction and closure, explanation, listening, self-disclosure, assertiveness and leadership, all highly relevant skills for those professions whose stock-in-trade is interaction with clients at the interpersonal level.

3. Curriculum structure and models of practice
A third indicator is the approach to the structure of the curriculum and the topics selected. So-called professional and academic studies must be structured to interrelate in their reference to practice whether this is college or placement based. Certainly, courses in the principles and practice of the profession concerned are the first line of integration with practice and must have an explicit relationship with courses or units in academic disciplines. This process of integration requires some model of professional practice, in broad terms, to organize the inputs into action. The so-called nursing process breaks professional practice down into four stages:
1. Assessment of client or patient need.
2. Planning to meet that need.
3. Implementation of the intervention decided.
4. Evaluation of the success of the intervention.

This is a version of the planning, implementation and evaluation model outlined above. The model extends these notions to include assessment as a necessary precursor of planning and as a stage which overlaps with evaluation in a cyclical cybernetic approach.

4. Approach to academic disciplines
The academic disciplines themselves will be taught not just to cover theoretical and empirical content but also to emphasize their method and approach to knowledge. This will, in scientific subjects, almost certainly require practical work where students have an opportunity to experience the reality of being, say, a psychological investigator. The methods and lessons learned through this practical work should then be applied to the decisions of professional practice.

Thus four indicators of the action-focus approach have been described:

1. **Differentiated** assessment of practical work.
2. **Structured** professional practical work in college.
3. **Integration** of topics across all modules into a model or models of professional action.
4. **Practical work** in academic courses to emphasize approach to knowledge and its application to practice.

I have set out the main features of an action-focus approach as a solution to the problems of the integration of theory and practice in professional courses. The relationship of the model to current concerns with competence and quality assurance have been discussed. Finally, four indicators of a curriculum organized along these lines have been described.

Nursing and social work

How then does reality measure up to these ideals and standards? It is beyond the scope of this chapter to review all curriculum developments in the professions to which the model might apply. I have decided to concentrate on two, nursing and social work, where there have been major curriculum initiatives over the last five years. In each case, the statutory body responsible for registration has decided to make major changes in the structure of basic education and training. In order to prepare practitioners who could cope with new needs and demands in a changing world, each body concentrated on the objectives and structure of initial training. Significantly, both saw the role of higher education as a crucial factor. However, while nursing saw a move towards or into higher education as crucial, social work saw it as necessary to curb the influence of higher education by insisting on a partnership between colleges and agencies as a necessary condition for acceptable planning and delivery.

The two professions were, of course, starting from different bases. Nurses' training was, typically, carried out in schools or colleges that were closely aligned with hospitals. Student nurses were conceived as part of the NHS workforce, albeit at an apprentice level. Completion of the basic training and consequent state registration was of little or no significance academically. The most generous credit allowed for this three-year preparation was one full credit in the Open University compared to non-graduate teachers who were given three full credits. Social work education and training, on the other hand, was typically undertaken in polytechnics and universities. Basic training led to the CQSW (Certificate of Qualification in Social Work) of the Central Council for the Education and Training in Social Work (CCETSW) and was coupled with a non-graduate Diploma, Bachelors, Postgraduate Diploma or Masters depending primarily on the qualifications of students on entry.

Each professional body set out its scheme in a comprehensive proposal document. That for nursing was described as *Project 2000*; that for social work as *Document 30: the Diploma in Social Work*. The main recommendations of *Project 2000* relevant to this chapter were the competencies proposed for all nurses and the structural alterations to the initial training course, the move towards higher education, and the status of the student enrolled on it. Strangely, the document says little about the curriculum itself other than to propose a division into a common foundation period followed by a specialized branch and to suggest that it should lead to academic as well as professional recognition. There is no explicit consideration of the problems posed by the integration of theory and practice nor any requirements which would lead to the fulfilment of the action-focus criteria. This neglect of specific curriculum guidance in a document which proposes radical changes in an educational system is odd but explicable in part by a division of labour between the United Kingdom Central Council (UKCC) concerned with the registration of nurses and the National Boards for England, Scotland, Wales and Northern Ireland. It is these Boards which actually validate courses as being professionally appropriate and it is these Boards which have issued detailed curriculum guidelines.

However, the guidelines from the National Boards have not advanced beyond the semantic conjunction approach characterized above. Suggestions are made about topics which should be covered with no recognition of the distinctions between description and prescription, knowing how and knowing that, and the levels of theory addressed earlier. Furthermore, while the importance of practice is emphasized, this rests upon minimum hour requirements and statements of competence which do not translate readily into assessment schedules. Nowhere is it laid down that there should be detailed assessment of practice and that this should be a major weighting in the academic award. Nor is it suggested that practice should be the focus of all studies or that disciplines might bring to practice an approach rather than necessarily substance.

In the absence of such advice, it is hardly surprising that the integration with higher education and the meeting of higher education standards becomes the priority. Curriculum planners tend therefore to move away from their previous emphasis on practical skills to pursue more academic goals. In so doing, they are in danger of regressing through the curriculum models outlined in this chapter and resting, at best, at the semantic conjunction approach. Students encounter academic theory, nursing theory and the exigencies of practice. Practice itself is typically assessed on a 'pass/fail' basis and is discrete from academic assessment of nursing and other theory. This is a pity since nursing, with its widespread emphasis on a process model, of assessment, planning, implementation and evaluation has a ready-made link from theory into practice.

The net result of *Project 2000* might well be to make the integration of theory and practice through an action-focus less likely. In the pursuit of academic recognition, colleges may have been diverted from their roots in practice. A close relation with practice at all stages of training is essential for professions whose purpose is to meet the needs of patients and there is some danger of this link being weakened through the well-intentioned push towards academe of *Project 2000*.

Social work, on the other hand, secure in its academic credibility, has had different priorities. The CQSW had been run, for a number of years, in parallel with a subordinate Certificate in Social Services. Typically, this qualification was sought by employees of social service agencies. Their course was planned and delivered by a partnership between employers and colleges (sometimes higher education but usually further education). This approach was perceived by employers as producing a competent practitioner whose capabilities matched the requirements of service. Colleges rose to the challenge of demonstrating that their teaching led to enhanced competence. Competence could include the capacity to be reflective not for its own sake but because the reflective, self-critical practitioner was more likely to solve problems through the generation of new solutions.

Fired with success in these courses and subject, like all professions to a pressure to demonstrate cost-effective competencies in its practitioners, CCETSW reviewed the two levels of qualification and the strengths and weaknesses of the methods of training. Their recommendations were for a new qualification, the Diploma in Social Work, which would replace the two certificates. It was argued that all courses should extend over three years (typically they were two in duration) and, crucially, that they should be planned and delivered as a *partnership* between employers and colleges. The document also produced curriculum guidelines and these include both competencies and curriculum content.

The results of these enforced partnerships are still emerging. However, there are early indications that they have been stimulating to the participants and very productive. They have certainly moved the social work curriculum closer to my action-focus ideal. For the first time, there has been a real negotiation between a competency-based approach, represented by employers and a more reflective theory-based education represented by colleges. (This is, of course, a gross oversimplification but is probably true to major trends.) In this planning, competence and its assessment have been given the central positions. But following from this has come a clearer identification of the relationship between academic material and the observation, planning, action and evaluation cycle of professional practice. Furthermore, the notion of competence has extended to recognize the functional value of a practitioner looking at the needs of clients and the possibilities of intervention from a number of perspectives. Typically, therefore, the new social work courses are more likely to meet the action-focus criteria. The concentration on competence and its assessment facilitates differentiated assessment and grading which can play a major part in the weighting of the linked academic award. Preparation for practice in simulated but structured college-based situations are encouraged as is the relating of theoretical material to practical problems. In such an environment the *approach* of academic disciplines may well be seen to be more potent than their temporary content.

These two snapshots of developments in professional training have been of necessity brief, superficial and, no doubt, oversimplified to make a point. However, their main message does have validity and should be salutary to other professions relatively young in higher education including physiotherapy, occupational therapy, chiropody, radiography and speech therapy not to mention older inhabitants such as teaching and even medicine.

Academic credibility can be a siren call if it undermines the close relation that there must be between professional training and practice. In particular, the partnership approach is commended since it gives formal recognition to the shared responsibility between practitioners and educators. The college will protect the integrity of educators; comparable status must be afforded to employers who have to maintain standards of delivery.

The action-focus curriculum has been proposed as the solution to apparently intractable problems of integration. A partnership between agencies and colleges for the planning and delivery of courses seems the optimum environment for it to flourish.

References

Cameron-Jones, M. (1989) 'Looking for quality and competence in teaching' in R. Ellis (ed.) *Professional Competence and Quality Assurance in the Caring Professions.* London, Chapman and Hall.

Ellis, R. (1980) 'Social skill training for the interpersonal professions' in W. Singleton, P. Spurgeon and R. Stammers (eds) *The Analysis of Social Skill.* New York, Plenum.

Ellis, R. (ed.) (1989) *Professional Competence and Quality Assurance in the Caring Professions.* London, Chapman and Hall.

Ellis, R. and Whittington, D. (1979) 'Skills in context: A model for the speech therapy curriculum.' Proceedings of the Fifth IUT Conference, University of Maryland.

Ellis, R. and Whittington, D. (1981) *A Guide to Social Skill Training.* London, Croom Helm.

Ellis, R. and Whittington, D. (eds) (1983) *New Directions in Social Skill Training.* London, Croom Helm/New York, Methuen.

Hargie, O., Saunders, C. and Dickson, D. (1981) *Social Skills in Interpersonal Communication.* London, Croom Helm/New York, Methuen.

Hume, D. (1748) *An Enquiry concerning Human Understanding.* Reprinted 1975. Oxford, Clarendon Press.

Ryle, G. (1949) *The Concept of Mind.* London, Hutchinson.

6

The Law Teachers' Dilemma

Diana Tribe and A.J. Tribe

Introduction

This chapter seeks to describe and evaluate contemporary changes in legal education in the UK, with particular reference to the development of skills and/or competencies as a formal part of the law undergraduate curriculum. Throughout the chapter, the polytechnics and colleges sector is separately identified from the university sector, although in 1992 the binary line will disappear and most if not all polytechnics will be known as universities.

This first section considers the development of the 'skills' movement which has taken place in undergraduate legal education in the past decade. This is then followed by a discussion of the problems associated with the definition, teaching and assessment of these skills.

There has been pressure over the last 25 years to integrate general interpersonal and study skills training within the academic content of all undergraduate degree courses in the UK. The Robbins Report identified this as a pressing need as early as 1963, yet in 1984 the University Grants Committee was still urging higher education institutions to take this problem seriously.

> The abilities most valued in industrial, commercial and professional life as well as in public and social administration are the transferable intellectual and personal skills. A higher education system which provides its students with these skills is serving society well.[1]

Resistance to the incorporation of skills training into the higher education undergraduate curriculum in the UK occurred in all subject areas, however, including law. One reason for this resistance was the firmly entrenched view of many lecturers that such work was not appropriate to 'high level' academic study at degree level and should thus be left for students to develop at the professional stage of training or when they were eventually in employment. However, the opposing view, that the development of skills in a higher education context *does* require a high level of academic rigour is gaining ground among lecturers in the polytechnics and colleges sector (and in a few universities) as staff are gaining experience of skills programmes. There was also a fear that academic staff, employed for their academic subject knowledge, would not have the expertise to provide the necessary skills training, even if such training was thought to be a desirable component of undergraduate education. This problem has to a certain extent been addressed through staff development programmes within institutions, though there is much to achieve yet in this sphere.

There has, however, continued to be pressure from outside bodies, as well as from intending employers (represented by the Standing Conference on Graduate Employment) to incorporate personal transferable skills into higher education, and, as a result, there has developed over the past 10 years a trend for those courses validated by the Council for National Academic Awards (until recently, the degree-awarding body for polytechnics and colleges in the UK) to include training in what are variously referred to as enterprise or interpersonal skills, which are taught alongside the academic material traditionally associated with undergraduate study. The Royal Society of Arts 'Higher Education for Capability' movement and the 'Enterprise' movement in the UK have each encouraged, and in some cases funded, curriculum innovation in the teaching and assessment of skills on undergraduate programmes (see Chapters 12 and 13). So, too, has the CNAA (for example its research into profiling and records of achievement as methods of assessing skills training programmes). Members of Her Majesty's Educational Inspectorate, who as arbiters of quality have become increasingly influential over the past decade in the polytechnic sector, have also used their influence to encourage the development of new assessment techniques to assess the personal and interpersonal skills of students, and the greater use of more varied teaching techniques to encourage student participation.[2]

Insofar as undergraduate *legal* education is concerned, the integration of skills teaching into the undergraduate curriculum has proceeded apace over the past five years, at least in the polytechnics and colleges sector. This may be because the subject content of law degrees lends itself readily to the development of skills training in such areas as interviewing, negotiating or document drafting. Moreover, the Law Society and the Council of Legal Education have also recently begun to demonstrate interest in skills training at the professional level, and have emphasized to providers of law undergraduate courses the importance which intending legal employers place on these skills.

Interestingly, the professional bodies (The Law Society and the Council of Legal Education), who regulate the subject content of qualifying/exempting law degrees for the professions in the six 'core' law subjects (Contract, Tort, Property, Equity, Crime, Constitutional Law) have agreed (1988) to a reduced law content in these subjects, and have become more flexible about methods of assessment (e.g. permitting a higher proportion of in-course assessment than was previously the case). This in turn has made it possible for the designers of undergraduate law programmes to be more innovative, in terms of course delivery, using some of the time, which was traditionally required for the transmission of law content, for skills-based activities. It has also become possible for novel forms of assessment to be used (such as peer or collaborative assessment) as part of the overall assessment package, and, at least at one institution, students leaving with a law degree will also take with them a record of achievement which identifies skills in which students have become proficient.[3]

Other academic areas which are often organizationally connected with law such as Business and Management Studies (in many institutions Law forms part of a business faculty, or school of study), have not been without their influence on Law degree curricula. Their use of case study material, active learning packages and the development of interpersonal skills in those areas, has been adopted by law staff, whilst in some institutions, such as Leeds Polytechnic, the Law degree programme is now a part of a larger modular business programme, the original skills objectives of which now also apply to the undergraduate law route.

A further influence on course designers has been student demand. As more and more applicants for undergraduate Law courses are becoming aware of the importance attached by employers to the 'well-rounded' graduate with skills other than the purely academic, students are now beginning actively to seek out courses which are advertised as providing the sort of training that they feel will prove useful to them, in what is currently (1992) a contracting Law employment market.

Research shows that the actual content of skills training on Law degree courses varies very much from one institution to another.[4] However, the skills covered usually fall into one of the following broad categories:

1. *Vocational skills for the legal profession* (sometimes referred to as clinical legal education). Here students are involved in training in a Law centre (or simulated Law centre) context, to develop the specific practitioner skills employed by legal professionals. The aim of this activity is to prepare students for their eventual employment as solicitors or barristers. Skills commonly included in such programmes include:

   - legal analysis
   - professional/ethical responsiveness
   - advocacy
   - litigation management
   - legal advice
   - legal document drafting

2. *General professional skills* (developed for general employment purposes). Skills such as these are designed to prepare students for all types of professional occupational contexts. Training in some or all of these employment skills is often incorporated into undergraduate Law courses (for instance, at Hatfield Polytechnic, all Law students can study a Modern Language or Business Practice as an integral part of their Law degree).

The rationale behind the integration of general professional skills into Law degrees is that not all students will necessarily enter the legal profession at the end of their undergraduate training. Indeed, the evidence suggests that only about 50 per cent will actually do so. However, the large majority will eventually enter into employment of some kind, either in Law or elsewhere, for which these more general professional skills will be appropriate. The types of skills normally included in programmes such as this will include:

- time management
- case management
- chairmanship
- negotiation
- client interviewing
- document drafting
- information technology skills
- foreign-language skills

3. *Life skills* (for personal development purposes). This is training which aims to help a student to maximize future potential, not simply in relation to employment, but also personal life. These are skills which it is claimed all undergraduate students need to develop as a fundamental basis for personal intellectual development, regardless of subject or occupational context. They include oral and written communication, self-management, information retrieval, word processing and research/study skills.

In practice, there is obviously a clear overlap between these three categories of skills training (for instance in order to be a competent interviewer of legal clients, good personal communication skills are essential). However, it is helpful to identify them in this way when analysing the undergraduate Law programmes at different institutions. The specialized clinical legal education courses are more easily identified than those which contain more general skills components, but all are features to some extent of modern legal undergraduate education in the UK, and some Law degree programmes include training which combines elements from each group (the Law degrees at Anglia, Hatfield, Huddersfield and Central London Polytechnics, and at Southampton College of Higher Education all fall into this category).

Of course, not all Law degree courses have developed skills components in this way. Curiously, those polytechnics which have traditionally offered the Law Society Finals Course (the second, and professional stage of training for Law graduates) have often been least involved in this area of curriculum development. Investigations by Macfarlane[5] and Tribe and Tribe[6] showed that skills training was included in the *formal* curriculum of only a limited number of public-sector institutions, although in many others skills coverage was informally encouraged (through debating, mooting or client interviewing) and integrated into Law subjects across the curriculum. In the early

1980s, universities such as Warwick, Kent and Brunel introduced specific clinical-practice programmes as a part of their undergraduate curriculum. These programmes gave students the opportunity to represent real clients before tribunals, and assessment of these representation activities contributed towards their final degree classification. However, clinical legal education is specifically oriented towards legal advice, legal representation and lawyering skills, and does not have the broad base of much of the more general occupational and personal skills work now developing in the polytechnics and colleges.

It is not coincidental that at the same time that these changes have been occurring in undergraduate legal education, there have been similar upheavals at the professional stage of training (which follows immediately after the academic undergraduate stage, and lasts for one year). The final examination for the Bar (which provides professional training for barristers) now includes a substantial element of skills training and assessment, and at the time of writing the new Bar finals course has just entered its second year of operation; this change has not been achieved without some difficulties. Despite this experience, however, the Law Society (which provides professional training for solicitors) has approved similar changes in its own professional examination, as a result of which the Law Society finals course will be replaced by the Legal Practice Course in 1993. A major re-appraisal of the basis of legal training has occurred here,[7] in which the emphasis placed on knowledge of substantive law has been replaced by an element of 'skills training' of the kind pioneered in Commonwealth professional legal education.

A final point here is that in some polytechnics, skills training is carried out in discrete curriculum components (which may be either optional or compulsory parts of the undergraduate programme). In others, however, skills training is included as an integral curriculum component, permeating all or many subject areas. Yet other polytechnics adopt both of these approaches so that there are specific legal skills training courses which contribute towards final degree classification, together with interpersonal and group skills training through the medium of subject areas such as Criminal Law or the Law of Contract. It should be noted however, that our evidence[8] suggests that differences between institutions in modes of course delivery derive from historical accident as much as from intentional curriculum design. Thus, the Birmingham Law in Context courses, where students are involved in simulated personal injury litigation, have been developed by staff with a particular interest in this form of teaching and who have a professional legal background. In other institutions, where staff with different academic interests are employed, such courses have not as yet been developed.

Teaching and learning processes

Which skills are taught?

The research referred to earlier has shown that there is a wide range of skills which it has been thought appropriate to include as a part of the undergraduate legal programme. Obviously these vary from institution to institution. However, it would appear that they cover the three broad areas of competence referred to above.

How are these skills taught?

Writing in 1987, Alan Blake described traditional law teaching methods as:

> a series of lectures with little or no student involvement and a tutorial programme . . . [which is] the only form of student participation that takes place during the whole of the student's academic legal education. The tutorial consists of analysing the answers prepared in advance to artificial Janet and John Doe problems, or esoteric essay questions.[9]

Blake is unduly pessimistic however. Over the past decade, there *has* been a shift away from the traditional didactic Law lecturing techniques towards a more student-centered (or in some cases student-led) approach;[10] indeed it is clear that this is necessary wherever Law lecturers are involved in developing student skills.

Thus, at Leicester Polytechnic, students on the Medical Law option in the final year share the preparation and delivery of lectures with the academic staff. In some cases, specific skills are taught in what has become known as a 'transactional context'; this means that a skill such as interviewing or drafting is taught in the context of a simulated action. Birmingham Polytechnic Law School led the field in this area with its Civil and Criminal Law in Context programmes, which have run in their present form since the mid-1980s. There are now several other degrees validated or accredited by the CNAA which have followed this lead, providing skills training through legal simulations. For instance, the fact management module on the second year of the Law degree at Anglia Polytechnic is based on a personal injury action, thus providing a meaningful link with the substantive law content of the negligence course taught earlier in the year. Training of this type has often been based on courses such as the Professional Legal Training Course (PLTC) in British Columbia which evolved in the early 1980s and was designed on the 'corkscrew model'. Rather than teaching skills and substantive law in discrete compartments, they are interwoven at increasing levels of complexity, through the various content areas of substantive law. In all programmes of this type however, 'active learning rather than passive information absorption is the hallmark of the teaching units'.[11] Although the PLTC is an outstanding example of an integrated *professional* skills training programme, there are similar courses in Scotland, Ireland, Australia and New Zealand which have been equally successful and equally influential in England.[12]

An alternative approach to the teaching of some skills has been that adopted by institutions such as Anglia Polytechnic where basic communication skills of writing and reading are taught in a compulsory free-standing first-year module, without any attempt to relate them to a specific legal context. The rationale for this approach is that the demands of a simulated legal context interfere with the acquisition of skills at this basic level. Similarly, at Leeds Polytechnic the foundation year skills course, taught free of context, is offered to all students on the Business Modular Programme, as an integral part of the Law degree.

Yet another approach which is now quite widely used, is to integrate the teaching of skills into the teaching of substantive curriculum areas.[13] Thus, at Huddersfield Polytechnic, group skills are taught and assessed as part of the Criminal Law and Tort programmes through the technique of seminar assessment. Here, students are assessed, not simply on their knowledge of Law, but also on the way that they operate as seminar group leaders and group members, and the extent to which their verbal communication skills meet certain predetermined criteria. They lead seminar and tutorial sessions, not simply in the time-honoured way of reading a paper, but actually taking over the management of, and responsibility for, the whole session. They prepare handouts, ask searching questions of their colleagues and draw conclusions as a result of discussion. In sessions such as these, the tutor acts as facilitator and resource, rather than as organizer. It has been found that this approach increases student preparation, participation and attendance, and has a positive effect on students' learning of the Law, as well as on their skills development.

How are these skills assessed?

Our survey in 1989 showed that the methods used for the assessment of skills vary very much from skill to skill within institutions, as well as between institutions. In some cases there is no formal assessment; all that is required for students to pass is their attendance. In others, assessment is based upon a mixture of attendance and written work, whilst in yet others this is combined with, or an alternative to, more innovative techniques such as filmed presentations, tribunal representation, or a comparison of the outcomes of negotiation exercises. In most institutions, several methods are combined in use, and in at least three (South Bank, Hatfield, Southampton) there is a schedule of component sub-skills which is used as a basis for the allocation of marks.[14]

What has become clear, however, is that there is a fundamental conceptual problem associated both with the delivery of skills training and its assessment, in that there is a shortage of objective criteria by which to judge students' performance. Put simply, the problem is: if we assume that it is, for example, appropriate to teach the skills of interviewing to intending lawyers we must identify the skills which make a good interviewer, and then identify the behaviours (or sub-skills) which combine to make up those skills. These behaviours (or sub-skills) will then form the basis for a teaching programme and for subsequent student assessment. We may argue, for instance, that in order to perform an interviewing task effectively, a student must be a competent listener, but this means that we must then identify the behaviours or sub-skills which will indicate this. Thus a breakdown of desirable listening behaviours might be as follows. An effective student interviewer:

- shows interest in the person who is speaking
- shows interest in the subject under discussion
- continues to listen when the subject becomes boring
- does not allow prejudice to reduce attention
- does not permit enthusiasm to carry them away
- is not critical of the other person's speech or method of delivery
- regularly summarizes what is heard
- checks for understanding
- does not allow emotional reactions to affect understanding
- concentrates when difficult ideas are being expressed
- creates the right environment for listening
- allows sufficient time for full understanding before reacting
- makes a final review of understanding of facts

Even if such sub-skills can be conceptualized in this way, the problem is still short of solution, since each sub-skill remains capable of further breakdown into component low inference behaviours. For instance the sub-skill 'shows interest in the person who is speaking', may be identified by such behaviours as:

- intermittent eye-contact
- head nodding
- smiling
- avoiding looking at watch
- avoiding interruptions from phone/colleagues

In any case, it may be the *balance* between the sub-skills, when they are combined together which is most important in the carrying out of the overall interviewing task.

   If one cannot identify with sufficient clarity exactly what students should achieve, it is difficult to assess whether, and to what extent, they have achieved it. The inarticulated idiosyncratic model 'I cannot define it but I know it when I see it' works, as Cort and Sammons have said,[15] in only a very limited way. Not surprisingly, although there are many skills training pro-grammes within law courses in the UK, it is rare to find that their objectives have been clearly defined in the way suggested above. The study of Cort and Sammons attempts such an analysis based not upon empirical study of what it is that professional lawyers do, but rather on an observation of student attempts to carry out lawyer operations. This results in the identification of six major competencies.[16] The Antioch Competency Based Model[17] takes this approach considerably further; here 53 lawyering tasks are defined, each of which is then split down into approximately ten observable behaviours per task. Each of these is then in turn divided into several sub-sets with marks specifically allocated to each sub-set on a ten point scale. Individual ratings are eventually combined to give a score for each student. A variation on this method is in use at Mercer University[18] where some of the original 53 competencies are identified as being essential for students to acquire, whilst others are only desirable, thus providing additional complexities in an already complex system. Whilst such systems appear to be systematically based, there is no set of objective criteria for the allocation of marks which still proceeds on a subjective basis; moreover, there is no provision for assessing the manner in which the sub-skills are combined to produce the total competency in question.

Another fundamental problem relates to the actual *grading* of skills activities by staff. Even supposing that skills can be identified and defined, what criteria should be used in allocating marks to their performance? What is the basis for distinguishing between 60 and 70 per cent in a negotiation exercise when so much depends on context (i.e. the strength of the other negotiating party) that it is only possible to make rough numerical judgements about individual performances. Additionally, academic staff need extensive training to be able to use a skills schedule such as the Antioch model, and the whole system is time consuming and expensive; it seems extremely unlikely that such a method would recommend itself to UK academics.

The difficulties referred to above in defining and assessing skills have meant that for many colleagues in the UK a written form of assessment in which students are asked simply to *reflect* on their acquisition of skills, was the natural and preferred method. Thus students might be asked to present a casebook outlining negotiation planning, tactics used and outcomes achieved as a basis for assessment. Although this may indicate something about an individual student's self-appraisal, it is not, though, an objective test of his/her actual negotiation skills. It is understandable that staff prefer assessment based on written work since it can be assessed by more than one member of staff, it can be repeated if unsatisfactory, and it can be sent to the external examiner in cases of doubt. Furthermore, there is a feeling among lecturing staff that such written assessment is in some way more 'objective' and 'reliable' than the assessment of practical work. However, with the advent of the Legal Practice Course, which will be introduced in some institutions by September 1993, colleagues are at last beginning to move away from these unsatisfactory practices.

Conclusion

Despite the conceptual and practical problems outlined above, the integration of skills teaching on undergraduate Law degree courses proceeds apace in the UK, if for no other reason than that such developments are seen as a necessary preliminary for institutions which wish to offer the prestigious and financially rewarding Legal Practice Course. Those polytechnics and colleges which can demonstrate a commitment to skills teaching and assessment as an integral part of their undergraduate programme of study, will be more likely to be chosen as providers of the new Legal Practice Course with its heavy emphasis on skills.

Evaluation of the effect of the integration of skills components into Law degrees remains largely at the descriptive, or anecdotal stage, and in some cases there seems to be an absence of academic rigour in the normal course appraisal mechanisms (annual monitoring and quinquennial review). HMI have been effective in appraising methods of course delivery, but their role has not really been to evaluate curriculum design.

At present, the brightest hope in this difficult area is the funding being offered by the CNAA as a part of the CASEL (Competences, Assessment and Education in Undergraduate Law Courses) project, the first stage of which (Assessing Competencies) is intended to assist institutions in evaluating the skills assessment work that is already being undertaken. Following a telephone survey of institutions, all law departments in the polytechnics and colleges sector, and some in the university sector, were invited to tender for funds which would be awarded for the development and implementation of reliable and valid methods of assessing legal competences. Five institutions were selected[19] in July 1991, and work on this first stage of the Project was due to be completed by July 1992.

One research project which will be carried out with CASEL funding will be to develop a collection of video-taped material which identifies the performance of certain skills at different levels of competence. Thus, video material of students performing certain pre-identified skills behaviours will be collected and analysed by the project team, and classified as being 'good', 'pass' or 'fail' standard. Other internal assessors will then observe samples of the video material to check the reliability of these identifications, prior to their appraisal by external assessors with professional legal experience, this external phase providing a measure of validity.

A library of video recordings of certain skills being performed by students will thus be collected and retained, together with written commentary in note form, for the training of future internal assessors. The aim here is to develop a shared understanding between staff and students as to the level of skills performance which students are intended to achieve during the course of their education. It is this kind of practical analysis of skills activities which has been missing in the past, largely due to a lack of resources to support its development. It is to be hoped that the CASEL project, and others like it, will be a stimulus to further much needed practical work in this area.

Notes

1. UGC/NAB (1984) *Higher Education and the Needs of Society.* Joint UGC and NAB Publication, London, HMSO.

2. HMI (1990) *A Survey of Undergraduate Legal Education: a report of twelve Law schools by HMI.* London, HMSO.
3. LL.B (Hons) at Hatfield Polytechnic.
4. Tribe, D.M.R. and Tribe, A.J. (1990) 'Taking skills seriously – skills assessment for the 1990s.' Paper presented to the CNAA/Hatfield Polytechnic Symposium on Skills, June.
5. Macfarlane, J. (1988) *An Evaluation of the Role and Practice of Clinical Legal Education with Particular Reference to the Role of Legal Education in the UK*, Chapter 5, para 5.2, unpublished PhD thesis, CNAA.
6. Tribe and Tribe, op. cit.
7. The Law Society (1990) *Training Tomorrow's Solicitors.* London, The Law Society.
8. Macfarlane, op. cit.
9. Blake, A. (1987) 'A strategy for legal education into the 1990s.' *The Law Teacher*, 21(1), 1–9.
10. Tribe, D.M.R. and Tribe, A.J. (1985) 'Paperchase revisited; The Huddersfield Experiment.' *The Law Teacher*, 19(2), 4–36. See also Weaver, M. (1983) 'Clinical legal education – competing perspectives.' *The Law Teacher*, 17(1), 1–10.
11. Cruickshank, D.A. (1985) 'The professional legal training course in British Columbia, Canada.' *Journal of Professional Legal Education*, 3, 111–32.
12. For an excellent survey see Cruickshank, D.A. (1985) 'Bar admission training in the United States, the United Kingdom, Ireland and Australia' in Matas and Macauley (eds) *Legal Education in Canada.* See also Nathanson, S. (1987) 'Putting skills and transactions together in professional legal education'. *J. Prof. Legal Educ.* 2, 187.
13. Tribe, D.M.R. and Tribe, A.J. (1990) *Skills Teaching on Law Degrees.* Proceedings of Conference held at the Institute of Advanced Legal Studies, February.
14. Macfarlane, op. cit.
15. Cort, H.R. and Sammons, J.L. (1980) 'The search for good lawyering: a concept and model of lawyering competencies'. *Cleveland State Law Review*, 29(3), 397–450.
16. Cort and Sammons, op. cit.
17. The Six Major Competencies are defined as: Oral Competency; Written Competency; Legal Analysis; Problem Solving Competency; Professional Responsibility Competency; Practice Management Competency.
18. Tyler, R. (1980) 'AALS Clinical Legal Education Panel; valuation and assessment of student performance.' *Cleveland State Law Review*, 603–6.
19. Central London, Hatfield, Newcastle and South Bank Polytechnics and the University of Warwick.

7

Developing the Knowledge Base: A Process Perspective on Professional Education

Michael Eraut

The professions and higher education

The professions constitute a sub-set of occupations whose boundary is ill-defined. Features such as length of training, licence to practise, code of ethics, self-regulation and monopoly feature in most discussions about the nature of professions but do not provide a workable definition nor remain stable over time. Hence Johnson (1972, 1984) argues that, instead of defining what constitutes a profession, we should regard *professionalism* as an ideology and *professionalization* as the process by which an occupation seeks to advance its status and progress towards full recognition within that ideology. Irrespective of what professionals actually do, their knowledge claims are strongly influenced by the need to sustain the ideology of professionalism and further the process of professionalization. Since higher education also derives its authority from knowledge claims, the history of the relationship between higher education and the professions has to be seen in this political context.

Since the Second World War, an increasing number of occupations have taken advantage of higher education, for two main reasons. First, getting a degree entry route established validates the profession's claim to a specialist knowledge base, and hence to professional status. Second, recruitment through the higher education system is critical for sustaining, let alone improving, the relative quality of a profession's intake.

Higher education has also derived considerable benefits from its relationship with the professions. The presence of professionally-focused courses has helped increasingly beleaguered institutions to argue that they do prepare students for employment and make a positive contribution to society. They have contributed to the expansion of student numbers, particularly in the public sector; and individual faculties and departments have been able to increase their relative power by incorporating areas of professional training which were previously outside higher education. Indeed, the widespread incorporation of paramedical training was strongly aided by the wish to sustain the number of Science students at a time of declining recruitment for degrees in pure Science (Jones, 1986).

Although both partners stood to benefit, there were many complicated negotiations between professional bodies and representatives of higher education, often involving other agencies as well. The professions sought to maintain their control over the licence to practise, while higher education sought to permeate new courses with its espoused aims of breadth, intellectual challenge and the development of critical abilities (Kerr, 1984). In a very real sense, these negotiations involved both partners in a reconstruction of the professional knowledge base. However, it is arguable how far this started from first principles. The resultant compromises could equally be described in terms of power-sharing between two distinct historical traditions.

The most obvious area of compromise is the structure of the training period. Three distinct patterns stand out. First there is the dual qualification system, favoured by Law and Surveying, in which a degree approved by the professional body is followed by a period of apprenticeship in professional practice and separate assessment for licensing purposes. This tends to be favoured by the more powerful professions, which can justify a long training period and argue that their knowledge base demands at least three years of full-time study. Its major disadvantage is the acute separation of theory from practice. Second, there is a concurrent system, in which periods of professional practice are built into the higher degree course. The power of the profession is considerably less, but may be asserted in two ways: through the assessment of the professional practice component or through the course-approval process, although neither is guaranteed in all professions. Concurrent systems offer greater opportunities for integrating theory with practice, but this potential is still underdeveloped. Some sandwich courses fit this more integrated pattern, for example those in Design. But others are only dual qualification systems in disguise: in Engineering, for example, there is little integration and undergraduate trainees are underused on many placements. Third, there is an increasing range of patterns associated with part-time study, some of which incorporate links with students' regular employment: Personnel Management and Management Accountancy use this as their major route to qualifications.

The negotiations over content have had equally pervasive results because the traditional higher education concern with disciplined, codified, propositional knowledge has usually triumphed. Either degree courses have been heavily weighted by components from 'recognized disciplines', or professional departments have been influenced by higher education norms towards giving research priority over developing professional practice. The result has been what Schön (1983) has called the dominant 'technical rationality' model of professional knowledge, which is characterized by a number of features:

> the systematic knowledge base of a profession is thought to have four essential properties. It is specialised, firmly bounded, scientific and standardised.
>
> (Schön, 1983, p. 23)

> the two primary bases for specialization within a profession are (1) the substantive field of knowledge that the specialist professes to command and (2) the technique of production or application of knowledge over which the specialist claims mastery.
>
> (Moore, 1970, p. 141)

> the concept of 'application' leads to a view of professional knowledge as a hierarchy in which 'general principles' occupy the highest level and 'concrete problem solving' the lowest.
>
> (Schön, 1983, p. 24)

Schön goes on to argue that this definition of rigorous professional knowledge excludes situations and phenomena which many professionals perceive as central to their practice. Knowledge of central importance to providing services to clients is accorded low priority in higher education or omitted altogether (see Chapter 3).

Behind Schön's position lies the view that the term 'knowledge' should be interpreted with the broadest possible meaning. Thus it should not be confined to codified, propositional knowledge but should also include personal knowledge, tacit knowledge, process knowledge and know-how. All kinds of knowledge are necessary to professional performance; and they should therefore be accorded parity of esteem in higher education. This viewpoint has also received some support from professional educators in the UK and from groups such as the Education for Capability movement (see Chapter 13) and the Enterprise in Higher Education initiative (see Chapter 12), which have their own perspectives. Hence the fundamental issue of different kinds of professional knowledge will be explored at some length before I finally return to discuss the implications for professional education.

Towards a map of professional knowledge

This chapter attempts to provide some guidance for those about to engage on the difficult task of determining the knowledge base of a profession. At this stage, any map is bound to be fuzzy and incomplete but nevertheless it is needed for several reasons:

- To correct oversimplified views in current circulation.
- To illuminate the debate about theory–practice links and the role of experiential learning.
- To highlight aspects of knowledge that hitherto have been somewhat neglected in higher education.
- To inform the growing debate about competence-based approaches to occupational standards and qualifications.

My task is complicated by the primitive state of our methodology for describing and prescribing a profession's knowledge base. Many areas of professional knowledge and judgement have not been codified; and it is increasingly recognized that experts often cannot explain the nature of their own expertise. A variety of methods and approaches have been developed by philosophers, psychologists, sociologists and government agencies, each with its own limitations. However, one central difficulty has been the lack of attention given to different kinds of knowledge. The field is underconceptualized.

Most of my attention, therefore, will be devoted to distinguishing between different types of knowledge, considering how they are acquired and discussing their role in professional action. I shall begin with *propositional knowledge*, the traditional basis of teaching in higher education; then move to consider the nature and role of personal knowledge, especially pre-propositional *impressions*. The longest section, however, will be devoted to various categories of *process knowledge*, a term I prefer to the more limited 'procedural knowledge' and 'know-how'. This will include discussions about how different processes make use of propositional knowledge and personal impressions. Finally there are some areas of knowledge which are more than impressions yet different again from propositional knowledge or process knowledge. These include moral principles and knowledge embedded in literature and the arts, whose particular characteristics I do not propose to address.

Propositional knowledge

Higher education is accustomed to maps of propositional knowledge, which it uses for the construction of syllabi. So I will give it only brief attention and avoid repeating what is already well known. Elsewhere (Eraut, 1985), I distinguished three sub-categories of propositional knowledge:

1. Discipline-based theories and concepts, derived from bodies of coherent, systematic knowledge (*Wissenschaft*).
2. Generalizations and practical principles in the applied field of professional action.
3. Specific propositions about particular cases, decisions and actions.

That paper went on to explain that such knowledge may get used in one of four modes – replication, application, interpretation or association – as a corrective to the common assumption that there is but one 'applied' mode of use. The last two modes, in particular, characterize the use of propositional knowledge in the situations we describe under process knowledge.

Two further issues should concern us when we consider the extent to which disciplined knowledge forms part of a profession's knowledge base. One use of disciplines is to provide a critical perspective when judging the validity of a profession's generalizations and practical principles (Hirst, 1985). Another use is when concepts and ideas from disciplines are drawn upon directly during deliberations about practical situations and actions. As suggested above, the use of such theoretical knowledge may not always be in the application mode stressed by the technical rationality model, but in the interpretative mode where it is more difficult to detect. Moreover, just because busy professionals do not use a particular idea, does not imply that they should not: that remains to be argued. It is also likely that a profession's awareness of possibly relevant research in a related discipline will be limited.

Virtually all discipline-based knowledge and most of the generalizations and practical principles of the profession will be publicly available, codified knowledge. So will the kinds of facts which appear in reference books. However, not all propositional knowledge is public. Personal knowledge contains propositions; and public theories and principles may give rise to personal interpretations. Finally, there is collegial knowledge, such as case material, which may not have been published but nevertheless has been organized, recorded and treated as true by people other than the author.

Impressions, personal knowledge and the interpretation of experience

All people acquire knowledge through experiences whose purposes have little overt connection with learning, through social interaction and trying to get things done. Such knowledge covers people and situations encountered, communications received and events and activities experienced through participation or observation. While some of this knowledge is sufficiently processed to be classified as propositional knowledge or process knowledge, much will remain at the level of simple impressions. Nevertheless, impressions gained from experience contribute to professional action in ways that are still only partially understood.

To pursue this problem further, I wish to examine the range of phenomena associated with two ideas in general circulation: those of 'personal knowledge' and 'experiential learning'. Since I will be traversing such a philosophical minefield without the appropriate qualifications I shall take as my guide Schutz's classic text *The Phenomenology of the Social World*. Schutz (1967), following Husserl, provides theories to explain how experience is apprehended and made meaningful; how configurations of meaning are constructed at higher levels; and how these become 'taken for granted' schemes of experience constituting the patterns of interpretation which provide order in our lives.

Each of us is embedded in a continuous flow of experience throughout our life. Discrete experiences are distinguished from this flow and become meaningful when they are accorded attention and reflected upon. The 'act of attention' brings experiences, which would otherwise simply be lived through, into the area of conscious thought, where treatment may vary from actual comprehending to merely noting or hardly noticing. Such attention may be given on a number of occasions, each conferring a different meaning on the experience according to the meaning-context of the moment.

However, these basic experiences become subsumed within a higher-level 'object' of attention when separate acts of attention are gathered together into a higher synthesis. We remember a table rather than a long series of occasions when it was encountered. Hence, higher levels of meaning can be built up layer upon layer; and higher meaning-configurations themselves become objects of attention if they can be apprehended as single entities. For example, a friend or colleague is apprehended as a person in the first instance, not as a selection of the encounters which contributed to our knowledge of that person. But if we need to think more deeply about the nature of that person, we can return to lower levels of aggregation or penetrate beyond those levels to particular incidents. As Schutz suggests, 'the reflective glance will penetrate more or less deeply into lived experience depending on its point of view'. The particular level of meaning which presents itself as not in need of further analysis is defined by Schutz as the 'taken for granted'; and what is taken for granted depends on the pragmatic purpose of the reflective glance.

The ordinary person perceives the world as ordered. This order seems natural and can be seen both as a synthesis of past experience and as knowledge of what to expect in the future. Schutz calls these patterns of order the 'schemes of our experience', including both experiences of the external world and inner experiences of the activity of our mind and will. These *schemes of experience* are normally taken for granted. We do not question them unless a special problem arises and even then we are unlikely to probe very deeply. They also provide the framework through which new experience is interpreted and in this way order the future as well as the past. But also, to varying degrees according to the intention of the person concerned, schemes will adjust and develop in the light of new information and new schemes may be constructed to handle new types of experience. Such development is readily apparent during childhood, when receiving effective education and in the early formative years of a professional career.

Returning to our earlier concern with types of knowledge, three important questions need to be addressed.

1. To what extent does the ordinary person's stock of knowledge constitute propositional knowledge?
2. What, if any, is the difference between the personal knowledge whose construction we have just been discussing and the largely codified propositional knowledge discussed under our discussion of propositional knowledge?
3. What are the implications for professional education?

Question 1 was pre-empted by my decision in mapping professional knowledge above to group types of knowledge into three major categories. This was intended to stress that, at least at the lower levels of personal knowledge, that which has been accorded little attention (and therefore only partially subsumed into higher configurations of meaning) cannot be regarded as either propositional knowledge or process knowledge. I referred to it earlier as pre-propositional, but even that would be making unwarranted assumptions. The term 'impressions' describes it well.

A more difficult problem arises, however, when we consider higher-order knowledge in the form of schemes of experience. Such knowledge undoubtedly includes propositions, but can it be fully expressed in propositional form? Personally, I think not; and I recall an epigram (source unknown) from the debate in the early 1970s between proponents of qualitative and quantitative methods of inquiry. To the well-known claim 'If you can't count it, it doesn't count', the qualitative reply was 'If you can count it, it isn't it.' If you do describe a scheme purely in terms of propositions, you have probably left something out; and it could be something quite important. This view of the limited scope of propositional knowledge is not only supported by scholars like Schön but also by those concerned with the arts. Even the field of artificial intelligence appears to be experiencing a paradigm shift in this direction, following recent failures to convert many areas of human expertise to wholly propositional form.

Question 2 recognizes that the educational experiences of graduates will have incorporated years of continuous encounters with propositional knowledge in its codified, public forms. So it can be safely assumed that a professional person's stock of knowledge will owe a great deal to the contributions of such knowledge. However, this will not be all. As stated at the beginning of this section, there are many experiences from which people learn without there being any intended educational purpose and without any codified, propositional knowledge being drawn to their attention. People naturally develop some constructs, perspectives and frames of reference which are essentially personal, even if they have been influenced by public concepts and ideas circulating in their community. Another proviso is that even schemes which are consciously and directly attributable to codified propositional knowledge become at least partially personalized through the process of being used. The personal meaning of a public idea is influenced both by the personal cognitive framework in which it is set (what propositions it is linked to) and by the history of its personal use (which also influences the meaning-contexts in which it is seen to belong).

Finally Question 3 addresses the implications of this analysis for professional education. These are greatest for those whose work involves regular contact with clients. First, aspiring professionals already possess a great deal of relevant knowledge as a result of growing up in a particular culture; but that knowledge needs to be brought under critical control by developing greater awareness of how it is used and re-examining many taken-for-granted assumptions. They also possess a lot of impressions which can contribute to their professional knowledge base, but still need to be further organized and processed. Second, they will continue to learn experientially throughout their professional lives, for example in getting to know other people; but they will need to be more aware of how they operate and to be able to supplement such knowledge with more deliberately-gathered information. Third, they need to recognize that other people learn experientially as well. In spite of its fallibility, they must learn to use experience rather than disregard it (see Chapter 9).

Finally, I wish to use the foregoing analysis to provide a definition of experiential learning to which I can refer in later sections. To avoid the truism that all learning is experiential, at least in some sense, I propose to restrict the term 'experiential learning' to situations where experience is initially apprehended at the level of impressions, thus requiring a further period of reflective thinking before it is either assimilated into existing schemes of experience or induces those schemes to change in order to accommodate it. Most models of experiential learning assume that this further reflection will happen, but that will depend on the disposition of the learner. Hence our ability to discuss the extent to which somebody has learned from experience. One reason why learning might remain initially at the level of impressions may be that there is often no specific learning intent; another is that the flow of experience and need for simultaneous action is so rapid that little further attention can be devoted to reflection until some later occasion.

Process knowledge

When people are asked to describe what professionals do or to examine the nature of professional action, the result will be a list of processes. Indeed, the quality of professional performance largely depends on the manner in which such processes are conducted. All professional processes make considerable use of propositional knowledge; and this will be a recurrent theme in this section. But nevertheless Ryle's (1949) distinction between 'knowing that' and 'knowing how' remains. In this context 'process knowledge' can be defined as knowing how to conduct the various processes that contribute to professional action. This includes knowing how to access and make good use of propositional knowledge.

There also exists a body of propositional knowledge about processes. People write books about them, especially in the area of management. But the purpose of these books is usually to provide guidance. If they attempt to provide blueprints for higher-level processes, their validity is immediately disputed. Indeed, it would be interesting to pursue the question of how it might be possible to determine whether such propositions were true. Our task here, however, is simply to note that the way people conduct professional processes can be only partially described by such propositions. 'Knowing how' cannot be reduced to 'knowing that'.

In order to illustrate the initial importance of process knowledge for professional action, I have selected five kinds of process for further discussion. These are:

- Acquiring information
- Skilled behaviour
- Deliberative processes, e.g. decision-making

- Giving information
- Controlling one's own behaviour

These five are interdependent; so also, I suspect, would be any additions to this list. My purposes during the following analyses of these types of process will be threefold:

1. To indicate how process knowledge contributes to professional action.
2. To prepare the ground for considering how and where process knowledge might be best learned.
3. To provide a basis for considering the merits of competency-based approaches to professional education.

Acquiring information

Processes for acquiring information involve the use of recognized methods of inquiry. However, not all professionals are thoroughly trained in all the methods they use. The reason, I believe, is that methods like interviewing and observation are often regarded as just commonsense: so exposure to the practice of senior professionals is more than sufficient training. Perhaps this explains why a significant minority of professionals do not communicate well with their clients?

Professional training will not remove the experiential element from information acquisition, nor is it necessarily desirable that it should. People still make tacit use of schemes of experience derived from their past; and will also acquire information simply by being present on a relevant occasion: such information often complements that which is obtained by more rational approaches. Even when reading a book one may learn many things other than those one originally had in mind. During a formal interview, one may pursue a planned list of questions and still learn as much from the unplanned aspects of the encounter. On the other hand, it is equally important to ask appropriate questions and to recognize relevant information when one comes across it.

An effective and efficient approach to the acquisition of information requires at least four types of knowledge:

- An existing knowledge base in the area concerned.
- Some kind of conceptual framework to guide one's inquiry.
- Skills in collecting information.
- Skills in interpreting information.

This could be characterized as a combination of appropriate propositional knowledge and the ability to select and implement appropriate methods of inquiry. Some methods such as interviewing, listening and observation are used in most professions, while others such as certain scientific tests are highly specialized in particular professions, for example, psychiatric interviewing, listening for a foetal heartbeat, observing a microorganism under magnification. Although propositional knowledge is vitally important in all these examples, none of these methods of inquiry can be learned from propositional knowledge alone. The 'knowing how' is as important as the 'knowing that'.

As suggested above, interpretation is a particularly important aspect of information acquisition; and it is useful to distinguish between three separate modes:

- Instant interpretation, as in recognizing a person.
- Rapid interpretation, as in monitoring one's progress in the middle of an interview.
- Deliberative interpretation, when there is time for thought and discussion, and even for returning to collect more information.

The mode adopted is affected by the expertise of the interpreter as well as the nature of the task. The expert translator, for example, will interpret a written foreign-language text in the rapid mode unless it is an especially difficult passage: whereas the novice may have to deliberate for some considerable time. There is also a shift from the deliberative mode towards rapid interpretation when people gain expertise in examining complex visual information, e.g. an aerial photograph, an electron micrograph, an X-ray image, an architect's drawing, an infra-red spectrum. When there are products to examine, deliberation is the obvious approach for the novice. But when the evidence appears during real-time incidents in a busy or crowded environment such as a casualty department or a classroom, there may be little time for deliberation. A live encounter passes in a flash. What is remembered will depend on the ability of the perceiver to notice and select the right information rapidly at the time of the encounter. There is no opportunity to start learning to interpret such incidents in 'slow motion'. Reflection has to take place after the event and may not be helpful without an experienced tutor who has observed the same incident and noted the significant evidence.

Pattern recognition may also involve making comparisons over time. Experienced professionals learn to detect changes in a familiar person or situation. This is particularly important in nursing where intuitive detection of change in a patient's condition often precedes more dramatic events or alerts nurses to the need for other sources of information (Benner, 1984). This capability appears to be experientially developed, though there may be a significant role for tutors in accelerating the learning process. It clearly depends on continuity of contact with the client with obvious implications for how nursing care is organized. Similar situations probably arise in other professions, for example, social work, environmental protection, military intelligence.

Different issues emerge when people combine evidence from a number of incidents and sources. For example, let us consider how a teacher acquires information about individual pupils in her class. Although teachers receive some information from records and comments from other teachers, their knowledge of individual pupils is based mainly on direct encounters in the classroom. These encounters are predominantly with the class as a group, but nevertheless a series of incidents involving individuals in whole class, small group or one-to-one settings are likely to be stored in memory, rather like a series of film clips. In so far as a teacher has made notes, these are likely to serve as *aides-mémoire* rather than independent sources of information. How is the information then used? Under conditions of rapid interpretation, teachers will respond to situations on the basis of their current images of the pupils; though these images may have themselves been formed by rapid assimilation of evidence with little time for reflection. Under conditions of deliberative interpretation, the most accessible evidence is likely to be carefully considered; but even that may be a sample of remembered encounters selected for their ready accessibility rather than their representativeness.

Psychological research on the information-gathering aspect of human decision-making has shown that a number of errors regularly occur, from which professionals are certainly not exempt (Nisbett and Ross, 1980). When retrieval from memory is a critical factor, incidents involving a person are more likely to be recalled if they are more recent and/or more salient: quiet unobtrusive people may not be remembered at all. Also sufficient allowance may not be made when a highly atypical sample of incidents provides the basis of the memory record. For example, a senior manager will rarely see junior employees at their ordinary work, a teacher in charge of discipline may only see pupils when they are in trouble, a clergyman sees parishioners in their Sunday best, and so on.

Misunderstanding is also likely to ensue from the strong tendency endemic in all of us to interpret events in accordance with our prior expectations. Thus earlier incidents may affect how later incidents are perceived. Worse still, informal second-hand reports or rumours may affect how the first direct encounters with a person are interpreted. People tend to see what they expect to see. Professional education needs to ensure that students are both fully aware of these pitfalls and able to review existing evidence and to collect new evidence in ways that avoid them.

Another information-gathering process of particular importance in social and community work, but not to be neglected in other professions, is networking. Effective performance can depend on having developed a wide range of contacts and sources of information, keeping it current and having the right relationship to be able to acquire authentic information in a hurry.

Finally there are a series of information-gathering processes associated with academic study and the extraction of information from documentary sources. These range from general library skills and study skills to the use of specialized references or techniques of textual analysis. The typology of Parker and Rubin (1966) is particularly helpful in this context.

1. Processes which expose the student to a particular body of knowledge: formulating questions, reading, observing, listening, collecting evidence, discovering principles.
2. Processes which allow the student to extract meaning from the body of knowledge: analysing, experimenting, re-organizing, consolidating, integrating.

3. Processes which enable the learner to affix significance to the knowledge: inferring generalizations, reconstructing, relating to other situations, testing for usability.

These go well beyond the acquisition of information to the extraction of meaning and to the cognitive processing of propositional knowledge, thus moving into my 'deliberative processes' category which is further discussed below.

Skilled behaviour

The term 'skill' is given a wide range of meanings, all earning a positive connotation of competence. The most appropriate dictionary definition is probably 'practical knowledge combined with ability'. I shall use what I believe to be its core meaning in discussions about knowledge and competence, and define skilled behaviour as a complex sequence of actions which has become so routinized through practice and experience that it is performed almost automatically. For example, much of what a teacher does is skilled behaviour. This is largely acquired through practice with feedback, mainly feedback from the effect of one's actions on classes and individuals. Feedback and advice from tutors or more experienced teachers is variable in quantity and quality, according to the system of initial training and the attitude of teacher colleagues to student or beginning teachers. Teachers' early experiences are characterized by the gradual progress towards automaticity of their teaching and this is necessary for them to be able to cope with what would otherwise be a highly stressful situation with a continuing 'information overload'. This automaticity is accompanied by a diminution of self-consciousness and a focusing of perceptual awareness on particular phenomena. Hence, knowledge of how to teach becomes tacit knowledge, something which is not easily explained to others or even to oneself.

Many similar examples can be found in other professions, particularly in the area of interpersonal skills and communication skills. However, unlike some commonly cited examples such as swimming or riding a bicycle, professional skills tend to involve a significant amount of rapid decision-making. For example, Jackson (1968) estimated that a primary teacher might make a thousand decisions a day. These decisions do not involve the deliberative processes discussed below, but are interactive decisions made on the spur of the moment in response to rapid readings of the situation and the overall purpose of the action. Such decisions have to be largely intuitive, so the person concerned will find it quite difficult to provide a quick explanation. This creates a dilemma that characterizes large areas of professional work. The development of routines is a natural process, essential for coping with the job and responsible for increased efficiency; but the combination of tacit knowledge and intuitive decision-making makes them difficult to monitor and to keep under critical control. As a result, routines tend to become progressively dysfunctional over time: not only do they fail to adjust to new circumstances but 'short-cuts' gradually intrude, some of which only help professionals to cope with pressure at the expense of helping their clients.

Apart from these minor modifications, routinized actions are particularly difficult to change. Consider, for example, my analysis of the problems facing attempts at educational reform:

> For teachers to change their classroom practice in any radical way involves both modifying their classroom persona and embarking on a learning task of enormous magnitude. Changing one's routines involves a great deal of unlearning before one can begin to reconstruct new routines; and the experience is like going back to being a novice again with all the difficulties of coping and maintaining classroom order but little of the tolerance and sympathy which is normally accorded to beginners. Even the intuitive decision-making is disrupted because one's 'navigation lights', those semi-conscious cues which alert teachers to the need to change the pace or the activity or to attend to certain pupils, are extinguished when the pattern of practice is modified. The experience of disorientation and alienation is profound; and unless teachers are given considerable psychological and practical support over a long period, they will revert to their old familiar practice.
>
> (Eraut, 1992)

Deliberative processes

Deliberative processes such as planning, problem-solving, analysing, evaluating and decision-making lie at the heart of professional work. These processes cannot be accomplished by using procedural knowledge alone or by following a manual. They require unique combinations of propositional knowledge, situational knowledge and professional judgement. In most situations, there will not be a single correct answer, nor a guaranteed road to success; and even when there is a unique solution it will have to be recognized as such by discriminations which cannot be programmed in advance. More typically there will be:

- some uncertainty about outcomes
- guidance from theory which is only partially helpful
- relevant but often insufficient contextual knowledge
- pressure on the time available for deliberation
- a strong tendency to follow accustomed patterns of thinking
- an opportunity, perhaps a requirement to consult or involve other people

These processes require two main types of information: knowledge of the context/situation/problem, and conceptions of practical courses of action/decision options. In each case, there is a need for both information and analysis. What does this mean in practice? We have already discussed the wide range of means by which such information can be acquired; and alluded to the phenomena of pattern recognition and rapid interpretation during the process of collection. Here, we consider the more cognitively-demanding activities of deliberative interpretation and analysis, for which professionals need to be able to draw upon a wide repertoire of potentially relevant theories and ideas. Also important for understanding the situation is knowledge of the themes, perceptions and priorities of clients, co-professionals and other interested parties. While some may be explicitly stated, others may be hidden, implicit and difficult to detect. Thus one of the most challenging and creative aspects of the information-gathering process is the elucidation of different people's definitions of the situation.

The other information-gathering task is equally demanding, the formulation of a range of decision options or alternative courses of action. This depends both on knowledge of existing practice and on the ability to invent or search for alternatives. Such knowledge of practice is mainly propositional knowledge acquired during training, but in need of regular updating thereafter. The research on change shows that busy people outside academe and the most highly specialized practices rely mainly on personal contact for such information rather than courses or professional literature. This may not be desirable but has to be taken into account. One problem for the professional is the difficulty of evaluating new ideas on the basis of limited information. All too often reports refer to work in contexts different from one's own and are written by advocates and enthusiasts. Thus the skills of acquiring and evaluating information about new ideas and new forms of practice are probably more important than the retention in memory of an increasingly obsolescent block of propositional knowledge.

If we confine our attention for the moment to processes like problem-solving and decision-making, much of the literature tends to suggest a rational linear model, in which a prior information-gathering stage is succeeded by deductive logical argument until a solution/decision is reached. In practice, this rarely occurs. Research on medical problem-solving, for example, shows that hypotheses are generated early in the diagnostic process and from limited available data (Elstein *et al.*, 1978). Further information is then collected to confirm or refute these hypotheses. Although described as intuitive, the process is essentially cognitive; but it allows pattern recognition and other experiential insight to contribute at the first stage. In less scientific areas, the need for continuing interaction between information input and possible courses of action is even greater. The information cannot be easily summarized and can usually be interpreted in a number of ways. There is also a need for invention and insight when considering possible actions, so new ideas have to be generated, developed and worked out. The process is best considered as deliberative rather than deductive, with an interactive consideration of interpretations of the situation together with possible actions continuing until a professional judgement is reached about the optimal course of action.

Such deliberation requires a combination of divergent and convergent thinking which many find difficult to handle, especially when working in a team. Some find it difficult to focus sufficiently to be good analysts or are too impatient to think things through, while others feel uncomfortable with any departure from routine patterns of thinking. The need for adopting several contrasting perspectives is also increasingly recognized; and this is one of the arguments for teamwork.

Giving information

Giving information to clients is a major part of the role of many professionals, and one in which it is frequently suggested that their performance could be improved. First, there is the obvious need to use intelligible vocabulary, which relates to attitude as much as competence because some professions use esoteric vocabulary to preserve their status and to give the impression of greater knowledge than they possess. Secondly, there is the need to ascertain what information is most needed by the client and to relate it to the client's goals and level of understanding. This may require a wider consultation and more attentive listening than clients are sometimes accorded. Thirdly, there is the need to translate information into a form which the client can understand. While these are clearly interpersonal processes, they draw on propositional knowledge in a variety of ways. Such knowledge is probably most developed in teaching, because teachers need both to understand children's conceptions and ways of thinking and to develop a repertoire of possible representations of every aspect of their subject (Gudmundsdottir, 1989; McNamara, 1991).

The main advantage of written communication is that it can be treated as a deliberative process. There is an opportunity to think things through and revise early drafts. Whether this is taken will depend upon priorities. Formal reports will be composed with great care, while correspondence with individual clients often becomes routine. The temptation is to assume that, as long as the content is correct, the mode of its communication is relatively unimportant. Yet, in addition to a basic linguistic competence and lack of ambiguity, the style and the choice of words can significantly affect how a document or letter is received and understood. Good written communication requires both time and skill.

Controlling one's own behaviour

Controlling one's own behaviour is best described as a meta-process. Thus it concerns the evaluation of what one is doing and thinking, the continuing re-definition of priorities, and the critical adjustment of cognitive frameworks and assumptions. Its central features are self-knowledge and self-management, so it includes the organization of oneself and one's time, the selection of activities, the management of one's learning and thinking and the general maintenance of a meta-evaluative framework for judging the import and significance of one's actions.

The value of this control process was highlighted by Argyris and Schön (1976) who demonstrated that for many professionals there is a significant gap between their espoused theories (their justifications for what they do and their explicit reasons for it) and their theories in use, those often implicit theories that actually determine their behaviour. This gap between account and action is a natural consequence of people's perceptual frameworks being determined by what they want or expect to see, and by people reporting back to them what they think they want to hear. The solution Argyris and Schön recommend is to give priority not so much to objectives – for then one reads situations purely in terms of one's own pre-planned ideas of how they ought to develop – as to getting good quality feedback. Unless one is prepared to receive, indeed actively seek, feedback – which may be adverse or distressing – one will continue to misread situations and to deceive oneself that one's own actions are the best in the circumstances. This process of obtaining feedback on one's practice corresponds to what others have called *action research* (Elliott, 1991). However it is not only obtaining good feedback that matters but making good use of it by being open to new interpretations which challenge one's assumptions.

The challenge to professional education

The traditional dual qualification system, combining a degree with a period of subsequent professional practice, fails to address many of the most difficult problems I have identified. The syllabus for the higher-education component is based on propositional knowledge and discipline-based methods of inquiry within a strictly academic frame of reference, thus largely ignoring the problem of developing and using such knowledge in professional contexts (Eraut, 1985). The professional requirement is defined in terms of satisfactory completion of a minimum period of practice in an approved work setting, including a minimum number and range of professional tasks, often supplemented by further examinations, written and/or oral, and evidence in the form of reports and logbooks. There may be little attempt to analyse the processes involved, to develop professional thinking, to clarify learning goals and to provide the appropriate kind of support. The prevailing assumption is that the professionals who run the system know what competence is and do not need to spell it out. They have little difficulty in recognizing incompetence, which is all that is really necessary. Neglecting such important aspects of professional education considerably reduces its quality and its effectiveness.

More serious still are the implications of my analysis for post-qualification education. Careful examination of the processes discussed above will show (1) that they characterize the actions of experienced professionals possibly more than those of novices, (2) that they demand thinking skills of a high order in addition to skilled behaviour developed through practice, and (3) that even for experts professional performance involves learning and there is always more to be learned. The support of a system of continuing professional education after qualification is essential for sustaining and improving the quality of professional work, and much of it will have to be based in or around the workplace. In this context, the precise stage at which professionals are deemed to have qualified will depend on what they are expected to do, that is on the organization of professional work. The appropriate question is 'qualified to do what?' and the appropriate answer cannot be 'qualified to do everything in the profession'.

For me, this mapping of the professional knowledge base provides sufficient grounds for a major re-think of current practice. The professions, however, will see it differently. They live in the world of *realpolitik*. and respond to political rather than academic pressures. But there also the professions are being challenged on several different fronts. It is important, therefore, to discuss the nature of those challenges before putting forward my conclusions. The first challenge comes from Europe. Traditions across Europe are very different, professions being more highly trained in some countries and in others rather less. Mutual recognition of qualifications is expected, so that idiosyncratic systems will need to be convincingly justified or else modified. Government pressure will be towards the less-expensive options, unless there is very convincing evidence that they cannot deliver competent practitioners. So claims about each profession's knowledge base will be subjected to increasing scrutiny. There will also be pressure for closely-related UK professional bodies to merge. On a longer time scale, there could even be some convergence between the higher education systems of different countries.

Second, there is the challenge posed by changes in financial practice in both private and public sectors. Many professional groups find themselves organized into cost centres which have to justify themselves according to financial criteria in addition to providing services to clients. Apart from giving the financial aspect greater prominence in professional decision-making, this is causing groups to consider different ways of organizing professional work. One result is likely to be the greater use of people with intermediate qualifications, for example, technicians, paraprofessionals or auxiliaries. There might even be some further differentiation within the professional group. Almost certainly there will be tighter job specifications.

Third, there has been growing public concern about professional competence, monopoly and accountability. The reputations of professions in this age of mass media are increasingly dependent on their weakest members; can the public be guaranteed that even the least capable can provide a satisfactory service? Without public confidence in all their members, how can their monopolies in providing certain services be justified? Would not competition bring the price down and widen consumer choice? This challenge, in particular, may force the pace in the development of continuing education; and it will become increasingly difficult for professions to sustain the policy that qualification is 'for life'. Accountability systems are often inaccessible and opaque, while self-regulation looks increasingly like self-serving. Which individual or organization is responsible when things go wrong? Who is answerable to the public for the policies and priorities of the profession as a whole? While many of these questions concern the organization of the profession, they also focus around the profession's interface with the public, for which most professional practitioners have had little 'professional' preparation.

Fourth, there is the challenge coming from the growing system of National Vocational Qualifications (Burke, 1991), which is planned to cover 80 per cent of all qualifications below degree level by the end of 1992. The National

Council for Vocational Qualifications (NCVQ) has a mandate to cover the professions as well but is proceeding cautiously while it has other priorities. Attention is likely to move to the upper levels after 1992, and several professional bodies are already engaged in discussions and pilot projects. The NVQ system will bring radical changes, because it has adopted a competence-based system of accreditation using assessments based on performance at work (Fennell, 1991; Jessup, 1991). So its adoption would correct the current overemphasis on propositional knowledge and give more attention to the processes which determine the quality of professional action. However, some of its other features might need modification before implementation at the professional level. One suggestion would be to consider using a wider range of approaches to the analysis of professional work. The current system of functional analysis breaks the job down into functional units, and the units into elements, each of which has to be separately assessed to cover a range of situations according to a list of performance criteria. The result is a very long document and an enormous assessment programme, even for qualifications at a sub-professional level. This is a natural consequence of focusing on behaviour alone. In contrast, an emphasis on professional processes of the kind discussed earlier would give a more economical structure to the qualifications, as well as providing close links to the modes of learning and the use of propositional knowledge. It would also attend to the thinking which underpins a professional's capacity to perform in a wide range of contexts and situations.

Another issue is the binary nature of the competence concept. A person is either competent or not competent, and no gradations such as 'just competent' or 'highly competent' are recognized, at least not for accreditation purposes. This implies that the only way to progress is to become competent in something new, when it might be more appropriate simply to do the same thing better. Capabilities associated with the processes I have identified as being essential to the quality of professional work can be continually developed throughout one's life. Thus I am more in sympathy with the five stage model put forward by Dreyfus and Dreyfus (1986): novice, advanced beginner, competent, proficient, expert. Even this model, however, neglects the impact of social and technical change on what counts as a good professional performance. That apart, it provides a useful basis for extending our discussion into the post-qualification period as well. The question then arises as to the point of development at which various levels of qualification should be awarded; and whether this might vary from one element of assessment to another. People might need to be proficient rather than competent in some elements, while remaining at only the advanced beginner stage in others. Spelling out the minimum essential requirements for qualification is essential, but beyond that a profile of achievement which acknowledged the need for further development would be less misleading and much more useful.

Finally, the NVQ system highlights the problem of reaching a compromise between three conflicting approaches to determining a profession's knowledge base:

1. To ascertain *the profession's preferred view* of its own knowledge base – this is rarely unanimous, likely to be based mainly on existing or recently developed training schemes and closely linked to the profession's search for autonomy and status.
2. To examine *professional knowledge currently in use* – this raises questions about the wide range of work contexts and whether to focus on experts or ordinary members of the profession.
3. To predict the knowledge base needed for *the profession's future role* in society – a difficult and controversial task, yet arguably better than settling for planned obsolescence.

There will be a degree of overlap between the outcomes of these three approaches, but still some significant differences of emphasis. NCVQ has chosen to focus on the second approach, using committees led by employers to resolve differences arising from the range of work contexts. This is a sensible decision but the danger of neglecting the third approach altogether will increase as the level of qualification rises.

Reconstructing professional education

This chapter has argued that three central questions need to be addressed by every profession:

1. What is our professional knowledge base?
2. What is best learned in higher education, what is best learned in professional practice and what is best learned through an integrated course involving both contexts?
3. What has to be learned before qualification, and what is best postponed until after qualification?

The first has been my central theme, while the second and third have been discussed only briefly. Now the concluding section brings all three questions together in order to formulate the principles on which, I believe, the reconstruction of professional education and training ought to be based. The foregoing map of professional knowledge, and my earlier writing on knowledge use, both argued that professional work of any complexity requires the concurrent use of several different kinds of knowledge in an integrated, purposeful manner. Yet this is difficult to achieve without significant interaction between formal teaching and professional practice, and specific attention to developing the appropriate modes of thinking. Process knowledge must be given a high priority but without neglecting the contribution of propositional knowledge to the process. This is not always best done by introducing propositional knowledge as and when it is required, because this destroys its coherence, leads to an uncritical, half-understood acceptance of ideas, and avoids practice in the appropriate selection of relevant knowledge from the repertoire. On the other hand, it is now well established that knowledge which does not get used in practice is rapidly consigned to oblivion in some remote attic of the mind. Learning takes time, so there is always going to be conflict between time spent on introducing new knowledge and time spent in putting it into use. This suggests rigorous pruning of the quantity of propositional knowledge in order to improve its quality. Alongside this is the need to postpone some areas of content until after initial qualification, when the learner will be better prepared to use it. Hence, we need to consider a qualification system rather than a single qualification.

What principles can we extract from this discussion?

1. A significant part of the initial qualification must be performance-based: otherwise professional accountability will be a sham.
2. Initial blocks of propositional knowledge should be kept as short as possible, unless there are many opportunities to use that knowledge in practice-related processes.
3. Process knowledge of all kinds should be accorded central importance.
4. There should be a clearly articulated approach to professional learning and development, linked to a system of initial and advanced further qualifications.

It should be noted that I am not recommending that the whole of the qualification be performance-based: that would be impractical and possibly undesirable. But I am rejecting the obvious compromise of a dual qualification system which separates professional practice and the development of performance capabilities from the teaching of propositional knowledge, claimed to be relevant to current or future practice. Such a system cannot properly develop process knowledge of central importance to the profession and its future. Moreover, it is based on a false epistemology which assumes a clear-cut distinction between theory and practice. This leaves the question of how much of the qualification should be performance-based and what should be the nature of that part which is not.

References

Argyris, C. and Schön, D.A. (1976) *Theory in Practice: increasing professional effectiveness.* San Francisco, Jossey-Bass.
Benner, P. (1984) *From Novice to Expert: excellence and power in clinical nursing practice.* Menlo Park, California, Addison-Wesley.
Burke, J. (1991) 'Competence and higher education: implications for institutions and professional bodies' in P. Raggatt and L. Unwin (eds) *Change and Intervention: vocational education and training.* London, Falmer Press.
Dreyfus, H.L. and Dreyfus, S.E. (1986) *Mind over machine: the power of human intuition and expertise in the era of the computer.* Oxford, Blackwell.
Elliott, J. (1991) *Action Research for Educational Change.* Milton Keynes, Open University Press.
Elstein, A.S., Shulman, L.S. and Sprafka, S.A. (1978) *Medical Problem Solving: an analysis of clinical reasoning.* Harvard University Press.

Eraut, M. (1985) 'Knowledge creation and knowledge use in professional contexts'. *Studies in Higher Education*, 10(2), 117–33.

Eraut, M. (1988) 'Learning about management: the role of the management course' in C. Day and C. Poster (eds) *Educational Management Purposes and Practices*. London, Routledge.

Eraut, M. (1989) 'Mid-career professional education'. Paper given to Greek Education Society, Athens, October.

Eraut, M. (1992) 'The acquisition and use of educational theory by beginning teachers' in G. Harvard and P. Hodkinson (eds) *Action and Reflection in Teacher Education*. Norwood, New Jersey, Ablex.

Fennell, E. (ed.) (1991) *Development of Assessable Standards for National Certification*. Sheffield, Employment Department, Standard Methodology Branch.

Gudmundsdottir, S. (1989) 'Pedagogical models of subject matter' in J. Brophy (ed.) *Advances in Research on Teaching*. Greenwich, New York, JAI Press.

Hirst, P.H. (1985) 'Educational studies and the PGCE course'. *British Journal of Educational Studies*, (3), 211.

Jackson, P.W. (1968) *Life in Classrooms*. New York, Holt, Rinehart & Winston.

Jessup, G. (1991) *Outcomes: NVQs and the emerging model of education and training*. London, Falmer Press.

Johnson, T.J. (1972) *Professions and Power*. London, Macmillan.

Johnson, T.J. (1984) 'Professionalism: occupation or ideology' in S. Goodlad (ed.) *Education for the Professions: Quis Custodiet?* Guildford, Society for Research into Higher Education and NFER-Nelson.

Jones, R.T. (1986) The Development of the Medical Laboratory Scientific Officer Profession: qualifying systems, professional politics and technical change. D.Phil. Thesis, University of Sussex.

Kerr, E. (1984) 'Education for the professions: the developing role of the public sector of UK higher education'. Paper given to Anglo-Swedish Higher Education Conference, Bournemouth.

McNamara, D. (1991) 'Subject knowledge and its application: problems and possibilities for teacher educators'. *Journal of Education for Teaching*, 17(2), 113–28.

Moore, W. (1970) *The Professions*. New York, Russell Sage Foundation.

Nisbett, R.E. and Ross, L. (1980) *Human Inference: strategies and shortcomings of social judgement*. Englewood Cliffs, New Jersey, Prentice Hall.

Parker, J.C. and Rubin, L.J. (1966) *Process as Content: curriculum design and the application of knowledge*. Chicago, Rand McNally.

Ryle, G. (1949) *The Concept of Mind*. London, Hutchinson.

Schön, D. (1983) *The Reflective Practitioner: how professionals think in action*. New York, Basic Books.

Schutz, A. (1967) *The Phenomenology of the Social World*. Translated by G. Walsh and F. Lehnert from 1932 original. Evanston, Illinois, Northwestern University Press.

Part 3

The Course Perspective

8

The Humanities: From Ivory Tower to Marketplace?

Elisabeth Lillie

The context

Students, asked why they chose a humanities course, typically give responses such as the following: 'They were my best subjects at school'; 'I had no clear ideas about career, but I had to do something and thought I might as well go on studying what I liked.' Reactions like these highlight the dilemma of humanities in the latter part of this century. Students want to do these subjects, largely because they are interested in them, but their studies do not necessarily lead them towards obvious career outlets. Widespread dissatisfaction with this state of affairs and with the isolationist or ivory tower image which the humanities have acquired has led to a range of initiatives and experiments in teaching. These are promoting learning for different kinds of purpose and linking humanities more closely to the marketplace where most of the students will spend their working lives.

Traditionally, humanities education has focused on particular disciplines, introducing the students to areas of knowledge and forms of experience as well as to methods of analysis. Much argument has been generated as to the precise nature of the disciplines and approaches to them, but, essentially, most humanities lecturers would agree that their subjects are about the study of human beings and their response to their environment in literature, philosophy, language, classics, theology or history. Politics and geography, depending on the orientation that a particular institution gives to these subjects, may also be included within the humanities. While a humanities education is seen as affording an introduction to one or more of these subjects, it is also considered as a formative personal experience. Individual students deepen their understanding of the society around them and become more insightful people, capable of using their minds with greater rigour.

This view stresses above all the benefits that accrue to the individual learner, but twentieth-century humanities are not allowed to rest content with such student-based definitions of their role. The humanities must today elaborate a rationale and respond to the urgent question of purpose in a wider social sense. It is not enough for them to be as one writer puts it 'essentially *human* in their capacity to develop human sensibility and moral and social awareness' (Squires, 1990, p. 52), in a tradition owing much to the influence of Matthew Arnold. A focus on the personal development of the individual is not perceived as adequate in an age which sees accountability in terms of practical and financial outcomes: 'The Government in no way implies that it undervalues the contribution of the arts, humanities and social studies to the future needs of the economy as well as in the transmission and enrichment of our national culture' (*Higher Education: Meeting the Challenge*, 1987, p. 7). However, a major concern in this statement of Government policy is 'the demands for highly qualified manpower' (p. 7).

There are other pressures too on the humanities. Those concerned with students cannot but be sensitive to continuing statements indicating higher rates of unemployment among certain of their graduates: 'Arts and social sciences graduates were, in general, more likely to be unemployed' (*Highly Qualified People: Supply and Demand*, 1990, p. 17), a statement which seems to confirm the pattern perceived by Boys and Kirkland for 1982 graduates (Boys and Kirkland, 1988, pp. 28–32). Significant exceptions were, however, noted in *Highly Qualified People* and 'the rate for language graduates was well below that for other arts subjects' (p. 18). Once in employment, humanities graduates, whatever their field, are not among the most highly paid: 'Arts subjects, languages and education all have lower than average earnings' (Dolton and Makepeace, 1990, p. 34).

Despite gloomy projections, strong support for the humanities has come from employers' bodies such as the Council for Industry and Higher Education. They recognize the positive role played in employment by humanities graduates whose education is considered valuable because of the training in thought and analysis, in balancing factors and weighing judgements in complex situations. Management is increasingly seen as using 'the humanities' own vocabulary of "imagination", "vision", "sensitivity", and "creativity"' to describe managerial virtues (*Towards a Positive Partnership*, 1990, p. 4). The wider role envisaged here for the humanities reflects the long-standing movement of certain recipients of a humanities education into state service at the highest levels of decision-making as well as in supportive positions. Today, the internationalization of business is requiring from central management teams something of the breadth and scope of vision once fostered for the diplomatic service by the humanities: 'international investment requires long-term judgements about social and economic trends . . . Many of the talents traditionally fostered for diplomacy are now needed by business' (*Towards a Positive Partnership*, 1990, p. 4). In view of the need to increase graduate numbers overall (Pearson *et al.*, 1989) there is much to encourage the humanities.

Initiatives and strategies

Three different bodies have done much to change approaches. The CNAA set out its 'Humanities and Employment' initiative in 1987 and placed its authority as a central validating agency and diffuser of knowledge behind the encouragement of work-oriented practices and curricula. In 1987, too, the Manpower Services Commission launched the Enterprise in Higher Education Programme (EHE), now run by Training, Enterprise and Education Directorate, Department of Employment (see Chapter 13). This has played an important role in providing funding and support on a national level for the introduction of a wide variety of enterprise activities into higher education. The RSA, through the different phases of its Education for Higher Capability Movement, has also exerted a strong influence on current trends, in promoting debate and information, as well as in the recognition of examples of good practice (see Chapter 12). All three bodies have helped to highlight the concept of transferable or generic skills, stressing that the competencies acquired in higher education are also key skills needed in employment. While central initiatives of this nature play an influential role, even before they were launched certain moves had been made on the part of institutions, linking humanities to more vocational disciplines and refocusing aspects of the curriculum towards the world of work.

Career-relevant combinations

Perhaps one of the most straightforward ways of preparing humanities graduates to enter employment is to make sure that their course includes a sizeable component in an area which is traditionally recognized as vocational. This was the route followed by humanities departments in the 1970s and 1980s as they offered their subjects in combination with a range of disciplines, most usually Management, Business, Economics, Computing or Law. Joint courses with Languages were the most usual, the language injecting an element of internationalism and mobility, but a number of universities and polytechnics also permitted other humanities areas to form a joint course with vocational disciplines. Less common combinations exist with Accountancy or the Sciences, Computing, Chemistry, Physics or Engineering. Sometimes, the humanities discipline remains largely unaffected by its vocational partner, notably in institutions offering a range of options for combined degrees. In other cases, particularly where Languages are concerned, the curriculum has undergone a very significant shift. Language programmes have in many institutions shed their traditionally literary focus, giving added emphasis to language competence, now re-oriented towards a discipline area such as Business, Economics or Politics. Difficulties were certainly experienced by a number of students whose prior education and mind-set were very much in the humanities mould when they met mathematically-based subjects. However, particularly in Business, in Management and Marketing, they also found much that was not so very alien to a humanities-trained mind. Of the options available, Business is still the most popular vocational partner with Languages.

The integration of Languages and Business Studies has been taken even further and international mobility increased with the creation of joint degree schemes with European partners. In these courses, study abroad of the vocational area through the medium of the foreign language leads to certification from both foreign and home institutions. Middlesex Polytechnic's European Business Administration was a leader in the field and other courses with Business, and also Accountancy, have followed.

Additional fields of expertise

Students who combine a humanities discipline with a vocational area of study have a target career in view and would normally expect to find employment there with relative ease. When students choose to devote their full time as undergraduates to the humanities, more concern is generated about their employment prospects, perhaps, in part, because the very diversity of potential career outlets creates anxiety. In a climate of economic recession, many employers seem, for the general run of recruits, to be looking for those with skills which make them immediately useful in some capacity or other. Recent informal contacts with regionally-based employers also suggest that they seek evidence that the humanities graduate is not just the 'arty' dreamer of the still prevalent stereotype but will be able to cope with the practicalities of employment. Educators have tried to meet some of these concerns by adding to the humanities discipline a small component of a career-relevant expertise such as computing or techniques of quantitative analysis, both seen as important by the Council for Industry and Higher Education (*Towards a Positive Partnership*, 1990, p. 6). Initiatives to generalize computing skills, so that graduates would no longer enter the marketplace ignorant of microcomputers or the most common packages, were widely promoted by the Council for Academic Awards and are also included in the brief of the Enterprise in Higher Education initiative (see, for example, *Enterprise in Higher Education: Key Features of Enterprise in Higher Education 1990–91*, 1991, p. 4). With the spread of computing in schools, basic work in simple word processing will become less imperative but at present it performs an important function in familiarizing students (and staff) with the necessary skills.

While computing sometimes remains a separate study, it more often than not comes to be integrated into the curriculum so that students perceive the relevance of computing techniques to their own domain and their motivation rises. An example of this which readily springs to mind is the introduction of computer analysis packages in relation to History, the latter drawing on statistical techniques.

There are interesting applications too in Languages. Translation exercises may be recorded on disc, so that the correct version of a translation may later be added. The students then have a comparative tool to pinpoint areas of error and assess their progress. The creation of personal word-banks also helps the acquisition of vocabulary and the process of translation, and offers an insight into the working practices of translators.

In many cases, then, what was originally perceived as an ancillary area has come to have real relevance for the way in which the subject is studied. Computing offers a means of analysis and work with the subject as well as a skill which will help graduates find employment. This presupposes that the level of computing relevant to study of the main subject is also that which will be useful in employment. A questionnaire survey of language students, who had taken basic computing in the University of Ulster as part of a postgraduate programme, revealed that some students would, with hindsight, have liked an even wider range of computing experience and techniques. While their computing had helped them into employment, once there, they had to rapidly acquire more extensive competence in the area. This response highlights a dilemma for educators: computing is very much a skill area taught in what must remain a fairly elementary form in terms of the discipline of computing. How does this element of training, essential for some types of employment and sought by students, fit into patterns and levels of study in undergraduate and postgraduate courses as traditionally defined? Should universities be more willing to accept a greater measure of 'training' within their programmes of study than at present?

Currently, humanities are having to face this issue within their own field, as language skills and European Studies are being widely introduced across degrees in preparation for the Single European Market. The level of knowledge attained in such options falls below (often well below) that expected of mainstream degree subjects. Yet, even the minimal expertise acquired is of importance both on a personal and national level. In offering Languages more widely, higher education is training students to meet the challenges of the world into which they will graduate, but in so doing finds itself in conflict with its traditional role of offering specialist study. Humanities (in particular, Languages and European Studies) are faced with the need to re-define the core of knowledge which is needed for this new category of student.

Inevitably, the curriculum for the purposes of such students will be more narrowly defined and topics will be selected to fit particular interests. New educational goals will inevitably lead to different targets of attainment and modes of assessment. As the level of competence reached in, say, Languages, as an ancillary skill, differs significantly from the norm for degree-level students, the nature of the student's work and final achievement must be clearly defined for employers in profiles of study.

Transferable skills

Transferable skills are variously defined but they are essentially those aptitudes acquired by students in higher education which are also essential to successful performance in employment. These competencies include the ability to work in groups and to interact satisfactorily with others in pursuit of a goal. General communicative ability, whether oral or written is considered vital, reflecting the importance of information within an organization or for a wider public. Self-knowledge and the ability to appraise oneself and one's performance are also stressed. This recognizes the life-long need for self-development as well as the capacity to measure achievements against the requirements of a particular situation and long-term goals. The cognitive skills traditionally linked to academic study are not absent but they are described in terms of problem-solving, the ability to engage with an issue and to analyse its various angles. The search for imaginative solutions is to be fostered as is the capacity to implement such solutions.

Institutions have responded in various ways to the need to introduce or highlight transferable skills in their humanities curricula. The discussion that follows on both transferable skills and enterprise owes much to a telephone survey conducted in October/November 1991 of a number of enterprise centres. Enterprise co-ordinators were also helpful in supplying further comments, copies of reports and publications.

The importance of consciousness raising among students is often seen as a key factor in the acquisition of transferable skills. Students must become aware of the goals which their education seeks to achieve, so that they may work towards their fulfilment more purposefully and become more active learners. They must realize the ways in which the skills acquired in a humanities education are relevant to employment. This educational concern also parallels the workplace, where to function efficiently people must be aware of the nature of their job and their role within the organization. To this end, specific skills are defined for these students so that they understand the attributes they are expected to acquire, whilst pursuing the curriculum in any given humanities discipline. This may be done through the creation of an individual skills portfolio, which will outline the specific competencies that will be mastered at various stages of the course. Less ambitiously, skills may be set out in relation to a particular project, possibly undertaken by a group of students. Uniting both subject knowledge and transferable skills is the concept of the learning contract where the student agrees at the start of a programme or unit to goals relating to both the subject expertise and transferable skills.

The highlighting of skills frequently leads to learning practices centering on groups, on the management of projects and on personal research. The results of the students' work will be presented to a wider class in a talk or, sometimes, a composite report may be drafted. Video work is often involved in the learning process, particularly in Languages, where students may, depending on the angle of the course, be involved in anything from mock TV discussions, interviews or documentaries to role-plays in business negotiation through the target language. Here, verbal skills of communication are emphasized but the initial preparation involves negotiation about task sharing, and then search and analysis followed by the creation, structuring and presentation of an argument.

The stress placed on oral presentation of research and other activities based on the spoken word reflects the importance of this form of communication in the modern world. These exercises may be seen, in part, as an evolution from the seminar paper, a class which in the past was not always an unqualified success. Such initiatives are also helping to address the problem of the low level of teaching of verbal skills in the humanities areas, an issue highlighted in a recent study on the teaching of personal transferable skills in courses in the UK (Gash *et al.*, 1990, p. 39).

Some activities undertaken under the umbrella term 'transferable skills' result largely from a re-focusing of existing practice. Report writing has been found to be a motivating variant of the undergraduate essay. The student will be set a career-related context and situation and asked to argue a case, to draw practical conclusions and add recommendations for action. Similar skills are being used as in the essay, the ability to scan and sift data, to analyse and structure, but the relevance of these skills to life outside higher education is emphasized.

The practice of negotiated learning allows students or a group of students to introduce into their course an area from outside the institutional curriculum. They agree with lecturers on a particular subject area, topic or project on which they will work. Students are in this way encouraged to take relevant initiatives and channel enthusiasms towards particular goals. This exercise has much in common with the long undergraduate dissertation, seen by many as an indispensable part of an Honours degree. It is, however, slightly larger in scope and it allows for greater variety in form of submission and assessment.

While report writing and project work draw essentially on a range of techniques traditionally taught by staff, other explicit work on transferable skills and orally-based activities is more novel. Many institutions offer specific training for staff in aspects of transferable skills and assertiveness and a number extend such skill and personal training courses to students. Even where no such explicit programmes exist for students, it does not mean that this training is considered unnecessary. Often it has been found that students react best to skills work and perceive it as relevant when it is undertaken by the subject staff rather than an outside unit (Gash *et al.*, 1990, p. 14).

The stress on transferable skills and student centered learning has provided more lively and motivating methods of engagement with humanities disciplines (Miall, 1989; Jackson and Prosser, 1989). The student comes to perceive that a humanities education not only offers an initiation into an area of human experience, but it also teaches more general cognitive and communicative skills which can be applied to a multiplicity of 'real-life' problems.

Forays into the marketplace

New approaches in classroom and curriculum may heighten awareness and equip students with skills and additional knowledge useful in employment. Such initiatives do not necessarily induce an immediate sense of the realities of the workplace or of the precise ways in which studies relate to the world outside university. To fill this gap, new forms of enterprise and work-related learning have been created for more vocational and commercial ends. Students use their subject expertise to undertake tasks and projects useful to outside agencies. Material produced in this way may even be saleable and marketed on a small scale. Much of this activity has been promoted or supported by enterprise units.

Entrepreneurial activity may be included as part or as the whole of a unit within the undergraduate curriculum. Lancaster University has firmly anchored enterprise in courses by designating one unit in their modular provision as an enterprise unit which students may include within their degree. This unit may take different forms, with a main focus on either one discipline area or alternatively on an interdisciplinary sphere of activity. Examples quoted by Lancaster include ongoing projects such as the production of booklets and guides for the Scottish National Trust and English Heritage which these organizations then publish and market.

Particular events on which the university may be consulted also serve as a focus for enterprise, allowing students to use these opportunities for purposes of course and personal development. Again quoting an example from Lancaster, an international conference for the Quaker movement gave rise to a number of enterprise-oriented projects in History. Two students prepared a history of the Friends Meeting House in Lancaster which was marketed as a booklet at the conference, while another student produced a video of a number of Friends Meeting Houses in the North West, also made available for sale at the conference. Work in History may have even closer links to industry as in the production of packages for companies to celebrate anniversaries and milestones in their past (Manchester Polytechnic). In English, students have been cited as undertaking readership surveys for bookshops or libraries or even research into the marketing of contemporary fiction or community publishing (University College of Ripon and York St. John, *Nexus* 2, 1991, p. 7).

The marketplace has connotations of commercialism but all student activity in it need not necessarily be linked to self-interest. The University College of Ripon and York St. John has included the application of theology within the concept of enterprise, focusing on learning in practical situations as distinct from a more theoretical study of the discipline. As part of an Urban Theology course, students co-operate with Network, an organization run by the Churches in the Chapeltown inner city area of Leeds, which offers support and training to young people in the community. The students have undertaken surveys and have identified local community needs, producing a Care Directory, cataloguing available facilities in church buildings (*Nexus*, 2, and discussion with Enterprise Centre). In this project, enterprise skills were targeted but the problems identified and the action plans devised extend the scope of the term.

Traditional student activities, related to their academic work, often previously undertaken in extracurricular clubs and societies may also now be more fully incorporated as enterprise activities into the academic curriculum.

Plays have been mounted with financial support from EHE using funding to take the production into more professional arenas than would have been possible on the students' own resources (Edinburgh Fringe, for example). One institution cited the case of a student marketing her own creative writing at the Cheltenham Festival of Literature (Cheltenham and Gloucester College of Higher Education). Employers and staff have always stressd the importance of such extracurricular activities as signalling commitment and initiative. For this reason, it seems a logical step to formally recognize their role in the student's education.

It has often been pointed out that many issues and problems in life outside education require input from different discipline areas. Enterprise activities too may draw on knowledge from 'more than one subject. Manchester Polytechnic, for instance, described a scheme for the production of teaching materials. Research was undertaken by History students who drafted information on the Industrial Revolution. This was put into a form suitable for presentation by Design students and was afterwards handed over to Teacher Education students for use in teaching practice. A project cited by the University of Lancaster was the organization of an eighteenth century music concert by a Music student and a History student. In these examples, different types of skill and co-operation are being developed. In the first case, the ability to use initiative in the furtherance of a wider scheme and to work to a particular organizational goal, transcending the individual input, is being fostered. In the second case, the enterprise was on a smaller scale developing the individual's skills and initiative in the pursuit and achievement of personal objectives.

The existence of enterprise activities in the undergraduate curriculum gives useful experience and reveals the multiplicity of ways in which academic study and work outside the university interconnect. At the same time, potential conflicts of interest exist between educational goals, practical constraints and commercial interests. A report of a project in the University of Durham (an area survey in Geography) signals this with a caveat about the danger of students being used as a source of cheap labour (Porter, 1991, p. 17). Entrepreneurial projects require careful selection and negotiation to ensure that they fully serve the students' educational concerns and the overall objectives of their degree programme.

Not surprisingly, these more applied learning situations are giving rise to new forms of assessment, to indicate levels of attainment and competence achieved by students. The learner is often actively involved in the process of grading through self-assessment, group assessment and peer assessment. These types of innovative system are not universally accepted but staff concerned with them are usually enthusiastic. In the University College of Ripon and York St. John, group assessment operates in relation to a number of team projects. Students devise their own criteria for evaluation and on completion of the project effect a grading. The marks given by the group for the unit stand, but it was stressed that the tutor plays an important role in enabling the group to evolve their criteria and in helping them to apply these criteria.

In some cases, the mode of assessment established follows rather more closely forms of evaluation used elsewhere on the degree. The enterprise units in Lancaster are examined by a report. This may be written for the organization with whom the student worked, and if this is the case, it will also be marked by university staff. In other instances, the project may be simply for the attention of the student's academic supervisor. If a booklet/video is produced, students normally prepare an additional commentary and report for the university.

Again, two different patterns of practice lead to the fostering of different skills. In the one case, group self-assessment permits a greater awareness of the criteria for judgement, and this heightened consciousness of the norms should lead to more competent performances. In the second example from Lancaster, the students are assessed on their capacity for presentation, analysis and reflection in relation to the particular example of action-based learning in which they have participated.

The fluctuations in model of assessment reveal a certain uncertainty on the part of academics (trained themselves in analysis, reflection and argumentation) as to the best mode of assessment of practical learning activities. One type of evaluation, peer assessment, reflects a frequent situation in life where people are constantly judged by colleagues and others with whom they come into contact. In self and group assessment, individuals or groups are being encouraged to rate themselves against target levels and criteria. Such exercises perform a useful function in raising consciousness, but whether or not one can be a good judge of one's own work from a position of quite limited knowledge and experience is open to question. Some institutions have decided that even innovative learning situations are best examined in a form closer to traditional practice. Assessment is made through written work, which permits the learner to stand back and reflect on the experience.

In the telephone survey and discussions, none of those questioned suggested that one yardstick for evaluation might be the actual commercial success of an activity or its usefulness in the eyes of the organization concerned. Such market-oriented criteria might, on one level, seem an obvious extension of enterprise activity, but they would bear little relationship to the traditional aims of evaluation in the humanities. In any case, success in working life is capable of many definitions, depending on whether the criteria employed are commercial, hierarchical, idealistic or humanitarian and these judgements relate to goals different from those of educational study.

Purposeful practice

One of the most obvious ways of preparing for a career is to undertake a period of relevant work experience in an outside organization. *In situ*, the student relates the theoretical to the practical and practises those interpersonal skills that group work, in particular, develops. A year or period abroad has long been standard practice for modern linguists enabling them (in theory at any rate) to benefit from constant exposure to, and practice in, the target language. Traditionally, they developed their skills through giving instruction in their own language in assistantships or they studied their subject at university. With the growth of more applied degrees, came practical work experience abroad in private industry or public-sector institutions.

The EHE initiative has given a further incentive to the purposeful use of the period abroad so that projects undertaken might serve a 'real life' as well as an academic purpose. In Manchester Polytechnic, to take one example, Language students (volunteers only) during their year abroad are involved in projects for clients at home, for the most part schools in the Manchester area. The students' task is to produce materials (booklets, videos) that can be used as part of teaching packages in the schools. To this end, a group of students based in Strasbourg are working on a teaching package about the European Parliament and are interviewing two European MPs on video. Placements in other areas of humanities are to be found in a variety of fields often reflecting relevant career outlets. Examples were quoted of work in media and broadcasting, the National Trust, local heritage associations, museums, the public records office and conservation groups.

Links with the working world are in many instances cemented and taken further through partnership formed between higher education and specific companies. Not only does this help with placement and to some extent graduate employment, but it also allows higher education staff to gain real experience in business practices and concerns. Links may also relate to specific curriculum goals such as computing as seen in the co-operation between Birmingham University and IBM. Advantages in industry/education partnerships are not all in one direction. Cases were quoted of business drawing on educational expertise and advice. In certain instances, business staff may be seconded to work in education on specific projects.

Knowledge gained through placement and contacts with outside agencies has even, on occasion, allowed staff to pinpoint areas of need, leading them to establish courses in new vocational fields. Nottingham Polytechnic cited the example of a placement in broadcasting, introduced as an option within a degree in communication studies. The success of this experiment in placement was said to be a key factor in the subsequent introduction of a BA degree in the area of Broadcast Journalism, in liaison with the BBC, Independent Radio and Independent Television.

Humanities and learning for the marketplace

In various ways, then, the humanities are re-orienting their teaching practices and curricula towards the marketplace of life. Humanities staff are not equally in favour of these developments. The Birmingham Polytechnic survey on the teaching of transferable skills discovered a range of attitudes, from very considerable enthusiasm and input at one end of the scale through to non-committal acceptance, non-cooperation and downright hostility (Gash,

1990, p. 52). Active innovators highlight new learning approaches, greater student involvement and motivation as well as the re-discovery on the part of students that learning may have real-life applications. Students also develop personal skills and acquire ancillary areas of knowledge (computing, statistical analysis). Often, students will say that computing and statistical techniques were key factors in securing their first post. Employers too are beneficiaries. Most immediately, they acquire students to undertake company projects which might otherwise lie dormant through lack of resources. For the future, they can look forward to graduates who are more personally skilled and adaptable in the workplace. They also reap advantages from the mutual exchange of knowledge and experience with higher education.

Yet, it is true that current reforms in practice raise anew questions as to the goal and nature of a humanities education. Technique and method cannot be divorced from knowledge, otherwise those leaving higher education will merely be 'smart, presentable, plausible idiots' (to quote a teacher surveyed in the Birmingham study) (Gash, 1990, p. 20). At the same time, in the past, study of humanities subjects has included methods of approach to knowledge and modes of describing that knowledge, the traditional forms of evaluation being structured essays and examination questions. The test of a good student was, in large part, the ability with which he/she had mastered the techniques of analysing and presenting his/her knowledge in response to a particular question.

In reviewing aspects of curriculum development connected with transferable skills, we have noted that many of the new exercises could be considered as developments of long-standing activities translated into an idiom reflecting today's practices and society. A different medium of expression need not necessarily imply lack of rigour or critical analysis. While considerable time is involved in the acquisition of the new techniques of oral presentation, the humanities have traditionally devoted time to particular techniques – witness the stress laid on the mastery of essay form. The late twentieth century is imposing new rhetorics of expression and description as well as tools of analysis, but these are the tools and language of the time.

In any case, the ivory tower of humanities was perhaps more apparent than real. The humanities have always led to jobs whether in teaching, administration or management. Today, the humanities disciplines must continue to serve students by taking cognizance of possible career outlets and by enhancing employability. Provided the necessary steps are taken to protect student interests, practical experience need not conflict with educational objectives. Indeed delivery in the marketplace may complement educational aims. Precision and coherence assume a new importance when it is likely that incorrect facts and poor presentation will lead to public ridicule.

By their very nature, the humanities disciplines have acted as a focal point for individual creativity and dissent, and for a searching assessment of particular norms and clichés. The humanities have always trained social critics and artists as well as custodians of the establishment. In the 1960s and 1970s, the questioning function of the humanities was perhaps more strongly stressed, in an almost Romantic opposition of artist or thinker and society. To some extent, current initiatives may be seen as redressing the balance in the direction of co-operation, cohesion and socialization. This is not to deny the importance of the ability to effect personal analysis, to maintain an unpopular interpretation, to swim against the tide and to combat injustice. Rather, it is to wonder if the development of intellectual independence necessarily suffers from the introduction of new modes of learning and a consciousness of the principles of human co-operation. Apart from the self-evident fact that critics and artists must almost always relate in some way to the world, the emphasis on human interface, and on discussion and investigative technique may actively enhance independence of thought and a capacity for reflection.

The humanities cannot be solely concerned with job training; an education in the humanities is valued because it offers something other than this. Yet, a humane education cannot ignore the type of culture by which it is surrounded. It cannot eschew the modern or neglect the nature of activity in the marketplace. Most students and graduates will have to earn a living, and they will have to exist within society and interact purposefully with it. Taking account of students' and society's needs and equipping young people for their careers may demand movement out of the ivory tower and into the marketplace but this need not constitute a betrayal of the humanities. Such a move may indeed even be part of what a humanities education should be about.

References

Boys, C.J. and Kirkland, J. (1988) *Degrees of Success: career aspirations and destinations of college, university and polytechnic graduates.* London, Jessica Kingsley.

Boys, C.T., Brennan, J., Henkel, M., Kirkland, J., Kogan, M. and Youll, P.J. (1988) *Education and the Preparation for Work.* London, Jessica Kingsley.

Bradshaw, D. (1985) 'Transferable intellectual and personal skills'. *Oxford Review of Education,* II(2), 201–16.

Brennan, J. and McGeever, P. (1988) *Graduates at Work.* London, Jessica Kingsley.

Burgess, T. (ed.) (1986) *Education for Capability.* Oxford, NFER–Nelson.

Dolton, P.J. and Makepeace, G.H. (1990) 'Graduate earnings after six years: who are the winners?' *Studies in Higher Education,* 15(1), 31–56.

Eggins, H. (ed.) *Arts Graduates, their Skills and their Employment: perspectives for change.* Basingstoke, Falmer Press. (In press.)

Enterprise in Higher Education: guidance for applicants (1989) Sheffield, Enterprise in Higher Education Training Agency Department of Employment Group.

Enterprise in Higher Education: key features of the Enterprise in Higher Education proposals 1988–89 (1989) Enterprise in Higher Education Training Department Group.

Enterprise in Higher Education: key features of the Enterprise in Higher Education proposals 1989–90 (1990) Sheffield, Enterprise in Higher Education Training Agency Department of Employment Group.

Enterprise in Higher Education: key features of Enterprise in Higher Education 1990–91 (1991) Sheffield, Employment Department Group.

First Year of Enterprise in Higher Education: final report of the case study evaluation of EHE (1990) Sheffield, Employment Department Group.

Gash, S. *et al.* (1990) *A Study of Personal Transferable Skills Teaching in Higher Education in the UK. Final Report.* Birmingham, Birmingham Polytechnic.

Hantrais, L. (1988) *Higher Education for International Careers.* Birmingham, AMLC in association with CILT.

Higher Education Developments: the skills link (1990) Sheffield, Employment Department Group Training, Enterprise and Education Directorate.

Higher Education: meeting the challenge (1987) London, HMSO.

Highly Qualified People: supply and demand (1990) London, HMSO.

Jackson, M.W. and Prosser, M.T. (1989) 'Less lecturing: more learning'. *Studies in Higher Education,* 14(1), 55–68.

Linklater, P. (ed.) (1987) *Education and the World of Work: positive partnerships.* Milton Keynes, SRHE/Open University Press.

Miall, D.S. (1989) 'Welcome the crisis! Rethinking learning methods in English Studies'. *Studies in Higher Education,* 14(1), 69–81.

Nexus (1990, 1991) The University College of Ripon and York St. John, 1, 2, 3.

Pearson, R. (1989) *How Many Graduates in the 21st Century? The Choice is Yours.* IMS Report No. 177. Brighton, Institute of Manpower Studies.

Porter, G. (1991) *The Derwentside Project.* Durham, University of Durham, Department of Geography.

Rigby, G. and Burgess, R.G. (1991) *Language Teaching in Higher Education.* Sheffield, Employment Department.

Southgate, B.C. (1988) '"Non-vocational?" Humanities and the world of work: a comment'. *Journal of Further and Higher Education,* 12(2), 51–4.

Squires, G. (1990) *First Degree: the undergraduate curriculum.* Milton Keynes, SRHE/Open University Press.

Towards a Positive Partnership: the humanities for the working world (1990) London, Council for Industry and Higher Education.

Wasser, H. (1990) Changes in the European university: from traditional to entrepreneurial. *Higher Education Quarterly,* 44(2), Spring, 110–22.

Whyte, G. (ed.) (1989) *Enterprise Education: Economic Development through Education and Training.* Cambridge, CRAC.

Wright, P.W.G. (ed.) (1990) *Industry and Higher Education.* Milton Keynes, SRHE/Open University Press.

9

Experiential Learning as Learning to Effect

Norman Evans

Introduction

Learning to effect can have many meanings. Here, it is taken to refer to ways in which the student's learning can be not merely effected but facilitated in ways calculated to enhance the quality of the student's experience of learning and the learning acquired. A central issue for higher education, that involves seeking a fit between student as learner, whatever his or her personal or occupational intentions, and how an institution organizes itself and offers its curriculum, whatever purposes the institution espouses. The theme in this chapter is that for some and probably an increasing number of students experiential learning, its assessment and accreditation can be a powerful contribution to securing that fit and hence improving the quality of the student's learning.

The connecting bridge between experiential learning and the quality of a student's learning is motivation. Experiential learning is that learning which has been acquired from experience. There is an obvious truth that formal teaching in lecture, tutorial, laboratory or project assignments promoted and provided by academic staff offers ample opportunities for students to learn from experience. Indeed, much discussion of pedagogy and methodology seeks to exploit those opportunities for students to enhance their learning. And much of that discussion concerns the motivation of students for learning and ways of strengthening it. But that is not the experiential learning which is the theme of this chapter.

Prior and current experiential learning

The attention here is concentrated on two categories of experiential learning. Each is different in origin but both share similar characteristics. Both reach deeply into students' motivation. (As will be mentioned later, both touch motivational issues affecting academic staff and even institutions.) Both are concerned with off-campus learning. One is prior experiential learning. The other is current experiential learning derived from experience provided by an institution as part of its provision of a course. The common component of both prior and current experiential learning is systematic reflection on experience. The difference is that prior experiential learning refers to learning acquired without any necessary connection with formal educational institutions, whereas current experiential learning is under the direct responsibility of an institution. A student on a sandwich course in which the learning derived from experience is not assessed should be acquiring current experiential learning. A mechanical engineer or unqualified social worker or office manager coming into higher education could have acquired prior experiential learning from their prior work experience. Both the latter are forms of uncertificated experiential learning, and need to be differentiated from prior learning which has previously been certificated. So, for example, someone with a Higher National Diploma in Mechanical Engineering or a nurse on the General Register for Nursing or a social worker with a Certificate of Qualification in Social Work may have that certificated learning taken into account for credit towards a degree in a relevant discipline as prior learning.

The central issue, therefore, that arises from experiential learning concerns finding reliable ways of converting uncertificated learning into certificated learning. For prior experiential learning, such conversion requires an individual to reflect systematically on some experience, and to express clearly what is claimed to have been learned from it in ways that can be considered for assessment and perhaps accreditation by academic staff. Those claims to knowledge and skill derived from experience must be supported by evidence relating directly to the claim being made and again must be acceptable to academic assessors. All of this is the direct responsibility of the person making the claim. Everything to do with judgements about the validity of the claim is the sole responsibility of the academics.

For the individuals concerned, this means isolating an experience which seems to have resulted in learning something new. It means formulating what that new learning was and then producing the necessary evidence to prove that the new learning was acquired. For the academics, it means using whatever assessment procedure seems appropriate. It could be that the previous examination paper is set as a challenge examination. It could be that the claim being considered could be considered against the content of a particular course unit or module. Obviously that is relatively straightforward where units or modules are written with learning outcomes or intentions alongside the syllabus description. Where a portfolio has been compiled by an individual, documenting both the learning claim and its supporting evidence, an academic assessor may require additional evidence. This may be necessary because, characteristically, experiential learning claims may demonstrate an imbalance between practice which is rich and theoretical understanding which may appear weak. Some required readings and an essay assignment can either produce evidence which can substantiate the validity of the claim or confirm that the claim is invalid. An interview may resolve such issues, either in person or by telephone. Whatever the approach, an academic must find ways of making a judgement which satisfies all the necessary criteria. This is essential to preserve the academic integrity not only of the assessment of experiential learning but of the institution itself.

For current experiential learning, the same principles hold good. The essential difference is that the work experience being offered to the students as part of a course is under the direct responsibility of the institution so that the learning intentions may well have been set in advance or determined during the early part of the work experience. In many cases, this is done through negotiations between the student, workplace supervisor and academic staff. The same sequence of reflection on experience to produce statements of learning supported by evidence has to be completed.

For prior learners, the motivation developed as a result of going through that sequence can be powerful. People can reveal to themselves that they have acquired considerable knowledge and understanding without realizing it. And this has a powerful motivational effect because it is self-revealed as a personal accomplishment. Confidence can be boosted so that embarking on a systematic programme of learning becomes not just a possibility previously unconsidered but an engaging and even enticing prospect.

Current experiential learning can also fire students with a new and sometimes different interest in learning more. Making the connection between theory and practice is one thing. But realizing that learning from and at work is not only possible but something to experience and that it can become countable towards the award of a degree is a motivating factor, difficult to reproduce in any other context. The proviso, of course, is that current experiential learning has to be assessed for academic purposes and integrated with the student's other academic assessments. Following such a period of work experience leading to assessment of learning, students are often better at learning during the remaining part of their formal course in the institution.[1] In both prior and current experiential learning, therefore, there is an obvious connection between experiential learning, its assessment and accreditation and the quality of the student's *subsequent* quality of learning.

Applications of prior experiential learning

Before exploring how the uses both of prior and current experiential learning can be used to enhance the quality of student learning in the context of higher education, it is important to notice the applications of prior experiential learning (PEL) are almost limitless. Access courses for higher education often include a PEL element. In further education, too, the assessment of experiential learning (APEL) is becoming ever more important. The Business and Technician Education Council, the City & Guilds and the Royal Society of Arts have all issued guideline documents to help institutions devise PEL schemes for their own courses and qualifications. The National Council for Vocational Qualifications has the APEL (it refers to it as APL achievements) as a central part of its policies for assessing competencies for National Vocational Qualifications. The Central Council for the Education and Training of Social Work (CCETSW) has APEL enshrined in its regulations for the recently established Diploma in Social Work. Both CCETSW and the United Kingdom Central Council for Nursing, Midwifery and Health Visiting both incorporate APEL for post-qualifying qualifications. The newly-established Training and Enterprise Councils are being encouraged by the Department of Employment and Training and Education Enterprise Directorate to deploy APEL activities. Employers increasingly are paying attention to the potential significance of employees' on-the-job learning (experiential learning in the workplace) in their search for ways of increasing the efficiency of their workforces. Employment Training Schemes and Youth Training Schemes have experiential learning components. The Management Charter Initiative has APEL as a requirement for its Certificates in Management, a requirement which will extend to its Diploma and Masters' level qualifications when they are fully developed. UK Government ministers make reference to experiential learning in some of their pronouncements. So there can be little doubt that APEL has rapidly assumed an important role nationally.

Experiential learning in higher education

Chronologically, higher education in the UK began developing in this field at the start of the 1980s. The case was there were many people who were unable to gain access to higher education because they did not have the formal entry qualifications, though they were eminently qualified to begin studying at degree level. That case was based on the assertion that many men and women learn from their experience of life, work and leisure and accumulate knowledge and skill which under scrutiny compares favourably with the levels of learning implied by formal educational qualifications. The case was based on the further assertion that, in certain cases, some of the knowledge and skill identified could merit recognition as equivalent to parts of a degree programme. In those cases, APEL might lead to admission with advanced standing. If that claim could be substantiated the implications for recruitment to higher education were obvious.

APEL is now soundly established in the UK, at least in polytechnics and colleges of higher education. Between 1985 and 1987, ten institutions were involved in the first development project funded by the CNAA which began to work out reliable procedures and assessment schemes for using experiential learning both for admission to degree courses and for admission with advanced standing.[2] That followed a preliminary inquiry also funded by CNAA, reviewing all entry regulations to check whether there were any good reasons for not introducing the assessment of prior experiential learning into higher education as an additional means of dealing with admissions.[3] After the establishment of CNAA's credit and accumulation and transfer scheme

(CATS) in March 1986, many institutions in the polytechnics and colleges sector took a sharp interest in APEL. This was because from the beginning of discussions about CATS at CNAA, APEL was included, and when these regulations were published, APEL was given national recognition since academic credit for APEL at both first degree and Master's level was authorized. From 1986, a steadily increasing number of polytechnics and colleges have developed their own CATS schemes, and every time APEL opportunities have been included.[4]

Universities are only just beginning to get involved with APEL in any formal sense. Sheffield, Nottingham, Warwick, Goldsmiths' College in the University of London and Kent are all collaborating in a TEED funded project under the title of the Potential of APEL in Universities, working along broadly the same lines as the CNAA project of 1986–87. And Liverpool University together with Liverpool Polytechnic and Chester College are working on a project for current experiential learning under the title of Work-based Learning For Academic Credit. The hope is that these projects will be the forerunners of developments in universities, as the early CNAA projects encouraged developments in polytechnics and colleges.

Experiential learning and admissions

The developments just described indicate that a new set of academic criteria is being used by a significant number of higher education institutions when considering candidates for entry to degree courses and for higher education awards. Such a development has considerable significance for moves towards a mass higher education system. Despite the uncertainties of demography, current moves in the UK towards a mass higher education are likely to lead to a relatively increased influx of two categories of entrants: older men and women who do not possess the formal educational qualifications for entry to higher education (some of whom will merit admission with advanced standing), and younger students who come through the vocational education route or who because of their learning styles can learn most effectively through a mixture of formal teaching and learning by doing. For the second group especially, the pursuit of academic subjects in a diet built on the traditional curriculum of formal lectures, laboratories and set assignments may not be appropriate. Experiential learning has much to offer some of them as a prime source of enhancing their learning achievements, since:

> Experiential Learning refers to learning in which the Learner is directly in contact with the realities being studied . . . direct contact with the phenomenon being studied rather than merely thinking about it.
> (Morris Keeton, 1978)[5]

This is why experiential learning can speak directly to the motivation for learning of many students.

Experiential learning as a link between higher education and employment

There is another reason why experiential learning is important in the context of the overall expansion of higher education. Formal education no longer has a monopoly of study leading to first degree and postgraduate awards. Many companies offer studies at those levels for their own employees. The Learning from Experience Trust has promoted the credit-rating of the in-house provision of more than 30 companies for academic credit towards Bachelor's and Master's degrees. In addition, a score or more of companies have arranged with CNAA or their local polytechnic to have their in-house education, training and provision credit-rated for academic value and then validated by academic authorities. In every case, the companies' in-house education and training schemes are scrutinized by academics, credit-rating values being recommended at either the first, second or third year level of an undergraduates' course or at Master's level and those credit-ratings are then validated by an institution with the authority to do so. Any company employee who has then completed a company course which has been validated may claim the amount of credit assigned towards the qualification being sought from any institution willing to accept that credit and with the academic organization which enables the individuals to complete the study programme for which the qualification will be awarded. Thus uncertificated learning becomes certificated learning.

Almost inevitably the question arises during negotiations in completing these arrangements: are there possibilities for employees' on-the-job learning to be accredited as well?

All these developments in APEL are part of an educational response to changing social, economic and domestic circumstances of increasing numbers of population. Most people in employment cannot afford to switch to becoming full-time students. Full-time study is increasingly expensive to undertake. Employers are more and more concerned to improve the effectiveness of their employees while being increasingly anxious about the costs involved in both releasing employees for part-time study and the additional costs involved through those people not being at the workplace. So both employees and employer have a direct interest in enabling the companies' own investment in education and training to be recognized academically, so that time, money and effort are exploited to a double purpose.

However, some of the implications of these developments for the quality of student learning need further comment. It is frequently the case that the type of negotiations conducted between a company and an academic institution leads to important curricular improvements for each. Companies will say that they are stimulated to improve their own programme as a result of discussion about the credit-rating and validation of their provision particularly over questions arising from assessment. More important though for higher education is that academics report the same. So the courses offered to regular students can be improved as academics learn from employers at first hand how their students can learn more through altering the content of courses, changing the emphasis of material and even the methodology. All of these possibilities in enhancing the quality of the student's learning stem from APEL.

In many cases, these developments under the APEL banner lead to arrangements between academic institutions and employers for a scheme of negotiated learning agreements or contracts for employees. Typically, a learning agreement is a result of a three-way negotiation between employee, employer and academic. The agreement will set down what learning is to be attempted, how it is to be achieved, what evidence will be used for assessment purposes and how it will be assessed. Such an agreement is likely to include APEL and credit derived from in-house courses. The vital point about these learning agreements, however, is that in this way employers can be assured that additional learning agreed will be of direct benefit to the company. If an employee as student learner knows that then the motivational factors are obvious.

Learning agreements of this kind are spreading into the mainstream work of some institutions for undergraduates. In Napier Polytechnic, a pilot project on 'Work-based Learning for Students on Sandwich Courses' began by involving courses in Hotel, Catering and Management and Business Studies with Commerce and Civil Engineering being added in the second year. Now, the project is spreading across the institution as its value for students, academic staff and employers is realized and is being documented. That project has included the coaching of students, academics and employers alike in the way learning agreements can be negotiated, and the setting out of what is to be learned during the period of work placement and how it is to be assessed academically, so that those assessments can be incorporated in final degree classifications. With Liverpool University's Science students, Liverpool Polytechnic and Chester College are working on a project entitled 'Work-based Learning for Academic Credit for Non-sandwich Course Students'. The students involved are volunteers and are spending one term of their three-year degree programme to undertake a period in work placements with four days per week off-campus and one day a week in the institution for tutorials, seminars and a half-day course on 'Employment in the 1990s'. There is no necessary vocational connection between their degree programme and work placement, the students receiving the same amount of academic credit they would have done had they spent that period on campus.

For both of these developments, it is the negotiated learning agreement which anchors the use of current experiential learning to clearly-defined academic standards. These are examples of developments which can be found in polytechnics and colleges and where institutions are collaborating with employers. All reports suggest that these arrangements are making a marked difference to students' experience of learning and their motivation for further learning.

Experiential learning and applicants to higher education

Learning to effect has to begin with applicants. There are two unresolved questions about applicants. How can we attract into the higher education those who have the undoubted ability to succeed but who either do not think of it or if they do think of it reject the thought because their experience at school has suggested to them that they are poor as learners on conventional programmes in conventional institutions? How can we best serve these students with not only an appropriate content of learning but with appropriate learning styles?

Experiential learning can contribute to solving the first conundrum about attracting non-traditional groups. The implicit message of experiential learning is different from the message most higher education institutions send to potential applicants. Instead of institutions saying implicitly, 'We accept you, provided you can show that you can cope with what we are offering', the experiential learning message is 'We value what you have accomplished so far. Come and let us see what those accomplishments amount to and let us together plan how you are going to use them to your best advantage. It is possible that we shall discover that what you have learned already can give you academic credit towards the degree you may want.'

Experiential learning can contribute to solving the second question by deliberately providing as options experiential learning through work-based learning programmes as a complement to formal tuition. As indicated already, the conceptual and technical issues have been settled in relation to work experience through negotiated learning agreements, planned to ensure that intended learning outcomes are clearly stated alongside the academic activities to be undertaken. Evidence of the attainment of those outcomes can be used for the assessment of the learning acquired. These arrangements meet two vital requirements for effective learning. First, they encourage students to accept responsibility for their own learning. They are additional educational modes. They can meet the preferred ways of learning for many students. In turn, they can have a positive effect on the way in which students tackle formal courses within the institution after a period of work-based learning. Students can become more motivated, moving from passive to active learning which teachers claim to seek to achieve in their students.

Negotiated learning agreements or contracts (as they are sometimes called) involving experiential learning meet a further important educational requirement: namely, academic staff are able to fulfil their obligations for ensuring that their students learn. Also, such contracts with students can help staff to discharge their professional responsibilities for monitoring student performance and making academic judgements about that performance, thus preserving the integrity of students' academic study. In other words, current experiential learning offered by an institution to its students under these carefully controlled arrangements can become normal mainstream academic work. It can extend the curriculum opportunities available by providing enhanced opportunities for students to learn when this mode of learning fits their preferred learning style.

Experiential learning and some institutional issues

If that is a sketch about the ways APEL can connect with an institution's life, then the picture needs more detail to substantiate the claim that experiential learning can enhance students' learning. At the admissions stage, guidance and advice about selecting learning programmes and how to make the best of the opportunities on offer become more important as the student entry becomes more heterogeneous and as the possibilities for students become more varied. This often confusing widening of educational opportunities is compounded where institutions are organizing their academic provision into modules and discrete units. The assessment of prior experiential learning offers an occasion for the advice and help many students need. Because the process of systematic reflection on experience is the essential basis for assessment of prior experiential learning, individuals frequently reveal to themselves all sorts of accomplishments which they either took for granted or undervalued or even did not know they had achieved. This often results in a changed self-image. Often, their view of their futures can change with an obvious influence on what they want to study.

Institutions and individual students confirm that something else can happen to individuals who have had their prior experiential learning assessed. Their confidence is boosted. Since they have revealed to themselves what they have learned successfully even though they may not have realized it, they can be more positive in their approach to formal learning in a higher education institution. Tutors are very familiar with the way many older students doubt their capacity to cope with degree-level work and worry as they look for assurance that they are coming up to scratch. APEL can often enable students to quieten that anxiety and get on with their studying with the enjoyment which comes from self-confidence.

Correspondingly experiential learning can widen the scope for admission tutors. Many have always taken seriously the attributes of men and women applicants who do not fit the conventional academic requirements for admission. But doing so systematically is a different matter. That is particularly important when it comes to admission with advanced standing, rather than to the beginning of a degree programme. Any admission with advanced standing must stand the most rigorous academic scrutiny. APEL provides that facility because of the way learning claims and evidence lead to assessment. So APEL can speak directly to those many potential students who do not approach conventional higher education but can and do with APEL acting as a magnet.

Experiential learning and its assessment can also serve as a catalyst for institutional development. The variety of personal circumstances of many of these kinds of applicants can affect the administrative, structural and regulatory framework of an institution. Many would-be students need to be able to study on a part-time basis, even on an occasional basis with facilities for mixed modes moving at will between part-time, full-time and occasional study. This can only be done when the academic work of the institutions is arranged on a unit or modular basis. Creating those arrangements is a major administrative and academic task involving re-writing of regulations not only for admission but for courses and programmes and their assessment. Administrators looking for ways of increasing student numbers may see APEL as a means of doing so, but such a development, if taken seriously, can prompt a wide range of institutional developments.

Obviously APEL is not, and should not be, expected to be of commanding interest to all universities, polytechnics and colleges. An inner-city location, a student profile in which mature students are prominent, a declared mission to attract non-traditional entrants, and a preparedness to develop programmes for professional people in collaboration with employing organizations will incline some institutions towards serving the students for whom APEL is especially appropriate. Those institutions who are so inclined can find that the stimulus of using APEL procedures releases powerful catalytic influences going beyond the regulations implications mentioned already. It becomes a matter of the institution's wider mission and how the institution is perceived by the general public.

Experiential learning and the curriculum

With experiential learning, the curriculum becomes critically important and in four ways. A message to possible students saying bring what you have and we will see where it can take you implies, firstly, an acceptance that while an institution can contribute to a student's learning, the institution will recognize that students have acquired learning which meets the standards of higher education without having been designed with entrance to higher education in mind. The institution has to accept that it has no monopoly over what counts as a valid 'higher' education experience. Secondly, and even more important, what students want to learn in the future may well be different from what is already on offer through existing courses so additional courses may be required. Thirdly, it implies providing different ways of learning, different learning styles to suit the best ways of learning for individual students. Fourthly, it begins to raise questions about the delivery systems used, whether formal tuition, distance learning, or the establishment of learning centres where video tapes, slides, and interactive PC programmes are available.

One of the clearest curricular implications of developing APEL schemes is the desirability for syllabus descriptions to be complemented by statements of intended learning outcomes. And this applies to any and every subject.

Where this combination of content description and learning outcomes is available, it acts as an assessment instrument for students and tutors alike. For the students, learning outcomes can be an invaluable diagnostic form of self-assessment. If intended learning outcomes are set down in documentary form and lodged in the library, any intending or enrolled students can look up a particular course where they may think that their experiential learning might produce academic credit and begin to test the validity of their possible claim for themselves. For academic staff, it means they have ready to hand an assessment tool when needing to make judgements about APEL claims for academic credit in relation to specific courses.

The development of learning outcomes is an important element of curricular development in its own right. It clarifies the purposes of any particular programme of learning. As it does so, it tests course content against the intended outcomes. And it can de-mystify the business of learning for both students and staff.

A curriculum organized to facilitate effective learning through making available the intended learning outcomes for particular courses or units rather than syllabus descriptions depends increasingly for its effectiveness on quality of guidance available to students. This need is increasingly recognized in institutions. The more varied the student body becomes and is confronted with an increasingly complicated array of opportunities offered through unit or modular course arrangements, the more the kind of help tutors give typically to full-time traditional 18+ students following linear courses is insufficient. APEL points this up. Determining students' most suitable programmes means having available generalist advisors who can listen attentively, and help students clarify what is best for them and with full knowledge of the institution itself and its courses. APEL can be a point of development for services of this quality.

Fourthly, experiential learning (both prior and current) can influence the curriculum through the possibilities it opens for student generated curricula which in turn can have a powerful thrust for effective learning. Apart from the School of Independent Studies Degree in the Polytechnic of East London and variants on independent study facilitated through learning agreements, there is no systematic approach in the UK to enable groups of students to negotiate courses of study with academic staff as part of an institution's regular activity. Since APEL presupposes that students bring significant learning achievements with them, and since the self-assessment facet of APEL can give students a more reliable sense of their future learning requirements, and since those requirements may not be readily available in the existing course programme, the motivation for learning can obviously be increased if they can learn what really interests them. The particular tough intellectual task of formulating a new course in outline, negotiating it, and learning how to make it substantial through discussions with academic staff, is an educational enterprise in its own right. So a student-negotiated course based on APEL amounts to a double enhancement of learning for the student: planning and negotiating it and then undergoing it.

Using experience as a component of the curriculum for student learning can extend the curriculum not merely in relation to the content of learning programmes but also to its pedagogy – the activities through which students can learn – and how the results of that learning are to be assessed. In each of those senses, APEL widens the curriculum. Learning derived from experience is in most respects different from learning according to prescribed syllabuses.

Experiential learning and some academic issues

Even if these claims about APEL acting as a stimulus for educational development are convincing, no claim has been made that its introduction is straightforward. Maintaining academic rigour must be central, a point which begins with academic staff. Staff whose own experience as students and as teachers in a higher-education environment predominantly of the traditional pattern of full-time study, perhaps in a residential community and often in specialist discipline studies, can sometimes find it hard to accept that students can learn effectively at undergraduate or graduate level without any reference to themselves or their colleagues. For some staff this can be seen as a threat to their professional role, even raising awkward questions about their personal significance as academics.

Even assuming that the validity of off-campus learning is accepted intellectually, the practice of APEL raises unfamiliar questions of assessment. If a teacher has not taught a student then clearly the evidence that student can present (to support a claim for assessment) is bound to be different from the evidence which the teacher relies on for those taught in formal classes. There is an additional complication. Adults learn eclectically, not according to the boundaries of knowledge organized in discrete disciplines. This poses a question as to whether experiential learning is considered for its course relatedness – does the evidence of experiential learning presented fit a particular course unit or module? Or can it be considered on its own merits in terms of evidence of a conceptual grasp which broadly matches the levels of understanding required for the same level of study under consideration? The description of learning programmes through learning outcomes to accompany syllabus descriptions clearly facilitates assessment of the former. But for the latter, academic, professional judgement must remain the sole authority.

It raises the fundamental question as to whether experience as the source of experiential learning can enable individuals to acquire propositional learning.[6] Some believe that propositional knowledge can result from systematic reflection on experience; others are more sceptical. The point is that it is not an either/or matter. Anyone who attempts to reflect on experience so as to state what has been learned almost inevitably finds themselves learning more about that past experience. The systematic reflection on experience is not an activity which can be static, applying only to the past. Beginning there, it fuses with the present so that additional learning is acquired, additional that is to what was learnt before. There is no reason why propositional knowledge should not emerge from these mental exercises and be documented as such. The first brochure of the Learning from Experience Trust included the following: 'Most people know more than they think they know, if only they knew that they know it.' Therein lies some of the value of experiential learning when brought into academic settings. Through reflection, tacit understanding can become conscious and, thereby, more amenable to deployment.

Assessments of experiential learning become specially important when they are considered for advanced standing in either graduate or postgraduate programmes. The tutor's professional academic judgement has to withstand especially rigorous scrutiny by academic peers where the stakes are higher than for admission to undergraduate study. Entry admissions are primarily decisions about ability to cope with the course. Admission with advanced standing involves judgements about an individual having, in effect, completed parts of the course before enrolling on it. This is where the institutional stance is so important. Unless the senate or academic board underwrites APEL with formal authority, through approved official documents incorporated in the institution's regulations, the use of experiential learning will lack academic and social legitimacy. An institution's responsibility towards the public is to ensure that its academic work is of the highest order. Only on that basis can the development of APEL in higher education be securely grounded.

All this requires a systematic provision of continuing professional development for academic, administrative and support staff to ensure that these sorts of flexible provisions produce a valid day-to-day experience for the students concerned.

Experiential learning as learning to effect

Significant learning has occurred when thinking involves alterations, additions and renovations to the furniture of the mind as contrasted with short-term memorization and reproduction. The case for APEL is that as a mode of learning, it can be a thoroughly creditable contribution to effective learning quite apart from the service it can offer to institutional development.

Systematic reflection on experience requires careful thought and determined work. When a topic being studied by individuals is their personal experience and the result of that study is an account of what was learned from that experience, then there is little doubt that the intellectual demands made to complete those reflective tasks satisfactorily make for an effective mode of learning. People can learn new things as they reflect on their experience. They can gain new insights. They can make fresh connections. They can recognize gaps in their knowledge which need to be filled. They may need a good deal of tutorial help along the way. But it is a thoroughly responsible commitment of academic staff time because it is effective pedagogically, in terms of what students learn as a result. And these points hold good both for prior experiential learning and for current experiential learning organized by institutions as an integral part of degree studies. The points hold good because students can be so powerfully motivated. And that is why for many students it can be claimed that experiential learning when incorporated into the work of academic institutions offers a superior education. In essence, experiential learning is a particularly striking form of learning to effect.

Notes

1. As evidence from Napier and Huddersfield Polytechnics testifies.
2. *The Assessment of Prior Experiential Learning* – Report of a CNAA Development Fund project conducted at the Learning from Experience Trust by Norman Evans (CNAA, 1988). Participating institutions were: City of Birmingham Polytechnic; Bristol Polytechnic; Essex Institute of Higher Education; Newcastle upon Tyne Polytechnic; Polytechnic of North London; Sheffield City Polytechnic; Stockport College of Technology; The Polytechnic, Wolverhampton; Middlesex Polytechnic and Thames Polytechnic.
3. *Access to Higher Education: non-standard entry to CNAA first degree and DipHE courses* (CNAA, 1984).
4. CNAA (1990) *CATS Newsletter*, June 1990.
5. Morris Keeton (1978) *Learning by Experience – Why, what, how? New Directions for Experiential Learning*. London, Jossey-Bass.
6. This touches the wider question as to the origins of knowledge in the context of the rapidly changing nature of higher education in the UK. For contemporary discussion see the *Higher Educational Supplement*, Peter Scott: Editions, 9, 16 and 23 August 1991.

10

Improving the Quality of Student Learning through Course Design

Graham Gibbs

Introduction

Research in Europe and Australasia has identified students' *approach to study* as a key variable in predicting student performance and the quality of learning outcomes. Whether students take a *surface* or a *deep approach* (attempting to reproduce subject matter or understand it) has a profound effect on the quality, structure and permanence of students' learning. This research has also identified the features of course design which foster a surface approach, often inadvertently, or which can be used to foster a deep approach through deliberate and purposeful course re-design. A project entitled *Improving Student Learning*, sponsored by the Council for National Academic Awards (CNAA) has studied a wide range of attempts to move students from a surface to a deep approach and has provided detailed case studies of the processes of change involved. This chapter describes the background research and one of the case studies in order to illustrate appropriate course design changes.

The chapter explores the potentially damaging impact on course delivery, and hence on students' approaches to studying, of the worsening staff: student ratio and increasing class sizes in the UK. It will point to course design strategies which hold out most promise of retaining quality in learning whilst the unit of resource declines. It also emphasizes that a focus on teachers' performance, highlighted by annual appraisal, observation of teaching and superficial teacher evaluation undertaken to satisfy academic audit, is unlikely to orient change appropriately. What is needed is a clear focus on course design with a conceptual grounding in research on student learning.

The CNAA project: improving student learning

Research on how students learn in higher education, how they develop and change, and what influences their approaches to learning, has over the past 15 years provided a coherent, rich and illuminating picture (cf. Ramsden,

1992). However, it has led to few changes in course design. The CNAA project was established to demonstrate the application of this research to the practical business of improving courses. Institutions responsible for over 100 courses applied to be involved and eight were selected to be funded to undertake detailed action research projects. The innovations based on principles from the earlier research into student learning were undertaken during the 1990–91 academic year and dissemination of the findings took place in the spring of 1992. The following sections selectively and briefly outline the research basis of the CNAA project.

Students' approaches to learning

Consider these two quotations from interviews with students. The first student is describing how he went about reading a book:

> I read it very slowly, trying to concentrate on what it means, what the actual passage means. I really try to read it slowly. There is a lot of meaning behind it. You have to really kind of get into it and take every passage, every sentence, and try to really think 'Well what does this mean?' You mustn't regurgitate what David is saying because that's not the idea of the exercise, so I suppose it's really original ideas in this one, kind of getting it all together.

In the interview extract below a student has just described taking verbatim notes in a lecture and has used the word 'learning':

> INTERVIEWER: When you use the word learning in relation to this course, what do you mean?
> STUDENT: Getting enough facts so that you can write something relevant in the exam. You've got enough information so you can write an essay on it. What I normally do is learn certain headings. I'll write a question down, about four, five different headings, which in an exam I can go: 'Introduction' and I'll look at the next heading and I know what I've got to write about without really thinking about it really. I know the facts about it. I go to the next heading and regurgitate.

These quotations illustrate extreme differences in intention: the students are trying to achieve different things. These two intentions have been termed a deep approach and a surface approach (Marton and Saljo, 1976).

- *Deep approach*
  The student attempts to make sense of what is to be learnt, which consists of ideas and concepts. This involves thinking, seeking integration between components and between tasks, and 'playing' with ideas.
- *Surface approach*
  The student reduces what is to be learnt to the status of unconnected facts to be memorized. The learning task is to reproduce the subject matter at a later date (e.g. in an exam).

It has been argued that while a surface approach may be common in schools, or perhaps in poor students in the first year in higher education, it is not really an issue beyond that. It is assumed to be a problem which automatically goes away with maturity and experience. This is not the case. Evidence of the prevalence of a surface approach is deeply disturbing. In the UK a surface approach is common in all subject areas, and more common in universities than in polytechnics (Ramsden, 1983). In higher education in Australia, students progressively drop a deep approach as they move through the three years of a degree programme. This phenomenon is more marked in colleges of advanced education than in universities, more common in science than in arts, and more common in undergraduates who do not intend to continue on to postgraduate studies than in those who do.

Student learning outcomes

The outcomes of student learning – what it is that they have learnt – also differ greatly in quality, and quantitative measures of student learning outcomes may reveal little about this quality. The first year of undergraduate courses in physics and chemistry commonly repeat much of the A Level syllabuses because although students who have got good A Level grades can substitute numbers in formulae, follow algorithms for solving standard problems and remember the definitions of terms, they do not adequately understand the concepts involved. When the quality of learning outcomes is examined through interviews this frequently reveals a very different picture than that revealed by examinations where students can accumulate marks for memorization.

There is now a considerable body of evidence of the lack of understanding of key concepts of students who have successfully passed courses, in a variety of subjects and at a variety of levels (cf. Dahlgren, 1984). For example, a study of a first-year undergraduate economics course found that few students had understood a range of other key economics concepts. Indeed, the quality of understanding of several concepts was actually poorer at the end of the course than before the course started. Results on a conventional exam, which rewarded regurgitation of information, revealed little of this failure.

The Structures Of Learning Outcomes (SOLO) taxonomy is a research-based measure of the quality of learning outcomes (cf. Biggs and Collis, 1982) and is a widely applicable framework for judging the structure of essays, answers to technical questions, medical diagnoses or students' accounts of their reading:

Level 1: Ignorance
The learner reveals no correct knowledge about the question.
Level 2: Unistructural
The answer contains one correct feature or item of information.
Level 3: Multistructural
The answer is list-like, containing a number of unconnected items.

Level 4: Relational
The answer relates components together to make a case or logical whole.
Level 5: Extended abstract
Level 4 with, in addition, a connection to a related area of knowledge beyond the explicit demand of the question.

These categories have an intuitive relation to degree categories. Level 3 answers gain a pass, or if the list is long enough, a lower second, level 4 answers gain upper seconds and level 5 answers gain firsts.

Approach and outcome

The significance of qualitative measures of outcome become apparent when they are used to measure the consequences of taking a deep or a surface approach to learning. In one study, for example, 69 students read a chapter and then wrote an account of it. They were interviewed about their approach and the structure of their account was analysed using the SOLO taxonomy, revealing the following pattern of results:

	Approach	
Learning	*Surface*	*Deep*
SOLO level 3	35	6
SOLO level 4	0	25
SOLO level 5	0	3

After Van Rossum and Schenk (1984)

In other words none of the students who took a surface approach produced anything other than a list-like answer, whilst most (28 out of 34) of those who took a deep approach produced answers involving logical arguments and relationships between ideas.

The consequences of a surface approach

As ways have been developed of identifying the quality of students' understanding, so it has been possible to study, under controlled conditions, the impact of a deep or a surface approach on the quality of learning outcomes. It has become abundantly clear that it is very unlikely that a student who takes a surface approach will gain a full understanding of a concept, an overview of a topic, a grasp of the main ideas in a chapter, be able to distinguish principles from examples, write an essay with a logical argument, or recognize the key ideas in a lecture. Essays, or summaries of chapters, written by students who have taken a surface approach, are quite different in structure to those of students who have taken a deep approach. A surface approach produces a multistructural essay (containing a list of unrelated items) while a deep approach usually produces a relational answer (integrating items into a structure) or an extended abstract answer (which goes beyond the immediate topic and applies ideas to a related issue or area).

It may be argued that full understanding is not always required, and that an ability to memorize without understanding is sometimes enough. Studies have shown that a surface approach does tend to produce marginally higher scores on tests of factual recall immediately after studying. However this small advantage is quickly lost. A surface approach leads to rapid forgetting and as little as a week later students who have taken a deep approach will score far higher than those who took a surface approach, even on tests of factual recall.

A surface approach is no more successful in passing entire courses or gaining qualifications. Both interview and questionnaire studies have shown that students who take a surface approach gain lower marks and poorer degree results and are more likely to fail. The effects are often quite dramatic. Given the limited correlation between students' A Level scores, intelligence and study skills and their performance in higher education, evidence of the link between students' approach to study and their performance is especially significant.

These studies have spanned subject areas as diverse as the humanities, Science, Computing and Social Science, in four different countries, using different research methods. They have spanned small specialist courses and large undergraduate degree programmes containing over 40 disciplines and over 2000 students (cf. Entwistle and Ramsden, 1983). The range and diversity of these studies leaves no doubt that a surface approach has a disastrous impact on the quality of learning outcomes.

Course design can foster a surface approach

If a surface approach is such a problem, then it is important to understand where it comes from. For some students, it seems to be a consequence of an unsophisticated conception of learning and a misunderstanding of the demands of the course. But most students can take either a surface or a deep approach. The examples given earlier in this chapter illustrating a deep and a surface approach did not come from two different students but from one student taking two different courses. He has simply responded strategically to the perceived demands of the two courses. What matters here is what it is about courses which can lead competent students to take such an extreme surface approach, with all the negative consequences this has for learning.

Many studies have looked at the relationship between the approach students take to their courses and a number of features of the courses in order to identify what it is about courses which affects students. Studies have involved laboratory experiments, the use of questionnaires and the use of depth interviews, in Sweden, the UK and Australia. Some of the studies have been very large, involving thousands of students and scores of academic departments across a wide range of subject areas and institutions.

The features of courses which are most likely to be found where students tend to take a surface approach are a heavy workload, relatively high class-contact hours, an excessive amount of course material, a lack of opportunity to pursue subjects in depth, a lack of choice over subjects and a lack of choice over the method of study, and a threatening and anxiety provoking assessment system.

As class sizes increase in the UK course delivery is moving towards European and American models, relying ever more heavily on lecturing as small group work becomes harder to resource. Students are being treated as a homogeneous mass and are being given less choice. Assessment is starting to be mechanized in order to save time, relying increasingly on methods such as objective testing which has difficulty in measuring understanding or rewarding the achievement of the higher levels in the SOLO taxonomy. Where open learning materials are adopted as a coping strategy, these often narrow the perceived learning task to one on mastering the text in the learning package. Where assessment taps understanding (as with more open-ended extended written work) it is much less frequent, providing less feedback and so increasing anxiety. The way many courses are responding to increased student numbers seems very likely to foster a surface approach in students.

Students' perceptions of teaching

Students have been asked, in studies, what they think good teaching consists of. Some think that the teacher should do all the work and make all the decisions. The teacher should select the subject matter, present it in teacher-controlled classes, devise tests and mark students on how well they have learnt the material which has been presented. What is to be learnt and what learning outcomes should look like is completely defined by the teacher (a 'closed' conception of teaching). Others think that while the teacher has responsibility for setting the learning climate, for making learning resources available, and for supporting students, all the responsibility lies with the student: responsibility for selecting learning goals, devising appropriate learning activities and for judging when learning outcomes are satisfactory (an 'open' conception of teaching). It will come as no surprise to learn that the former, 'closed', conception of teaching is held almost exclusively by students with conceptions of learning concerned with memorization, while the latter, 'open', conception of teaching is held by students with conceptions of learning concerned with understanding.

The issue then is whether students see 'closed' teaching as good because they have a reproductive conception of learning, or whether they have a reproductive conception of learning because they have been experiencing 'closed' teaching. I believe the latter explanation and that implicit in course design and teaching methods are underlying assumptions about what learning and knowledge itself consists of. Students pick up these implicit assumptions and adopt them.

One consequence of the kinds of teacher-centered courses which are being used to cope with large classes is, therefore, likely to be the development in students of a closed conception of teaching and a reproductive conception of learning. It is already becoming commonplace for students in large courses to express very conservative views about innovations in teaching and great anxiety if alternatives to lecturing are suggested. Some student-centered innovations are having to be abandoned due to opposition from anxious students. I believe their opposition is rooted in their unsophisticated understanding of what teaching and learning consist of and which the conventional course delivery methods have induced. Even third-year undergraduates can be terrified of independence in learning because they have experienced undiluted teacher-centered methods for the previous two years.

Course design for a deep approach

Studies have identified a number of factors which are, in effect, the obverse of factors which foster a surface approach, such as intrinsic interest in the subject and freedom in learning. Freedom may involve choice over content or method of learning or scope for intellectual independence. A crucial additional factor is 'perceived good teaching'. What 'good teaching' consists of has been identified through many studies of teaching processes which are associated with a deep approach. Four key elements have been identified and none concern lecturer's classroom performance:

1. *Motivational context*

   A deep approach to learning is more likely when students' motivation is intrinsic and when the student experiences a need to know something. Adults learn best what they need to learn in order to carry out tasks which matter to them. Students are likely to need to be involved in selecting what is to be learnt and in planning how the learning should take place if they are to experience 'ownership' of it. The motivational context is established by the emotional climate of the learning. While a positive emotional and motivational climate may be a necessary condition for deep learning, anxiety and instrumentalism may be sufficient conditions for surface learning. Conservative approaches to teaching large classes lead to alienation and low motivation.

2. *Learner activity*

   Students need to be active rather than passive. Deep learning is associated with doing. If the learner is actively involved, then more connections will be made both with past learning and between new concepts. Doing is not sufficient for learning, however. Learning activity must be planned, reflected upon and processed, and related to abstract conceptions. Conservative approaches to teaching large classes treat students as passive.

3. *Interaction with others*

   It is often easier to negotiate meaning and to manipulate ideas with others than alone. The importance of discussion for learning is not a new idea, though there is precious little discussion in much of higher education. Interaction can take many forms other than conventional tutorials and seminars, and autonomous student groups and peer tutoring can be very effective. Studies have even shown that in peer tutoring the student who does the tutoring learns more than the student who is tutored, confirming the everyday experience that the best way to learn something is to teach it. In large classes discussion is disappearing as seminar groups become ever-larger and tutorials become rarer.

4. *A well-structured knowledge base*

   Without existing concepts, it is impossible to make sense of new concepts. It is vital that students' existing knowledge and experience are brought to bear in learning. The subject matter being learnt must also be well structured and integrated. The structure of knowledge is more visible to, and more useful to, students where it is clearly displayed, where content is taught in integrated wholes rather than in small separate pieces, and where knowledge is required to be related to other knowledge rather than learned in isolation. Interdisciplinary approaches also contribute to a well-structured knowledge base. While conventional lectures may be able to convey the structure of a subject, they do not involve students in actively relating past and current knowledge into structures.

   (Biggs, 1989)

The extent to which course design, teaching and assessment methods embody these four elements will determine whether they are likely to foster a deep approach. Problem-based learning, for example, embodies all four of these elements. It has been found that while deep approaches to learning decline over time in traditional medical schools (which tend to involve heavy lecture programmes and rote memorization for the first two years), they do not in a medical school using problem-based learning.

Fostering a deep approach

This section identifies nine strategies for improving the quality of student learning by fostering a deep approach. These strategies overlap in several respects and many innovations embody features from several of the strategies. The important features of these strategies are the extent to which they embody the four elements introduced above: a motivational context, learner activity, interactions with others and a well-structured knowledge base. The key features of these strategies are elaborated by Gibbs (1992a).

Strategy 1   Independent learning
Strategy 2   Personal development
Strategy 3   Problem-based learning
Strategy 4   Reflection
Strategy 5   Independent group work
Strategy 6   Learning by doing
Strategy 7   Developing learning skills
Strategy 8   Project work
Strategy 9   Fine tuning

The way these strategies embody the four key elements which foster a deep approach can be seen most clearly by looking at the example of Strategy 3. Problem-based learning involves learning through tackling relevant problems. The goal is learning, not solving the problem; the problem simply provides an engaging context within which learning takes place. This is distinct from learning how to solve problems, in which what is learnt is problem-solving skills, and also distinct from applying knowledge to problems in project work where the learning takes place first and is only then used in the context of a problem. In problem-based learning, there is no prior presentation of subject matter. Students discover what they need to learn about through being confronted with problems, and then learn what they need to in order to be able to tackle the problem. In some applications, the nature of the problem has to be identified by the students who are simply confronted with a situation or evidence and asked, in effect, 'What is problematic about this?' In some applications of this method, there is no emphasis on actually 'solving' the problem. Problems are simply exploited for their learning potential, after which students move on to the next problem. The main features of the strategy are:

- *Relevant problems*. Problem-based learning is most common in professional courses such as Medicine and Engineering where students are given real-world problems of the kind a professional would be faced with. In well-developed applications, the problems are carefully designed to involve all the important parts of the syllabus. Students may select and negotiate their way through problems in order to make sure that they 'cover' the syllabus.
- *A 'need to know'*. What students go off and learn about is determined by what is necessary to tackle the problem. This generates a great deal of highly focused motivation.
- *Integration of knowledge*. Real-world problems are very often large scale and interdisciplinary. Students do not experience knowledge in artificially discrete packages.
- *Interaction*. Problem-based learning almost always employs groups of students working co-operatively, sharing ideas, dividing up the learning to be done, briefing each other and solving problems co-operatively.

Problem-based learning therefore involves all four elements which foster a deep approach.

It is important to recognize that these nine strategies are not those commonly being used as class sizes increase, a point which will be pursued below.

Case study

The CNAA project *Improving Student Learning* undertook action research with a wide range of courses with the intention of fostering a deep approach and improving the quality of learning outcomes. The following case study illustrates the ways in which the above strategies were employed in a Law course.

Business Law, Wolverhampton Polytechnic

The case study concerns a one-semester Business Law module in the first year of a BA/BSc Business Information Systems modular degree programme. It is a relatively small course, involving students in about one-quarter of their time for half a year, involving a total of 150 hours learning. The module runs twice a year and the case study looked at its pilot operation and its operation involving changes introduced as a result of the pilot.

Instead of the conventional approach of a lecture and a seminar a week, the course involves setting students up into learning groups and giving them a series of six projects to undertake. The class contact of two hours a week is used to brief and review the group tasks, to support the development of the groups, to develop research skills and to share learning across the groups. Very short lectures are used to introduce the topics addressed by the projects but almost all the content of the course has to be collected by the groups themselves. The following is a description of the programme for the class session for Week 3:

The Waiting Game
Group Game (Structures)
Discussion within groups of progress made on the second project
Plenary session on the second project
Introduction to Employment Law (with group exercises)
Signing of project 2 contract

The six projects (listed below) involve activities in real-world contexts rather than wholly academic tasks.

Project 1. A series of short questions and tasks to establish co-operative group work and identify the nature and uses of legal source material. Questions include: '*Obtain a street map of Wolverhampton and the 1990* Yellow Pages. *Plot the location of Solicitors on it. What conclusions can you draw?*'
Project 2. The design and construction of a computerized legal advice giver, accompanied by a detailed written analysis of the area of law concerned.

Project 3. The production of a report explaining the rules relating to the formation of registered companies.

Project 4. An analysis of media stories with a Business Law dimension.

Project 5. The design and administration of a questionnaire to evaluate public knowledge of an area of law relevant to consumers and entrepreneurs.

Project 6. An interview with an individual concerned with problems in the area of Business Law, and the preparation and presentation to the individual of a report analysing the relevant Law and proposing a legal resolution to the problem.

The first of the projects is formatively assessed and the other five are summatively assessed. Group project reports are graded and the group members then peer-assess relative contributions to the project and award moderated grades to each other based around the tutor's grade. There is no exam, unlike parallel conventionally taught Law modules.

Students keep a 'learning log' in which they record reflections on their learning of Law. The way students research topics independently is illustrated by this extract from a student's learning log:

12.3.91   Bought The *Express and Star*... found a range of legal topics, but one that interested me was the death of a woman when doors in a Do-It-Yourself store were not securely placed. Does it relate to Health and Safety at Work or the Tort of negligence? Anyway the court case is tomorrow at 10.00 a.m.... I think I'll appear to see whether the action will be brought in under negligence or under a breach of a condition of the Health and Safety at Work.

13.3.91   Appeared at the Court...

3.4.91   Used facilities in Central Lending Library and travelled to DTI in London, various Banks and Business Enterprise Schemes to gather information on the next task.

18.4.91   After the lesson the group went to a small business centre for information on companies. We also went to a business centre in Lichfield Passage.

Students read Law textbooks and consult Law Reports as well. This contrasts with the type of research undertaken on the parallel conventional Law module:

[They have given us a book guide. I think there is a book on the list discussing Marx. I'll probably read the minimum amount necessary... read the introduction and conclusion and skim through the bits in between]

INTERVIEWER: Where are you getting your understanding from?

STUDENT: Well from the lecture notes. Well ideally you are meant to use the lecture notes as a starting point. We get a book list. In an ideal world you would go off to the library and pick up books on the book list. Unfortunately it is not an ideal world.

A 36-page workbook explains how the module operated and provides instructions for the projects. Students keep a log of their learning activities and record the hours they spend on the module.

The findings

One might suspect that first-year students might not undertake the independent work required for a course like this. However, the projects were assessed and there were no other assessment elements and so students could not avoid doing independent work. According to their logs, they spent an average of 153 hours on the module (with a range of 94–268 hours on a module planned as 150 hours' work) and complained that it involved far more work than their other modules. They averaged 74 per cent attendance at class meetings.

The crucial issue here is whether students approached their studying differently on this course than on a parallel conventionally taught Law course. At the start of the two courses, there were no significant differences between students' approaches (as measured by the 'Approaches to Studying' questionnaire). By the end of the semester, students on the parallel Law course 'Law, Justice and the Individual' were taking a surface approach to a significantly greater extent than on the Business Law course and taking a deep approach to a significantly lesser extent. Students' approaches could be clearly identified in interviews. The following is an example of a student taking deep approach on the Business Law module:

> You give us something to do which we have not done before, make us go and find out about it. I know that's harder to do but at the end of it when you've done it you feel much better because you feel you've achieved much more. With other assignments, you feel like you are not interested in it because you think you have done it before, you've covered it before . . . You're looking for understanding, basically . . . so you know that we understand what we have written about. We have not just gone away and copied it or it has just gone in one ear and out the other.

This contrasts with the following examples of students taking a surface approach on the conventional Law module:

> Well basically it was dictation . . . we just sit there and [the lecturer] just reads through his notes, we make our notes and . . . basically just take the notes and to a large extent switch off.

> It is all writing down and we don't have much time for discussion . . . it's mostly dictation. You can't possibly think about what is being said. It is just a question of trying to decipher it later on.

While students on the Business Law course changed their approach (away from a surface approach and towards a greater deep approach), they did not change at all on the parallel 'Law, Justice and Society' course, so the differences were not simply a matter of maturation or increasing sophistication. These students were responding to the design of the course.

Students' grades were examined to see if they were related to their approach. Students worked in teams on assignments and gained a team grade which was peer-moderated. The average approach scores (on the 'Approaches to Studying' questionnaire) of team members were therefore examined to see if they correlated with average grades of teams. There was a large and significant positive correlation between deep approach scale scores and grades and no correlation between surface approach scale scores and grades. Neither the percentage of class sessions attended nor the total number of learning hours students spent on the module correlated with grades. In other words, the only predictor of performance was their deep approach scale score: the extent to which students attempted to understand the material.

These marked positive effects of the design of the course on student learning were not evident the previous year when the course was being piloted. The main changes which were made after the piloting of the module which are likely to have been influential in this change were:

- Much more attention was paid to the formation and support of the learning groups, which increased co-operative interaction.
- Regular multiple choice tests were dropped as it was felt that they disoriented students towards a surface approach.
- Brief overviews of topics were provided in briefings at the start of each team project as a way of providing a sounder knowledge base for the independent work.

These modifications illustrate the importance of fine tuning in making such innovations effective.

Students' group coursework projects were analysed using the SOLO taxonomy. There was a very close relationship between the extent to which students took a deep approach and the SOLO level of their projects. In other words, the greater the extent to which they took a deep approach, the more sophisticated was the structure of content of their project reports. Students who took a deep approach also gained higher grades.

The important features of the innovation in this case study were the motivating nature of the problems and projects, active learning, interaction between students in project teams and in class, and the integrative way knowledge was acquired. There was also a good deal of fine tuning of classroom techniques and assessment so that processes and desired outcomes were congruent.

All this 'research' evidence, including questionnaire data, interview data, data from students' logs and analyses of the outcomes of student learning using the SOLO taxonomy, was undertaken by a lecturer. The only outside assistance this lecturer received was a briefing and documentation at the start of the year and a meeting to interpret the results at the end. It illustrates a lecturer engaged in rigorous action research using a coherent rationale with a firm base in research on student learning. This contrasts with some models of quality assurance in which a lecturer passively receives the results of standard student feedback questionnaires at the end of the year telling her that her use of audio-visual aids is 'satisfactory'.

Strategies for coping with large classes which foster a deep approach

The course design strategies listed above which foster a deep approach might at first glance appear anachronistic at a time of rapid increase in student numbers and of the disappearance of one-to-one tutorials or indeed any significant individual support for students. While these strategies may have been usable in the heady well-resourced days of the 1970s, they are surely impossible to employ today. In fact, the case studies in the CNAA project cost no more to run than their conventional counterparts. Indeed it was a condition of courses' involvement in the CNAA study that innovations were no more expensive to run than the courses they replaced.

But there is a more important argument here than about the relative costs of strategies. Whatever strategies are adopted, lecturers and institutions will have to deal with the special problems larger classes involve. As class sizes increase, students face any or all of the following problems (Gibbs, 1992b):

1. Lack of clarity of purpose.
2. Lack of knowledge about progress.
3. Lack of advice on improvement.
4. Inability to support wide reading.
5. Inability to support independent study.
6. Lack of opportunity for discussion.
7. Inability to cope with variety of students.
8. Inability to motivate students.

Motivation has in the past come from personal contact with lecturers and involvement in small group discussion. When students' imagination was fired, library and other resources could give it free rein. In large classes, in the absence of either personal contact or small groups, and with inadequate resources to fuel motivation, students are frequently disengaged and passive.

If we were to look at the methods adopted in North American higher education to tackle these kinds of problems, we would find very different kinds of solutions to those which foster a deep approach. In the main we would find 'control' strategies (Jenkins and Gibbs, 1992). Subject matter is specified in advance, often in terms of behavioural objectives, and tested with multiple choice questions, often computer marked. Motivation is generated through frequent testing with an emphasis on quantitative results (the grade point average). Access to reading is provided by text books and discussion may not be supported at all. Table 8.1 contrasts 'control' and 'independence' strategies for dealing with large class problems. It is easy to see which of these is more likely to foster a deep approach. It is also easy to see which are more closely allied to conventional course delivery techniques.

Table 8.1 'Control' and 'independence' strategies

Problem area resulting from large classes	Characteristic methods adopted	
	'Control' strategies	*'Independence' strategies*
1. Clarity of purpose	Use of objectives	Use of learning contracts
2. Knowledge of progress	Objective testing	Development of student judgement and self-assessment
3. Advice on improvement	Assignment attachment forms	Peer feedback and assessment
4. Ability to support wide reading	Use of set books and learning packages	Development of students' research skills
5. Support of independent study	'Follow-the-instructions' projects	Independent group work
6. Opportunity for discussion	Structured lectures	Independent student-led seminars
7. Variety of students	Pre-tests plus remedial self-instructional material	Variety of levels of support mechanisms including peer support groups
8. Student motivation	Frequent testing	Problem-based learning

It is apparent from this analysis of solutions to the problems of large class teaching that few of the solutions have got anything to do with teachers' classroom performance. However in North America, a large proportion of quality assurance consists of student feedback on teachers' classroom performance and there seem to be moves in this direction in the UK with lecturers' teaching being appraised by classroom observation and talk of lecturers' pay being linked to assessment by students through lecture feedback questionnaires.

Improving student learning

If an individual lecturer wanted to take immediate steps to improve the quality of student learning, what could she or he do? Many of the implications outlined above involve relatively major changes in course design which might involve the co-operation of others, approval and resources, not to mention a long-term perspective on change. Nevertheless, there is scope for individually initiated improvements. The following list is offered, derived from evidence concerning what fosters a surface or a deep approach.

- Review assessment tasks to ensure that good marks cannot be achieved by regurgitation of factual information, but only by understanding.

- Clarify your assessment criteria and make them explicit so that students are in no doubt that mere memorization will not be rewarded.
- Provide examples of what the outcomes of taking a deep approach (and a surface approach) look like, by copying reports, essays or exam answers and discussing what is wrong and right about them. Orient students towards higher-level goals by providing models of these goals.
- Look for opportunities to increase the amount of exploratory discussion which students engage in. If you lack the teaching resources to offer tutorials, set up autonomous discussion groups or learning teams, or set assignments which require team work.
- Look for opportunities to introduce active learning where it was previously passive – during lectures, for example.
- Try turning flat content into problems and puzzles so that engaging with it is inherently interesting. Look for ways of making reading and routine work engaging by surrounding it with questions and interesting contexts.
- Look for scope to allow students in on decisions about what and how they study. There may be more leeway, within existing curricula and exam regulations, for students to study what interests them, and to undertake assignments of their own choosing, than you think.
- Look for opportunities to encourage reflection, for example through requiring students to write self-assessment comments on their lab reports or essays before they submit them, and through the use of reflective journals, discussed in seminars.
- Look for opportunities to deal with subject matter in larger, more interdisciplinary lumps rather than always in small specialist lumps.
- Take every opportunity to encourage students to discuss what good learning and good teaching consist of, rather than always discussing substantive subject content.
- In evaluating your course, use questionnaires based on research into student learning (cf. Ramsden, 1991) rather than questionnaires which focus on teachers' lecturing performance.

Conclusion

This chapter has argued that the key variable when examining the quality of student learning, that of students' approach to learning, is profoundly important in determining the quality of learning outcomes, and is very extensively influenced by aspects of course design. These aspects do not have much to do with teachers' classroom performance. As class sizes increase, pressures build up which seem to force course design in directions which foster a surface approach and which will inevitably worsen the quality of learning outcomes. However, alternative course design strategies exist which both address large class problems and foster a deep approach. If quality in learning is to be maintained, we must pursue these course design strategies rather than focusing on teachers' classroom behaviour within unchanged conventional courses.

References

Biggs, J.B. (1989) 'Does learning about learning help teachers with teaching? Psychology and the tertiary teacher'. *The Gazette* (Supplement), 26(1). University of Hong Kong.

Biggs, J.B. and Collis, K.F. (1982) *Evaluating the Quality of Learning: the SOLO Taxonomy*. New York, Academic Press.

Dahlgren, L.O. (1984) 'Outcomes of learning' in F. Marton *et al.* (eds) *The Experience of Learning*. Edinburgh, Scottish Academic Press.

Entwistle, N.J. and Ramsden, P. (1983) *Understanding Student Learning*. London, Croom Helm.

Gibbs, G. (1992a) *Improving the Quality of Student Learning*. Bristol, Technical and Educational Services.

Gibbs, G. (1992b) *Problems and Course Design Strategies. Teaching More Students* (No. 1). Oxford, Oxford Centre for Staff Development.

Jenkins, A. and Gibbs, G. (eds) (1992) *Teaching Large Classes: maintaining quality with reduced resources*. London, Kogan Page.

Marton, F. and Saljo, R. (1976) 'On qualitative differences in learning: I. Outcome and process'. *British Journal of Educational Psychology*, 46, 4–11.

Ramsden, P. (1983) 'Institutional variations in British students' approaches to learning and experiences of teaching'. *Higher Education*, 12, 691–705.

Ramsden, P. (1991) 'A performance indicator of teaching quality in higher education: the Course Experience Questionnaire'. *Studies in Higher Education*, 16, 129–50.

Ramsden, P. (1992) *Learning to Teach in Higher Education*. London, Routledge.

Van Rossum, E.J. and Schenk, S.M. (1984) 'The relationship between learning conception, study strategy and learning outcome'. *British Journal of Educational Psychology*, 54, 73–83.

Part 4

The National Perspective

11

Credit Accumulation and Transfer and the Student Experience

Gaie Davidson

Credit accumulation and transfer (CAT) is a relatively recent term in UK higher education. It arose at national level in 1986 when the Council for National Academic Awards (CNAA) piloted a scheme of 'portable credits' among the five London polytechnics. In this scheme, students can enrol directly with the CNAA who, acting as a broker, will accredit learning gained across a spectrum of formal and informal experiences (CNAA, 1991b). Students can climb a ladder of levels, ensuring progression through their studies to attain a variety of awards: 120 credits at Level One, which is equivalent to a first year full-time student load, enables students to reach for a certificate; with another 120 at Level Two, they can look to a diploma and a further 120 at Level Three enables them to lay claim to a degree (CNAA, 1989). Such a scheme is similar to the 'Californian model' of ladders for which the Vice-Chancellor of Oxford 'expressed enthusiasm', where students can cross and climb the learning ladder in a manner that suits individual requirements (Reed, 1991).

The CNAA CAT scheme, however, is only one step on a rung of flexible educational innovations. Early this century, the University of Harvard inaugurated a system of 'elective' courses which replaced the established prescribed syllabus (Squires, 1986). Not only were students permitted to form degrees by selecting from a range of related courses, they could also include in their award comparable learning gained outside academe. Within a short time, this 'modular' system became the standard educational pattern throughout the country.

According to Harold Silver, British interest in modularity arose in the 1960s when new pedagogical and curricular issues were high on the academic agenda (CNAA, 1990a). Early in the 1970s, several polytechnics developed modular structures, notably Oxford Polytechnic and the City of London Polytechnic (CNAA, 1991a). Another rung on the flexible ladder was the introduction of unit structures. Several distinctive models exist. Most commonly encountered is that operated throughout the London University federation (Theodossin, 1986) and the distance learning example provided by the Open

University which serves mainly mature students. Finally, the CNAA opened the door to transbinary credit transfer when it introduced CATS in 1986.

Module, unit, CAT and semesters

Units, modules and CAT schemes

Each of the steps outlined above are indices of the gradual move towards a more flexible provision of learning within UK academe in the last quarter of a century. The terms that are employed, however, vary and some have quite distinct meanings. Unit systems, for example, do not necessarily require departments and faculties to adopt standard size units nor is there a necessary expectation that units will be examined upon completion or exchanged between faculties or institutions. Within the London federation, a particular exchange scheme applies which permits movement between the colleges. A consensus that the standard length of a unit is a year, with a provision that half units may be offered, facilitates collegiate credit transfer. Agreement that full-time students may study no less than three units a year and no more than four permits a degree of flexibility throughout the system yet maintains consistency.

Several years ago, the unit structure at Liverpool University enabled mathematicians to offer common units to students within a number of faculties, thereby avoiding duplication. In October 1991, the unit arrangement that was promoted among the School of Dentistry and the faculties of Science, Engineering, Medicine and Veterinary Science was embraced by the remaining faculties in Liverpool (October 1991).

Modular schemes tend to distinguish themselves from unit-based ones in that an institution adopts a standard size unit which is assessed either during or immediately upon completion. The Open University (OU) is an example of this type of scheme. Since its incipience, the OU has been open to students with a desire to learn. It offers them discrete modules which, through distance learning, may be accumulated at a pace which suits their particular lifestyles.

Both unit and modular schemes introduce a degree of flexibility into administrative arrangements. Students may move between institutions, faculties or departments which share a common unit system and thereby take advantage of a broader selection of courses. Modular schemes, which have fixed points when students can plan their next stage of learning, regularize flexibility. Standard size modules facilitate delayed choice and, if they are less than a year in length, increase the number of selection points.

The CNAA Credit Accumulation and Transfer (CAT) scheme differs from unit and modular schemes because it is not a structural arrangement. It advances many of the ideas that are found in such schemes, but moves one step further by accrediting learning wherever it is gained and whenever it is or was acquired.[1] Students can learn from several locations, have learning that was acquired prior to registering for a course accredited, study full-time, part-time, at a distance or by a combination of modes. In a paper issued by the CNAA in October 1990, the CAT approach is described as follows:

> The principle underlying the Scheme is that appropriate learning wherever it occurs, provided it can be assessed, should be given credit towards the Council's awards. Thus a student can obtain an award by an accumulation of academic credit gained from more than one source subject to having their programme of study approved in advance and assessed by a competent authority.
>
> (CNAA, 1990b)

The principles of CAT neither require nor demand modularity or unitization. There is no organizational structure inherent in the processes of accrediting learning from a variety of sources and permitting students flexible study arrangements. Just as unit and modular schemes have existed for a number of years without CAT principles, so too can the CAT scheme exist without modules or units.

Modules, units and credit accumulation

An interface between modular and unit structures and CAT occurs when considering how best the principles of CAT may be administered. Slicing learning into separately assessed slivers enables students to accrue their credits at a pace which best suits their individual circumstances. Some traditional students may wish to take a fast journey through this part of their educational career and accumulate their credits in three years or less of full-time study. Others may wish to learn at a steady part-time rate, vary part-time study, move between full-time and part-time enrolment, or interrupt their studies for a year or so. Credit accumulation in this manner is most easily facilitated when specified learning is assessed immediately upon its completion, as within modular systems.

> ... modularisation can assist credit transfer by employing learning components representing measured portions of a programme and by assessing the student's achievements in those components immediately upon completion.
>
> (Theodossin, 1986)

One of the dangers of accumulating learning over a period of time is that it may become outdated. A glance at recent scientific and technological developments testifies to the growth of knowledge in both areas which quickly outstrips earlier work. In other areas, such as Political Science, Law and Environmental Studies, lecturers point to the direct and indirect impact of recent European Community legislation on their subjects. Gradually accumulated programmes require interrogating for contemporaneity and those parts which have become outdated need refreshing. Other subjects, such as Modern Languages, require constant practice. Students who interrupt their studies need to polish their language skills before continuing to progress through the levels. Attention to these issues is part of the logic of effective CAT.

Modules, units and credit transfer

Transferring credit for learning gained at one venue to another is most easily managed when it is discrete. Such an arrangement enables admissions officers to estimate the compatibility of learning acquired elsewhere in terms of content contribution to a pathway, level, credit point and, where appropriate, grade.

Learning which gains full credit in one institution may contribute only partially to a pathway in another. One can imagine a drama unit which claims full credit in a Film and Drama degree at institution X but which might contribute only half a unit to an English degree at Institution Y. In a Chemistry with French degree, it is possible that the language units which were studied at Level Three might be included in the degree classification, but not so in a French Honours pathway where the classification was only calculated on students' performance in Levels Two and Three units and the language units in question were placed at Level One.

There are occasions when credit which is deemed specific in one pathway might only be considered general on another. For example, a specific Sociology unit which was deemed sufficient to enable a student to gain advanced standing into Year Two of a Social Work diploma might only warrant general credit towards entry to a Geography degree. A similar decision might be made when credit becomes outdated. An 'E.C. Directives' unit studied in 1973 might have contributed specific credit to a Politics of the E.C. pathway for five or six years, but later might contribute only generally to the same pathway because of more recent directives that had emanated from Brussels.

Each discipline and each institution is likely to safeguard its reputation by designing regulations that permit entrance or advanced standing to be at the discretion of admissions officers to named pathways. Some units may have a longer 'shelf-life' than others, but only those people in charge of validating pathways can evaluate at any one time the amount and type of credit that various forms of learning may contribute.

There are several inherent dangers in credit transfer that institutions wish to avoid. First, specific learning should only contribute once to an award. To avoid the pitfall of double counting, a number of universities are considering specifying students' anticipated learning attainments in terms of *learning outcomes*, as opposed to syllabus input. Second, learning needs to form a coherent, academic programme. Most institutions prefer to design their academic programmes in terms of pathways, composed of core and optional units, which lead to named awards. A number of departments in institutions, such as some departments of continuing education, are exploring the possibility that students may negotiate individual learning contracts with

Table 11.1   Standard length size unit[†]
Answer to Q2a: *Have you identified a size of standard course unit? If yes, give length in weeks*

Scottish, Irish, Welsh Universities (weeks)		English universities (weeks)	
Aberdeen	12		
Bangor	12	Leeds	12
Heriot-Watt	10/12	Leicester	12
Queen's, Belfast	15	Liverpool	12
Stirling	15	Nottingham	14
Swansea	12	OU (p/t)	15/16[*]
Ulster	12	Sheffield	12

† The most common semester length course unit is 12 weeks. From my interviews, I would suggest that this frequently refers to 12 teaching weeks housed within a 15-week shell which allows 3 weeks for assessment and examinations
* OU courses run from February to October

them. Such customized programmes are an essential part of the CNAA CAT approach. In both circumstances, students' learning must form a viable whole, not just a disparate collection of credits. Finally, those members of staff that are developing CAT and modular programmes focus attention upon the progression of learning from one level of study to another – especially on those units which require certain prerequisite knowledge so that students can master subsequent learning, and on the complementarity and integration of the elements that together form the programme of learning.

Semesters and CAT

Institutions that have a variety of unit sizes encourage non-coincidental learning completion points and these hinder transfer possibilities. Over time, if they wish to facilitate CAT, unitary-based institutions tend to recommend that the various pathways are composed of standard-sized units. Small length units make learning difficult to identify and, if assessed immediately upon completion, fracture the academic calendar into numerous examinable points. Long units, on the other hand, limit the number of points at which students can transfer or alter accumulation pace.

In reply to a questionnaire sent out on behalf of the author by the Committee of Vice Chancellors and Principals in 1991, 13 universities answered that already they had adopted a standard length unit size. Table 11.1 shows that 12 learning weeks within a 15-week learning and assessment shell is the most common unit pattern. From interviews with administrative and academic personnel at a number of universities, it appears that, providing fractions and multiples of units are permitted, such an arrangement is viewed as the 'best fit' for the wide range of subjects that a common course structure needs to accommodate.

Further evidence from the author's study of 'CATS in the British Universities'[2] shows that learning patterns coincide within individual disciplines across the system, more than they do across disciplines that are within the same institution. For example, in the majority of universities visited by the author, at most points in the curriculum humanities subject specialists are more likely to prefer two end-to-end units which equal an academic year than half-year or semester-length units. A look at Science subjects reveals that specialists in these areas often prefer units of less than a semester length. However, across many subjects, learning is likely to be spread over several units towards the final period of study as students work on projects or outside placements.

In general, semester systems tend to be least resisted by disciplines whose offerings are not dependent upon year-long teaching units. In an attempt to meet the challenge of the increasingly flexible educational scene, many subject specialists are currently considering novel ways of evaluating learning that is 'in progress' or that could be seen as 'sections' in a cumulative assessment scheme. Assessment which includes continual monitoring, portfolio evaluation or project work, for example, is less likely to puncture the academic session with severe discontinuities than are a series of the traditional three-hour unseen examinations. These arrangements are expected to promote the smooth learning curve desired by both learners and teachers whilst simultaneously ensuring that quality is assured and high standards are maintained.

Currently, 20 universities are considering either semester length units within the present term structure or altering their terms to correspond with semesters (Table 11.2). Eleven others have already agreed to semester length units. Leeds, Liverpool and Sheffield universities, which have all set target dates for when they will modularize their systems (see Table 11.4) have each agreed standard semester length course units of 12 learning weeks. Nottingham has set a 14- and 16-week pattern in which 12 weeks in each semester are devoted to teaching, but assessment periods differ between the two.

From current discussions within many institutions, 12 teaching weeks within a 15-week shell, which includes an assessment period, is the pattern which appears to be that most commonly considered at present. When institutions are closer to organizing the practice of semesters, it may be that solving the weight of administrative matters that need attention at the end of the academic session may mean that variants on the Nottingham model will appear more frequently.

Summary of module, unit, CAT and semesters

In summary, for both the accumulation and transfer of learning, discrete units greatly enhance the possibility of gaining learning from more than one

Table 11.2 Universities with semester-shaped units[†]
Answer to Q3: *Which of the following patterns of university year will you adopt?*

Considering semester length units (b) with present terms retained (c) with terms altered to correspond with the semesters				Agreed semester length units (b) with present terms retained (c) with terms altered to correspond with the semesters	
Birmingham	b/c				
Bradford	b/c				
Bristol	b				
Brunel	b/c			Leeds	b/c
Cranfield	b			Liverpool	b/c
Durham	b	English universities		Nottingham	b/c
Leicester	b	(excl. London)		Sheffield	b/c
Manchester	b/c			Southampton*	b
Salford	b				
Southampton*	c				
Sussex	b				
UMIST	b/c				
Goldsmith	b				
LSE	b/c	London		QM Westfield*	b
QM Westfield*	c	University		RH & BN	b
Aberdeen	c				
Swansea	b			Bangor	b/c
Queen's, Belfast*	c	Scottish, Irish,		Ulster	c
Heriot-Watt	b/c	Welsh universities		Queen's*	b
Dundee	b/c			Stirling	b/c

† Total number of responding universities = 56
* Universities that appear in both columns

source. Standard size units enable the maximum transfer arrangements within and between institutions and end of learning assessment permits ease of varied modes of accumulation. Currently, semester length units appear to be the 'best fit' units since they can accommodate longer and shorter units thereby unifying an institutional provision. It is at the juncture of the rationales of providing standard sized units, which are assessed at the completion of learning and which are semester length, that the philosophy of CAT and administrative arrangements meet.

CAT schemes in UK universities

As a scheme which was set up to assess and accredit learning, CNAA CAT advises students on credit rating their qualifications and experience and centrally registers those who cannot be based at an institution of higher

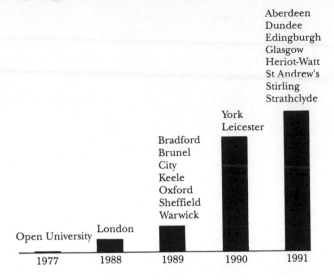

Figure 11.1   CNAA agreements with universities (in the case of Oxford, the agreement is with the Extramural Department)

education. It acts as an academic broker for industry, collaborates with professional bodies, and helps to develop links between consortia of institutions (CNAA, 1991a).

Initially, CNAA CAT schemes focused upon centrally registering students and accrediting a broad spectrum of learning that they had culled from a variety of locations. In recent years, CAT schemes have expanded to become an institutional policy, first among polytechnics and lately among universities. By 1991, 19 universities had signed agreements with the CNAA which outlined a series of ways in which they would co-operate with the CNAA's CAT scheme for entry, advanced standing and credit rating (Figure 11.1). In response to a further question in the current UK university CAT-scheme study, 'Are you Adopting a Credit Rating Scheme?', a total of 27 universities answered that they were adopting the CNAA CAT or SCOTCAT[3] scheme (Table 11.3). This response indicates that although 19 universities have signed formal CAT agreements with the CNAA, many more institutions are willing to accept students who have gained credit for learning in places other than the institution into which they wish to enter or transfer than those who have signed formal agreements. It could be argued that the swell in the numbers of those universities who are prepared to adopt the CAT credit rating scheme demonstrates that a national framework is emerging through consensus and practice among higher education institutions. Such a consensus and parallel practice will facilitate a greater degree of flexible learning than has heretofore been seen in the UK.

Table 11.3   Universities adopting the CNAA CAT or SCOTCAT scheme[†]

Birmingham	London S*
Bradford*	Manchester
Bristol	Nottingham
Brunel*	Open University*
Durham	QM Westfield
East Anglia	Sheffield*
Hull	Surrey
Kent	Sussex
Lancaster	Swansea
Leeds	Ulster
Liverpool	UMIST

[†] Eight Scottish and six other English universities have also signed agreements; see Fig. 11.1.
* These have signed a CNAA CAT/SCOTCAT agreement

Rationales for CAT schemes

One wonders why so many polytechnics and universities have embraced CAT schemes. The arguments are several (see Chapter 9). For those who embrace access, it is a scheme which breaks the traditional boundaries of learning and bridges educational walls by allowing people with non-traditional qualifications to enter education. Secondly, those who cannot or do not wish to study full-time are not excluded. Thirdly, those whose circumstances alter once they are enrolled in higher education institutions may adjust their educational programme to suit their other circumstances. Fourthly, those who, at 18, were too poor to continue or had other commitments which prevented them from continuing formal education may recoup their chances later. Fifthly, people may integrate learning from a wide variety of places with that gained within higher educational establishments. Finally, for those who have reached retirement, but who wish to remain educationally active, they may do so. The access argument itself, however, is not simple.

A number of pressures operate to encourage institutions to increase access to higher education. First, there is the social pressure that comes from looking at the demographic picture of those within higher education institutions and finding that it is drawn from too small a social class pool. There is a social justice argument to extend access to all those who could benefit from formal learning. Secondly, there is a subject pressure. Certain subjects, namely Science and Information Technology, have not, for some time, been recruiting at a sufficient rate to fill the places needed by industry and commerce. Third, the UK is rapidly falling behind other Western European states and industrial countries in the percentage of the population who enter tertiary education. The UK is likely to lose its competitive edge if a larger percentage of its adult populace is not educated to a higher level. Social, educational, political and economic reasons are forcing the doors of higher education open.

It is not surprising that those institutions, like the Open University and schools and centres for continuing education, who have always operated open-door policies, question the basis of the changes in access policies currently demonstrated by many major institutions. Are polytechnics and universities opening their doors to more people and altering their teaching patterns because they have altered their philosophies too, or are they merely looking to create new markets? Are flexible learning schemes being adopted because institutions put students first or because it will enable them to expand and maintain economic viability? Do institutions really wish to accredit work-based learning because they wish to accredit learning wherever it occurs or because there is a political will to erode the distinction between education and training?

How institutions are responding to the pressures to open their doors to more students varies. For those Vice Chancellors who believe in the social justice argument of access, often the mission statements of the institution contain a commitment to access that is easily identified. Others, who are responding to change in a more practical manner, look to administrative arrangements that will enable their institutions to weather the gale-force winds with a good chance of success. Most recognize that the form of education they currently have is insufficiently flexible to take the increase in student numbers that is predicted. Many recognize that their admissions procedures are unsuited to applicants with non-standard qualifications. Others are aware that the timetable currently in operation may be unsuitable for mature students. All are concerned that the quality of their provision and the prestige upon which institutions rest their laurels must be maintained. Currently, there seem to be few answers as to how universities will meet the projected increase in student numbers if there is not to be a matching increase in funds to the universities. Whether the move towards more flexible offerings which has gained momentum over the last 20 years contains answers to the practical issues as well as sustaining the broader principles behind access is yet to be established.

The interim results of the UCACE study into 'Credit Accumulation and Transfer in the British Universities' indicate that at the end of 1991, 29 universities claim to have developed, or are in the process of developing, modular systems (Table 11.4). Respondents to the question of modularization answered with varying views of modularity in mind. Universities such as Nottingham, Sheffield and Leeds strongly adhere to the principle of CAT. In the case of Nottingham, the early stages of opening the university doors focused upon developing a network of further and higher education establishments that formed an access consortium. From this initial position, the university embraced a principle of flexible provision which grew and blossomed from the accessible roots that it had cultivated. Similar cases are made by Sheffield and Leeds. Universities such as London and the Open University, however, rightly lay claim to having, for many years, modular

Table 11.4 Modularizing universities*†
Answer 'yes' to Q1: *Has your university:*

[a] established a modular scheme? (n = 22)	[b] begun to modularize? (n = 9)	[c] agreed in principle to modularize? (n = 9)	[d] discussed modularizing at senate? (n = 9)	[e] none of these? (n = 5)
Stirling (1965)				
Aberdeen				
UCL				
SSEES (1991)				
RHNB				
QMW				
LSE				
King's				
Imperial				
Birkbeck				
Senate H				
Sussex (1992)				
Surrey (Sc 1991)				
Reading			Durham	
(Ag+Sc 1990–91)	Bradford	Birmingham	Lancaster	
OU (1971)	UEA	Bristol	Oxford	
Newcastle	Leeds (1993)	Kent	(Gen. B. Fac.)	
Loughborough	Leicester	Manchester	Salford	
Liverpool	Southampton	Nottingham (1992)	UMIST	Aston
Hull	Warwick	Sheffield (1994)	Dundee	City (PG)
Exeter (1991)	Bangor (Sc 1991)	Goldsmiths'	Glasgow	Essex
Cranfield	QUB (1992–95)	Heriot-Watt	Cardiff	York
Brunel	Ulster (1992)	Swansea	Lampeter	Edinburgh

* Target date for the university to modularize
† Key: Ag = Faculty of Agriculture; Sc = Faculty of Science; Gen. B. Fac. = General Board of Faculties; PG = postgraduate study

systems. Their unit structures have facilitated credit transfer (in the former) and credit accumulation and transfer (in the latter). Other institutions, for example, Liverpool, are expanding a unit system promoted within their Science subjects for many years to the rest of the system. Shortly they will introduce an academic calendar based upon semesters (12 learning weeks housed within a larger shell which includes assessment time) and later plan to express their curriculum in terms of CNAA CAT points and levels.

The self-labelling by institutions of either having or moving towards modular systems when, in reality, a diverse set of institutional arrangements are exhibited by them, points to the confusion and interchangeability of terms that is currently occurring in UK higher education. It also points to the comparability of certain structural arrangements and certain philosophical positions.

As noted in the introduction, modular and unit structures facilitate a number of flexible arrangements, but do not embrace all of the principles of CAT. CAT is based upon accessibility to, and recognition of, learning that can be acquired in many places. It promotes boundary crossing. It challenges the idea that learning only occurs within institutions set up solely for educational purposes. It suggests that learning can occur throughout people's lives, not only when they are aged between 18 and 21 years.

Unit and modular structures, in that they divide learning into smaller size pieces, set the structural conditions for people to ask whether pieces of learning cannot be, or have not been, learnt outside universities. They enable people to ask whether a piece of learning could not be gained from another course, another faculty, another educational institution, a non-educational institution, or outside an institution. Flexible structural arrangements enable people to start asking a series of questions that may lead them to espouse CAT principles. Flexible structures are not solely useful stepping stones to holding CAT doctrines. In that CAT principles could best be practised in systems that permit the greatest flexibility, it can be argued that unit and modular systems, where they provide fixed points of entry and exit, permit students to accumulate their awards in ways that best suit their particular circumstances. Where unit size is standardized, students can move from one pathway to another, should they find their learning best suits a certain route. Where units are calibrated to a national norm, transfer of learning, from one department to another, from a nearby polytechnic to a neighbouring university, from the workplace to the educational institution, can be facilitated. Unit and modular systems, therefore, best facilitate the CAT approach although, in themselves, they do not necessarily embrace it.

How institutions are adopting more flexible provision depends greatly upon their size, history, motivation and policy. In Table 11.4, those universities which have a single target date set next to their titles are restructuring their total provision simultaneously. The arguments for this 'big bang' approach are several. For those who espouse CAT principles, their view is that the enormous upheaval that rearranging the administrative and academic framework entails is preferable to the chaos that would ensue should they try to run two disparate systems. The argument made by the Director of the Integrated Credit Scheme (ICS) at Liverpool Polytechnic would support this stance. When introducing the scheme in 1990, a new registry was set up which, in organizational terms, complemented the flexible principles that are enshrined in the ICS. There are some universities, however, which, for various reasons, have to adopt a rolling flexible programme. For these, there are limited horizons that students registered in the interim period can hold and considerable trials for administrative staff who must cope with staff and students operating quite different systems. For those universities which are conducting a pilot exercise by asking one department or faculty to change the mode of delivery and form of learning, there may be considerable risk avoidance for the majority of the institution, but great stress for the experimental group who have to work against the predominant philosophy.

The combination of related terms and concepts is not necessarily the same in those institutions furthest along the flexible route. Liverpool University has found it best to talk about units, subsequently about standardizing unit size, then about introducing the idea of semesters and finally about considering CAT schemes. Whether the term 'modules' is ever used is, as yet, not known. Liverpool's methods have been most successful in bringing into their institutional scheme the School of Dentistry and Faculties of Medicine and Veterinary Science because it has gradually reformed its structure by employing past terminology and extending an existing structure. Often, those disciplines whose degrees extend beyond three years and which are divided into pre-clinical and clinical years find it difficult to adjust to a system that was initially modelled upon a three-year degree. The commitment of its new Vice Chancellor to access encouraged the University of Nottingham first to develop a philosophy of access and then to bolster this philosophy by practice, through forming a 22 access consortium with other educational institutions in the surrounding community, and subsequently moving to semesters and CAT. Sussex University found that what they thought was an avant-garde 'green field campus' approach of the 1960s could not accommodate, in the 1980s, the demands of students in the American Studies programme to intermit. A study of their regulations led a senate working party to a more flexible programme provision at an early stage. Only latterly has the University decided to look again at semester patterns, which it initially shelved, at a time when other institutions are also considering such moves.

The manner in which universities move along the flexible path influences not only the degree of institutional disruption experienced, but also the type of learning that students experience.

CAT schemes and student-focused learning

Unit, modular and CAT systems benefit students by shifting the focus of learning away from the lecturer and onto the learner. The obvious advantage of such moves for the students is that their needs are considered paramount in the learning exercise. Several issues need to be considered, however, regarding whether the ideal philosophy and practice of CATS can be attained and what pitfalls need to be avoided.

In order that students may wisely select or re-select specified pathways or build customized programmes of study, they must have access to well-designed, accessible information systems. Institutional guidance and counselling services must be available to them so that, armed with the information gathered from a retrieval system, students can discuss the advisability of continuing or changing a chosen route, altering the pace of learning or studying units offered in a variety of locations or by distance-learning methods.

To a certain extent, the manner in which units are timetabled determines the spectrum of study programmes students may build or select. Liverpool Polytechnic offers units from 9 a.m. to 9 p.m. Several universities are discussing such a venture, but many wish to keep a '9 to 5' schedule for full-time students and an 'unsocial hours' schedule for part-time students. Such a distinction does not fit the CAT approach, which permits movement between full- and part-time study and advocates no distinction between students registered on either mode.

From interviews with registrars at universities developing flexible systems, many institutions are altering their provision by designing timetables which give priority to the availability of core and optional units required within the institutions' named pathways and subsequently assigning remaining units to vacant timetable slots. Giving priority to pathway units inevitably restricts the number of new combinations that students can form from available units or the complement of units they may choose to build customized programmes. It must be remembered, however, that CAT does not imply that students have a right to study whatever they want when they want. In any institutional provision, what is offered and when it is offered will always be limited by staff expertise, numbers of students wishing to study a unit (and whether priority is given to those for whom a unit is a core element in a selected pathway), room availability, and other practical considerations. A fear has been expressed by some staff that, should students suffer further reductions in their financial support, some may select units that are offered at times which do not coincide with those when they can boost their income with additional paid work. The academic coherence of study programmes will not necessarily coincide with choices primarily guided by fiscal necessity.

The possibility of learning from more than one location and in institution-based and distance form extends the range of unit choice offered to students. Already the Open University has agreed some co-operative arrangements with individual universities. The Department of History at Warwick University receives OU students for one-year full-time study as part of their degree programme. Recently, the OU has expressed great interest in extending its co-operative ventures with other institutions which are prepared to teach or award students who have a combination of credits gained from more than one source.

Moves out of and into pathways or forming new paths from a combination of credits gained from more than one source require students to have a good knowledge of their performance on the learning they have so far gained. Such information is available if student transcript or record of achievement systems are in place, but difficult if such information is hidden in the archives of a number of departments.

In order that students may take advantage of the flexibility of CAT systems, a funding system that allows institutions to enrol students on a full-time, variable part-time and mixed mode basis, and among a number of institutions needs to be designed. From the institutional perspective, universities need to be able to estimate their projected student numbers in full-time and part-time mode and in the various programme areas currently used for funding so that a coherent programme can be offered and best use made of staff and plant resources.

The student perspective

From the student perspective, the range of flexible systems discussed here offer a number of advantages. Students can alter their academic direction once enrolled on a course, alter the pace of learning, combine learning from different locations – educational or other – and include portfolios of learning gained prior to registering at an institution. Such advantages sound superlative to students whose careers have not followed the standard route. Adjusting a system so that it offers opportunities to other than a small exclusive group is part of a sound social philosophical practice. To this non-standard cohort, however, there are disadvantages to flexible study. For students who change path or alter their pace of learning, they may be faced with repeatedly trying to integrate with a new cohort of peers who already have established their friendship bonds. For those combining learning from several institutions, they may be faced with different institutional practices; for those forming portfolios, they may come across staff who are unfamiliar with assessing such work; for those with non-standard entrance qualifications, they may find that admissions officers neither have the time nor the expertise to process their submission.

It may appear that the changes discussed in this chapter only apply to non-traditional students, since it may be assumed that traditional students are well served by the existing system. It could be argued otherwise. At the 1991 degree ceremony for the Faculty of Humanities at the University of Kent, over 50 per cent of the students graduated with customized degrees. This is possible through the unitary-based part one of the degree which offers students a broad selection of subject combinations. If, under a current, partially unitary-based system, with half of the students able to choose their own tailor-made routes, it is possible that a much larger number would do so if the system were so designed. One can ask whether such options are good. Do students form packages of units which are academically suitable? Does the academic viability of each individual selection take many hours to be approved, examined and awarded? Do these selections meet employers' needs?

Information received from existing flexible systems indicates that few students choose non-approvable packages of learning. What most commonly occurs is that they select variants on existing pathways to meet the requirements of particular career goals. This developmental aspect of existing provision is one which, it can be argued, is an advantage to staff and students. A recent degree in Environmental Policy and Management at the

City of London Polytechnic (validated 1990–91) was developed in response to a demand by students to look at the legislative, political and social aspects of the environment. Throughout the five co-operating departments, members of staff greeted the development with enthusiasm. Particularly in Level 3 (equivalent to year three) those whose research complemented the core units were able to offer option units which employed some of the material they had collected in their investigations. Further developments in this area are now under discussion for postgraduate awards.

Developments over the past 20 years indicate that, from students' viewpoints, the doors to learning have opened further and further. At the Open University, students first experienced the opportunity to enter tertiary education without formal prerequisite knowledge and paced learning to their personal requirements. Continuing education departments offered part-time degrees in the evening and at weekends before stepping into the modular field and now the CAT one. London University developed a federal unit system which embraced all the member-colleges and facilitated internal credit transfer. Recently, modular structures, as developed in the polytechnics, have offered the opportunity of putting together customized study packages. CAT now offers students various entry and exit points which permit them to attain the level of learning they require at a pace that suits them and not be defined as failures if they do not conform to an imposed institutional norm. The possibilities appear boundless. However, unless students receive the correct information at the correct time and in an accessible form so that they may make wise choices, it is unlikely that all these developments will blossom. If CAT is treated as a bureaucratic device instead of a living subject, it is in danger of not responding to developments and becoming petrified in its developmental form. If student funding does not mesh with the flexible offerings that universities are developing, then students are unlikely to take advantage of the new possibilities on offer. Should universities be unable to fund new information retrieval systems, transcripting services and guidance counsellors, the goal of flexibility is unlikely to flourish. For the CAT to be realized in practice, a great deal of hard work, good will and appropriate financial support has to be forthcoming.

Notes

1. APL and APEL are both aspects of CAT. APL stands for the accreditation of prior learning and APEL refers to the accreditation of prior experiential learning. See Chapter 9.
2. The study is funded by the Universities Funding Council through the Universities Council for Adult and Continuing Education and is administered at the University of Kent at Canterbury.
3. The SCOTCAT scheme differs from the CNAA CAT scheme in that it is designed for the four-year Scottish Honours degree. Students can exit after three years of full-time study with a general degree. In the third year of work, students are

required to gain 60 Level 2 credits and 60 Level 3. For further information see CNAA Committee for Scotland *Guide to Transfer of Credit between the SCOTCAT and CAT Schemes (Paper CTS/91/40)*.

References

CNAA (1989) *Credit Accumulation and Transfer Scheme: A guide for students registered centrally with the scheme.*

CNAA (1990a) *The Modular Option.* Information Services Discussion Paper 5. December.

CNAA (1990b) Mimeo ref: *(DRP/DP/1722).*

CNAA (1991a) *Higher Education News*, 13, 12–13. Spring, 1991.

CNAA (1991b) *Fact Sheet*, 2.

Reed, J. (1991) 'New module army'. *Oxford Magazine*, Michaelmas Term, No. 76.

Squires, G. (1986) *Modularisation.* CONTACT Paper No. 1. Manchester.

Theodossin, E. (1986) *The Modular Market.* Bristol, The Further Education Staff College, pp. 45–56.

12

Creating Capability for Change in Higher Education: The RSA Initiative*

Susan Weil

Introduction

This chapter focuses on the Higher Education for Capability initiative, launched by the RSA[1] ten years after the publication of the *Higher Education for Capability* manifesto. This was at the same time as the Enterprise in Higher Education initiative (Chapter 13). These programmes have been among the first attempts at a national level to stimulate major reforms in the curriculum and pedagogy of higher education. Each has sought to draw attention to teaching and learning processes and practices that are conducive to the development of broad-based transferable skills and qualities, and the capacity to know how to continue learning throughout life.

The broad terms, 'capability' and 'enterprise' were used by the two campaigns to underline the importance of these learning outcomes in higher education. Each of the two programmes has sought to stimulate debate and developments that re-interpret the purpose of higher-education courses in ways that go beyond specific knowledge or professional concerns. Each has also drawn attention to the need for significant changes within institutions and the system as a whole to underpin this re-definition of purpose (see also Wright, 1990). These initiatives provide valuable case-study material about national interventions – by a government agency and by an independent body – into what might be termed as the 'sacred domain of the don' (see also Price, 1987). Moreover, these have occurred at a unique time in UK higher-education history, when government and funding forces combined with other kinds of changes – economic, technological, demographic, social, political – to create fertile ground for innovation and change within institutions at all levels.

---

* The views expressed in this chapter are made in a personal capacity and should not be read to represent an official position of either the RSA or the Higher Education for Capability initiative.

In this chapter, I shall describe key features of the general RSA Education for Capability campaign (as initiated in 1979), and of the shift of emphasis brought into play in 1989. At this latter time, three new initiatives were launched, targeted at schools, further education and higher education (HE). It was at this point that primary emphasis was placed on 'learner responsibility and accountability, individually and in association with others' as the basis for developing the capacity of students to deal more effectively with challenges presented by changes within society. After outlining the HE strategy, I shall offer examples of developments stimulated at the staff–student interface and across the HE curriculum. These raise issues about the broad notion with which this book is concerned: 'learning to effect'.

Four interrelated sets of educational ideas will then be related to the notion of capability, as embodied by the campaign. I shall conclude by focusing on institutions that are trying to create the capability to learn, change and challenge the 'world as given', not merely with regard to students but also staff and institutions. Throughout, I shall be identifying ways in which the capability initiative has been harnessed to broad social and educational purposes, particularly within the context of the current shift from an élite to a mass system of higher education. Its capacity to transcend the more instrumental and utilitarian agenda with which it has sometimes been associated will therefore be demonstrated (Thompson, 1984; Barnett, 1986; Handy, 1986a,b; Barnett, 1990).

The RSA Education for Capability campaign, 1979–89

The RSA campaign was launched in 1979 with *The Times* publication of a 'manifesto', signed by 250 well-known figures in industry, commerce and public life.[2] This called attention to the disproportionate emphasis placed by the education system on 'comprehension and cultivation', even for those, 'who pursue a scholarly path'. The need for greater emphasis on preparation for life in the outside world was asserted (RSA, 1980).

More specifically, the following principles were set out as central to any programme designed for education for capability, whatever its level:

1. The demonstrated competence is increased, particularly through active methods of learning which develop the existing interests, skills and experience of the learners.
2. The capacity to cope is developed by encouraging learners to find solutions to problems that they have personally identified in contexts relevant to their lives.
3. The creative abilities of learners are drawn upon and expanded through doing, making and organizing.
4. Learners are encouraged to get on with other people and to initiate and engage in co-operative activity.

5. Learners are involved according to their maturity, in negotiating with their teachers what it is they need to learn.
6. Programmes are accessible to a wide range of learners.
7. Methods of assessing and giving recognition to successful performance are appropriate to the nature of the activity undertaken.
8. The aims and objectives of programmes are understood.
9. There is coherent programme design with effective execution.

A national recognition scheme was established, whereby examples of ways in which teachers integrated the development of these capacities into their curriculum and pedagogy could be brought to wider attention. During the first 10 years of the campaign, interest and activity were generated largely in schools. However, a few individuals working to establish these principles within HE became involved and in fact won the RSA recognition award. One of these was John Stephenson, Head of the School for Independent Study at the then NorthEast London Polytechnic. He was later to direct the HE initiative, in association with the present author.

Three new initiatives, 1988–91

There was a limit to what the original campaign could achieve with one Fellow and a committee. However, government initiatives were beginning to stimulate new approaches to the curriculum and teaching and learning within schools and further education (FE).[3] A new emphasis was being placed on the quality of the process and outcomes of student learning. In particular, there was greater importance being given to independent learning, and its relationship to the development of specialist knowledge and effective performance in life and at work. From an RSA perspective, these initiatives could be seen to be responsive to the concerns of the original signatories to the manifesto.

At the same time, these developments could be dismissed as politically motivated, instrumentally driven and as an attack on liberal educational values. Those who had long been associated with the RSA campaign prided themselves on using cross-sector debate and case studies of capability practice to counteract what might be called 'either–or-nery' thinking in and about education. The Recognition Scheme, for instance, had tried to demonstrate through example how traditional dichotomies in educational debate need not be conceived as such. These would include, for example, education and training, liberalism and vocationalism, subject-centeredness and student-centeredness, intellectual and social development, and theory and practice. (Examples of capability-led curricular change that illustrate the breaking down of such dichotomies are provided below.)

The campaign emphasized the value of such tensions being resolved through a creative dialectic, rather than through exclusion of one emphasis in favour of the other, often on grounds of status and quality. In other words, the concern was to evolve new meanings of quality in the curriculum that accommodated the 'both–and' rather than the 'either–or' nature of such debates. This, however, was not always understood or perceived to be the case by the campaign's critics (Thompson, 1984).

The time was, therefore, considered ripe to re-establish the RSA as the honest broker in such matters. Throughout the 1980s, the need for a 'neutral forum' for educational debate was becoming more sharply defined. In 1988, the RSA launched three new educational initiatives. Each was targeted at a specific sector of education, and had its own sponsorship, directorate and steering committee. The original Education for Capability steering group was maintained as an overarching body. The details of the strategy adopted for HE will be described below. First, however, it is important to identify the shift in emphasis in the capability philosophy that characterized this new stage.

The new stage: a stronger emphasis on self- and group-managed learning

The rationale and practice of the School for Independent Study (SIS) at North East London Polytechnic had long been an influence on the capability campaign through Tyrell Burgess, Sir Toby Weaver, and other original signatories who had been associated with the SIS establishment in 1974. John Stephenson's decision to leave his post as Head of School to direct the RSA's higher-education initiative led to a strengthening of that influence.

The principles of the original campaign (as set out above) continued to be associated with the capability approach. However, self-managed and group-managed learning was made the fulcrum principle of this new stage. It was argued that comprehension, cultivation, creativity, and abilities to co-operate, to cope and to continue learning in a rapidly changing world were more effectively developed if students were made more responsible and accountable for their learning, individually and in association with others.

In the *Higher Education for Capability* launch document, the following form of wording was adopted:

If students are given opportunities to be more responsible for their own learning, individually and with others, and to explore the relevance of their studies to themselves and the society in which they live and work, they will develop their abilities to:

- acquire and apply knowledge and skills
- communicate ideas and information
- listen to and collaborate with others in mutually planned activities
- set achievable and relevant goals
- assess the effectiveness of their actions
- be critical of, and be creative in, their thinking and actions
- see both success and failure as opportunities for learning
- take account of their feelings and intuition

– show respect and concern for others
– reflect on their values.

The campaign believes that students who have experienced capability programmes can achieve excellence in their specialist studies whilst developing their potential for making effective and humane contributions in a diverse and changing society.

The Higher-Education Strategy

In higher education, particularly, the aim was to push the horizons of educational debate beyond the overt political arena. This was especially important, given the simultaneous launch of the Enterprise in Higher Education initiative. The strategy adopted can be described as a 'top-down, bottom-up, sandwich' approach. On the one hand, there was a need to focus attention on the purposes of education, and on the value and validity of capability approaches, especially in the push for expansion and diversification of the system (cf. Baker, 1989). Equally, attention was to be drawn – at all levels of the system – to the challenges that capability principles and practices posed for heads of institutions, employers, professional and validating bodies, and funding councils, as well as course designers, teachers and students (Stephenson and Weil, 1992a,b).

At the same time, there was a concern to seek out existing practices that gave meaning and substance to the debate and made the reality of these challenges all the more explicit and took capability thinking and practice forward. The activities of the campaign took many forms. Initial 'consciousness-raising' seminars were held at the RSA, attended by most Directors and Vice-Chancellors, as well as leaders from industry. Heads of institutions were also urged to invite the RSA directors to meet with groups of their senior managers and academic staff. These provided the opportunity for the RSA Directors to learn more about existing capability-related curriculum innovations. These visits also helped to stimulate greater strategic awareness of wider questions about higher education, and to take debate beyond the focus of particular disciplines and government action. (Over 70 institutions were visited during the first 18 months of the programme.)

In addition, regional and national conferences were held, always with transbinary institutional partners.[4] A regular newsletter was established, each one relating to a particular challenge (such as to employers) or theme (such as quality). A software program began to be developed as the basis for a RSA database that would create new possibilities for cross-institutional access (via JANET) to capability resources, people and examples. Specialist network groups were established as examples of capability in practice were sought from each six specialist fields. These included:

Art and Design (Stephenson and Bromley, 1992)
Engineering/Technology (Weil and Bridges, 1992)

Teacher Education (Weil and Bridges, 1992)
Humanities and Social Sciences (Weil and Melling, 1992)
Maths and Sciences (Emanuel and Weil, 1992)
Business and Management Education (Weil and Frame, 1992)

Over 400 examples of developments offering different interpretations of capability principles and practices were received from across these subject areas and the sector.

In addition, special inquiry meetings were set up, to address particularly the challenges of educating for capability in relation to the following:

Employers
Professional bodies
The management of change
Validation and assessment

Meanwhile, provision was made for the continuation of the project beyond the initial three-year contract period, by the RSA in association with Leeds University and Leeds Polytechnic, where the activities of the next stage were to be organized.

By the end of this initial stage, the database was ready for trials, and had received funding from the CNAA. The final publication of the project, *Quality in Learning* was virtually complete (Stephenson and Weil, 1992a).

Examples of capability in practice

Obviously, the influence of the RSA campaign on curricular and institutional reform cannot always be easily be disassociated from that of the Enterprise in Higher Education initiative. However, examples received by the campaign were drawn from many institutions that had no enterprise funding. Moreover, the notion of learner responsibility and accountability, individually and in association with others, became the discriminating factor in the selection of examples used to raise wider issues. For instance, an example of a lecturer who 'taught communication skills' or who gave students projects and problems on which to work would not have been considered to represent a capability approach.

The examples below illustrate developments that have been identified through the campaign.[5] They also signal some of the wider questions raised by a shift in emphasis within higher education towards greater student responsibility and accountability, individually and with others.

The humanities
Within the humanities, value has long been placed on the development of a student's capability for analytic thought and the critical interpretation of literature. The essay, the seminar, the examination paper have tended to be accepted as vehicles for and evidence of such capability. However, new intellectual currents such as Feminism and post-modernism give rise to new

forms of questioning about educational processes and outcomes. Diminishing resources, expanding student numbers with large proportions of non-traditional mature students, and new political pressures to justify the validity of study in these areas (e.g. CIHE, 1988, 1990) combine with disciplinary developments to generate the possibility of new educational developments.

In the particular conditions of the 1990s, the capability campaign has provided a respectable terrain within which to consider the implications of these multiple forces for student capability: what does it mean, and how might it be developed and assessed and for what purposes? For example, the notion of the autonomous learner accords with values deeply within the humanities, but it can be argued that teaching methods and the stances of teachers have not always been attuned to its expression and development to full potential within programmes (see also Weil and Melling, 1992).

A development undertaken by one School of Humanities, in response to the RSA initiative, deliberately set out to examine these issues critically. In doing so, the staff questioned the validity of the vocational–liberal divide for study in the humanities. Students on this particular BA(Hons) course have the opportunity of developing what might be called a 'multi-faceted' capability. They are encouraged to relate interests embedded in their prior experience (within and outside the course) to techniques and knowledges outside the humanities. Courses such as 'the concerto', 'colour, nature and culture', the 'politics of equal opportunities', 'forensic science: fact or fiction', 'science and sociability' and 'climactic change' are just some of the offerings through which students can explore wide-ranging interests and concerns, as defined by themselves rather than the 'logic' of a syllabus or the dictat of the expert.

The Science Faculty is central to this development, working in partnership with the Humanities Department. As such, new meanings of coherence are being constructed through deliberate 'boundary crossing'. New angles of vision are being stimulated for staff and students. For example, this development has challenged the Science Faculty to re-think its entry criteria and the role of knowledge in Science degrees. Moreover, course experience is not walled-off with different forms of assessment to suit different purposes. Instead, students are responsible for integrating their learning through projects. These projects are student-determined, either individually or in groups. They are intended to provide opportunities for students to make sense of these crosscurrents of learning that are made accessible through this major cross-faculty initiative. Furthermore, non-traditional and creative forms of production are actively encouraged. Evidence of critical and analytical thought, as well as of student initiative can be provided through short pieces of fiction to desk-top publishing, exhibitions, photographic essays as well as the more traditional essay.

This capability-inspired development illustrates the ways in which new terrains – that are not 'either–or' but distinctive fusions of 'both–and' – can be defined. As the course tutor pointed out in his original RSA submission:

[This development] is not vocational training in the narrowly defined sense nor is it an uncritical response to the ideology of the enterprise culture. Rather, it seeks to link the academic acquisition of knowledge to its wider social purpose: that is, the production and reproduction of knowledge. The specialist objectives of the programme can be extended beyond the traditional confines of the degree and in ways which empower students to act within the wider culture.

Students and lecturers are thus actively grappling with definitions of knowledge that are appropriate to a humanities education. The experience of staff and students doing this alongside each other is deliberately intended to stimulate student autonomy, initiative and creativity. This example also illustrates how student centeredness and subject centeredness need not be placed in opposition. Intellectual skills and qualities continue to be developed, perhaps more rigorously than previously, through their exercise in unfamiliar and creative domains. Skills and qualities that are oriented to social interaction and action can also be as validly nurtured. As in this case, these need not be driven by technical or instrumental requirements, but rather on terms that are understandable within the academic community's own values and culture, as well as that of the students. The latter has proved particularly important to the situation of this urban polytechnic, given the significant numbers of students who have traditionally been under-represented in higher education, by virtue of their age, gender, ethnicity, race and social/educational backgrounds.

Engineering

In engineering, the notion of what is meant by a capable engineer has been the subject of considerable debate since *The Finniston Report* was published (HMSO, 1980). This has been intensified by needs for new kinds of generic skills within the profession itself, such as to be 'market conscious, commercially adept, environmentally sensitive and responsive to human needs' (Engineering Council, 1985). The pace of technological change makes it essential that engineers are capable of continuous learning and of managing change. They must maintain their specialist knowledge and skills while coping with new demands on the profession. This sometimes requires them to jettison deeply-rooted ways of understanding the world, and of relating to others. Few engineers function as autonomous professionals, instead being required to work in groups, often with other kinds of specialists with whom effective communication and co-operation are essential. The role of the engineer in the world is further influenced by changing social awareness, such as of ecological and environmental issues. Pressures to recruit and retain students are intensified by the overall shift to a mass higher learning system, against a backdrop of diminishing resources.

The ideas and principles associated with the Capability Campaign have been of considerable interest to those concerned with engineering education.

More content, longer courses, and programmes with a larger lecture content are inadequate to the scale and nature of the challenge faced by the profession.

Capability-related developments within engineering often challenge traditional attitudes and behaviours within the accrediting professional bodies. All the same, the RSA received evidence that some people involved in engineering education have been willing to risk loss of accreditation if coverage of required areas of the syllabus rather than the development of capability was the predominant concern of the professional institution. Indeed, initiatives are being undertaken that ensure the provision of learning opportunities whereby students are actively learning how to learn, are working with others, are tackling genuine engineering problems in a real social and economic context and are actively appraising their own and others' learning processes and outcomes.

A wide range of capability-related activity in engineering was drawn to our attention through the campaign. For example, work based projects that focus on 'real' engineering problems and make use of learning contracts have become more common. These can entail everything from students serving as consultants or resource people for an employer on challenges they are facing, to building a bridge and designing a highway. Interdisciplinary design projects are also an increasingly important component of engineering programmes.

In some engineering programmes, there is a growing emphasis on students negotiating with students, while remaining accountable to tutors and internal validating procedures for the process and outcomes of their decisions. For instance, there are examples of staff and students assuming the roles of client and consultant, or of negotiating projects within the framework of a 'ghost company'. In other words, in capability approaches such as these, the process of learning has become as important as *and fused with* the substantive academic task of learning content and scientific principles. It can be argued that an emphasis on process can in fact improve the quality of the latter. For example, learning how to learn and how to manage the planning and completion of complex tasks within realistic time frames, and understanding more about the real perspirations and passions of achieving such things with others become central to the development of specialized knowledge.

Teacher education

The pace of change in teacher education increases. Teachers are obliged to re-equip themselves with attitudes, behaviours and skills that enable them to manage the challenges of their profession, as are relevant to their work with students, with trainee teachers, with the wider system, and with the community. Pressures to be proactive are great and conflicting messages are considerable. For example,

> On the one hand, there is the trend towards criterion-based assessment
> and standardized testing of predetermined lists of competences and strict

guidelines that restrict professional autonomy and diversity in the interpretation of prescriptions and guidelines.

On the other, new emphases on appraisal, student-directed learning, relevance in the curriculum, and active learning can provide opportunities.

For many, a capability based approach – with its twinned emphasis on responsibility and accountability – offers a sound educational basis in its own right, as well as a viable response to the challenges of so much change.

(Weil and Bridges, 1992)

For example, the use of student profiling is becoming more common. This entails student and staff in ongoing reflection and documentation of learning aspirations, activity, processes and outcomes. Profiling – an ongoing record of learning aspirations, activity and achievement – provides a focal point for building actively on experience, within and outside formal programmes. At the same time, the outcomes of learning – intended and otherwise – are kept in view, and the student is challenged to provide evidence of how their understanding, attitudes, and competencies have been challenged and changed. Profiling provides a valuable vehicle for improving communication and partnerships, amongst the array of players now involved in the teacher's initial and continuing development: schools, higher-education institutions, tutors, supervisors and local education authorities.

Profiling itself therefore involves students taking responsibility for their learning and being accountable for it in specific ways with regard to certain criteria, processes and competences. It provides evidence of performance against agreed criteria. These may be predetermined, such as by the Council for the Accreditation of Teacher Education (CATE), by the values and aims of a particular programme, as well as by the interests, concerns and experiences of students. Profiling can also be combined with other capability approaches, such as the use of learning contracts. These can provide a framework within which students can become responsible for the coverage of requisite content as determined either by a course team or professional body. For example, developments brought to our attention often involve students working in groups to tackle essential dimensions of the syllabus on terms that have meaning for them, within the context of their own lives and their expectations and hopes for the course. Accountability is often, but not always, underpinned by assessment strategies that take account of individual and group learning processes and learning outcomes.

Further, profiling is challenging teachers to think in more complex terms about learning outcomes for which students might be made accountable. The following kind of statement is beginning to be used to clarify staff educational assumptions and values, as well as their expectations of student performance:

> students will demonstrate their capacity to make complex decisions in the area of home–school partnerships, and to take account of different cultural values in their work and relationships with parents.

The student would thus be expected to provide evidence to support this learning outcome, through the profiling process.

Experience has shown that such interpretations of responsibility and accountability, individually and with others, are most effective when they are central to course and final assessment requirements. Otherwise, students learn quickly that the emphasis on significant learning and development, as explored through the profiling and contract-based project approaches, becomes marginalized.

Capability: four interrelated domains of educational ideas

The notion of capability, and its emphasis on 'learner responsibility and accountability, individually and with others' can be interpreted as representing four interrelated domains of educational ideas.

1. *Capability as transcending the realm of the familiar:* Within the examples above, there is a considerable emphasis on the values and importance of HE preparing students for the 'unfamiliar'. Stephenson distinguishes between students becoming trained to become 'dependently capable' or 'independently capable'. On the one hand, they may be able to deal capably with familiar problems within familiar contexts. On the other, an independent capability enables them to tackle as well unfamiliar problems in unfamiliar contexts:

> the speed of technological, economic and social change means our jobs and circumstances change more frequently and less predictably than before. The explosion in the expansion of specialist knowledge (doubling every 8 years by one estimate) puts a premium on giving people confidence in their own ability to learn and shows how futile it is to try to sustain the formal transmission of knowledge model in higher education.
>
> (Stephenson, 1990)

The examples above illustrate how students are being challenged to cross traditional boundaries: for instance, between disciplines, between the institution and the outside world, between their life and work experience and their learning on progammes, between theory and practice (see also Weil and McGill, 1989).

2. *Capability as being responsible and accountable:* Here, the term is used to emphasize the processes and practices that enable students to be and become capable through their programmes. Profiling, student-centered interdisciplinary projects, and learning contracts, opportunities for active and interactive learning that build on prior experience offer some examples. Opportunities to 'be capable' are assumed to enhance the capability of the student.

The campaign's emphasis on 'responsibility' stresses the importance of students building programmes and programme components around their aspirations, needs and interests. It emphasizes the centrality of their decision-making in the educational process. These considerations are becoming more and more important, given the growing diversity of students on any one module or programme. The educational and social backgrounds, and consequently their different starting points for learning, are becoming ever more varied, and therefore the need for more flexible and student-centered approaches is growing.

The emphasis on 'accountability' underlines the importance of negotiation and validation, as well as critical reflection. That for which students take responsibility needs to be consistent with the intellectual and practical requirements of the intended reward, as well as values and aims associated with particular programmes and institutions. Such processes of negotiation and validation need not be instrumentally driven, with all learning outcomes predetermined. Instead, they need to be seen as iterative, since students continue to learn from their experience.

The actual experience of taking responsibility for continually reviewing and reflecting on one's learning processes, directions and outcomes, and being able to 'give an account' of oneself as a learner and of one's learning, should be a distinctive feature of a capability programme in higher education. Space and time for such activity needs to be built into programmes, such as through 'making sense modules' where the processes and outcomes of learning become the content on which to build further learning. The quality of challenge, support and dialogue offered to the student in relation to activity becomes critical (cf. Wildemeersch, 1989). It is through these arenas that a student's stance becomes open to the possibility of personal and social transformation (cf. Salmon, 1989).

3. *Capability as empowerment:* A person who is capable tends to be seen as having the power to do something, on the basis of certain qualities and skills. Research on quality in student learning emphasizes the importance of students deciding what and how they are to learn academic material (Marton *et al.*, 1984; Ramsden, 1988). Their active engagement with such decisions is strongly associated with what is called a 'deep approach' rather than a 'surface approach' (see Chapter 10) to learning. In the latter, the idea of learner responsibility figures very little.

The emphasis in the RSA literature is on the disempowering nature of certain kinds of learning experiences, and on the empowering nature of a capability approach. Words from the higher education initiative launch document (see above) such as, 'alone *and* with others', being able to 'relate their learning to their own development and the world in which they live', and on 'learner responsibility and accountability', emphasizing possibilities for individual and collective self-determination, convey the kinds of actions and interactions that are assumed to 'empower'. The critical question that must be asked is empowerment for what and for whom?

4. *Capability as performance:* To some extent, the answer of the campaign and those who have been influenced by it would lie in the nature of a person's

performance in relation to aims and objectives that have been jointly determined. Moreover, performance involves a multi-faceted capability. Capability as embodied in performance may, for example, on the one hand be narrowly defined. Examination performance could be seen to test analytic and creative powers as well as those of recall. On the other hand, capable performance in many professions can be seen to involve not only these intellectual capacities, but also intuition, creativity, social awareness, the memory, effective listening, teamwork with others, and abilities to make judgements on the basis of conflicting and complex (and limited) evidence and to take account of different value positions in one's decisions and actions.

Creating capability and change in higher education: the emerging leadership challenge

The obstacles that maintain capability-type approaches at the margins of the HE system are many and are increasingly well documented (Wright, 1990 and Chapter 13; Stephenson and Weil, 1992a,b). Responsibility and accountability for bringing about student-centered learning approaches – now part of the rhetoric of expansion – cannot rest with course designers, teachers and students alone. It rests equally with managers, professional and validating bodies, funding councils, employers and others.

Many obstacles lie within the structures and processes that uphold the prevailing culture, embodied in a host of assumptions, behaviours, and habits and traditions of attaching value. For example, if research selectivity exercises attribute low status and priority – as measured in funding terms – to applied research as compared to so called 'pure research', the hierarchy of theory and practice is subtly reinforced. If publication records are seen to be what counts in terms of promotions and institutional rewards, investment in the scholarship of teaching and learning that promotes the development of capability will remain a low priority. If funding is attached to quality assessments based solely on discipline and Honours degree-based criteria, the development of new forms of curricula will be curtailed. If employers' recruitment patterns continue to favour those who have not invested in the capability-related developments called for by organizations such as the Council for Industry and Higher Education (1988), students and staff will read between the lines and adjust their behaviour accordingly.

So how do we create institutions where learning to effect is central to the lived experience of the institution and all who come into contact with it? A growing body of experience suggests that there is value in seizing the initiative. It is more resource intensive to bolt a capability-driven approach to teaching and learning onto more traditional systems of course design and delivery than to create the space where the use of existing resources can be re-thought from totally different angles and the potential for and commitment to change can be built.

This shift of awareness in particular institutions has come about from a process that I call 'managing up' (Weil, 1992). People who have been at the forefront of capability developments and change within institutions have had to devise dynamic and innovative ways of creating strategic awareness and commitment to a learning orientation across the institution. The new wine does not fit into the old bottles. Therefore, it is essential that a culture is created where traditional ways of thinking, behaving and attaching value can be held constructively in question and opportunities to learn from the experience of others are maximized. Managing upwards – against the weight of traditional ways of thinking, behaving and attaching value within institutions and in the wider system – demands consciously-planned, long-term fundamental-change strategies. It also entails the creative and opportunistic seeing and seizing of opportunities for change. For example, course validation and review systems and procedures have been found in those institutions that were CNAA validated to eat up massive amounts of resources of staff time. They can also become little more than elaborate rituals whereby energy is focused on either spotting or covering up problems and on the production of detailed documentation that has little relevance to the actual experience of staff and students on that course.

Broader commitment to and experience of capability approaches, combined with the development of credit schemes, modularization, the accreditation of prior learning, franchising and other such innovations, against the backdrop of diminishing central resources, are throwing up the inter-relatedness of educational, organizational and management challenges. In such institutions, quality assurance systems are beginning to be re-thought and re-designed to stimulate fresh perspectives, new forms of dialogue, and the constructive exploration and development of new roles and responsibilities for all staff, students, and managers. Since time and money are at a premium, the challenge is to use the resources traditionally invested in quality assurance systems and procedures in ways that will prove more meaningful and relevant to cultural change within institutions.

The design of a total learning environment that challenges and supports staff and students, and continuously develops the capability of people and the institution to learn and change, needs to be the concern of all, and not merely those within specific subject areas. Institutions that want to make the notion of capability central to their identity will require quality systems, forums and processes that can stimulate and support debates about 'educational coherence', and 'educational gain' in relation to the institution's mission. These explorations need to be made part of the lifeblood of the institution and not merely the focus of one-off events or committee debate.

Those institutions that have embraced capability-related approaches to teaching and learning as part of their identity and purpose are discovering that vision statements are more important than mission statements. Moreover, more than senior management need to be involved in creating, communicating and winning commitment to a vision. Visions also need to be translated into what these might mean 'on Monday morning' so that they are understood in the context of particular disciplines, circumstances and departmental cultures, and in terms of the different attitudes, behaviours, responsibilities and roles required of staff and students.

Culturally appropriate approaches to performance review need to be devised that support capability-related institutional and professional development, while taking account of political and funding imperatives. For example, the emphasis must be on more than measuring progress, based on throughput measures and targets. Institutions have to 'educate' others about how performance review can also do justice to the complex processes and forces that influence the quality of 'educational gain' in higher education, and stimulate the creation of a learning culture. Systems of reward and recognition need to support the development of a 'capability culture'.

Finally, generating and winning commitment to new visions – such as what 'educational gain' is to mean within a particular institution – is seen to be a long-term process of learning and development. This must be iterative, and requires new spaces for debate across traditional disciplines. The traditional working party or academic committee or validation event may not be appropriate to such purposes. In other words, key features of a capability approach at course level need to be mirrored throughout institutions. The continual and dynamic negotiation of responsibility and accountability becomes central to how all staff relate to one another, not just in the corners of student programmes. Valuing and building on prior experience needs to become as important a consideration with staff as it is with students, so that they can take responsibility for their ongoing learning and development. So too are their needs for self-determination and autonomy. But at the same time, there are needs for greater accountability, such as for effective team working across traditional boundaries: academic and administrative, levels, subject and institutional.

My own work with institutions suggests that as the critical mass of confidence and risk taking spreads, and a sense of empowerment increases, the courage to 'manage up' into the political system becomes greater. Institutions that wish to remain at the forefront of shift from an élite to a mass system of higher education realize that if they wait for permission, little will happen. Instead, through their actions they are discovering that they can push the boundaries of thinking and practice, and create agendas that become more and more difficult to ignore, in light of the espoused aspirations and commitments of politicians.

The RSA capability initiative has perhaps done little more than to stimulate and give substance to an argument about how learning and quality might be enhanced. This argument was framed from the beginning in terms of systems and institutions, as well as in terms of students and teachers. This, I believe, has helped innovators to look beyond their own parapets, and to create new needs and opportunities for significant institutional and cultural change.

Dick Beckhard (Beckhard and Pritchard, 1992) speaks about the difference between incremental and fundamental change. The latter requires both learning and doing to be equally valued. It also requires: leadership at all levels of institutions and people managing up, not just down; the continual negotiation of responsibility and accountability; the creation, communication and understanding of the vision for the institution, and what this will mean in terms of the day to day lived experience of all who come into contact with it; processes that generate ownership and commitment by the professionals involved while allowing for creativity and autonomy; and their empowerment through the development of skills and confidence, and a sense of shared social purpose.

The sets of educational ideas set out in this chapter, and as elaborated through the examples, can be incorporated in programmes that are kept at the margins of programmes and institutions. They can be used instrumentally in support of a 'credentialled' society at the expense of a learning society. Alternatively, the experience, enthusiasm, and confidence that involvement in capability approaches can generate can provide the seedcorn for the more fundamental changes that will be required if the shift from an élite to a mass system is to be sustained and opportunities for learning to effect are to be created for students, for staff, for institutions, and the wider system.

Notes

1. The RSA was founded in 1754 as the Royal Society for the Encouragement of Arts, Manufactures and Commerce. The *RSA Journal* describes the organization as,

   independent of special interests . . . a seedcorn for new ideas and an agent for change since its foundation. Today the RSA offers a forum for people from all walks of life to address issues, shape new ideas and stimulate action.

2. See Burgess, T. (1986) for the full *Education for Capability* manifesto and list of signatories.
3. Examples include the establishment of the General Certificate of Secondary Education (GCSE), the Technical and Vocational Education Initiative (TVEI), the introduction of the new National Curriculum and the National Council for Vocational Qualifications (NCVQ).
4. Conferences were held with Manchester University, Manchester Polytechnic and UMIST; Wolverhampton Polytechnic in association with Birmingham Polytechnic and University of Warwick; University of Strathclyde and Paisley College; Leeds Polytechnic in association with Humberside Polytechnic, Bradford University and Huddersfield Polytechnic; University of Bath.
5. The examples of course developments described in this chapter are drawn from a wide range of evidence brought to the attention of the Campaign, through visits, conferences, specialist group meetings, and formal submissions in response to the 'Call for Examples'. A comprehensive account can be found in Stephenson and Weil (1992a), where full acknowledgement of contributors is also made.

References

Baker, K. (1989) 'Higher education – 25 years on'. Secretary of State's speech at Lancaster University, 5 January 1989. London, DES.

Barnett, R. (1985) 'Higher education: legitimation crisis'. *Studies in Higher Education*, 10, 241–56.

Barnett, C. (1986) 'The burden of the past: the organisational failure' in T. Burgess (ed.) *Education for Capability*. Windsor, NFER-Nelson.

Barnett, R. (1989) *Responsiveness and Fulfilment: the value of higher education in the modern world*. Abingdon, Higher Education Foundation.

Barnett, R. (1990) *The Idea of Higher Education*. Milton Keynes, SRHE and Open University Press.

Beckhard, R. and Pritchard, W. (1992) *Changing the Essence: the art of creating and leading fundamental change in organizations*. London, Jossey-Bass.

Boud, D. (ed.) (1988) *Developing Student Autonomy in Learning*, 2nd edn. London, Kogan Page.

Burgess, T. (1986) *Education for Capability*. Windsor, NFER-Nelson.

Candy, P. and Jaques, D. (1988) *Learning for Action: course development for capability in higher education*. Oxford, SCED Occasional Paper, No. 51.

CIHE (Council for Industry and Higher Education) (1988) *Towards a Partnership*. London, CIHE.

CIHE (Council for Industry and Higher Education) (1990) *Towards a Partnership: the humanities for the working world*. London, CIHE.

Emanuel, R. and Weil, S. (1992) 'Capability through science and mathematics' in J. Stephenson and S. Weil (eds) *Quality in Learning*. London, Kogan Page.

Engineering Council (1985) *Raising the Standard*. London, Engineering Council.

Handy, C. (1986a) 'The new industrial society' in T. Burgess (ed.) *Education for Capability*. Windsor, NFER-Nelson.

Handy, C. (1986b) 'Implications for education' in T. Burgess (ed.) *Education for Capability*. Windsor, NFER-Nelson.

HMSO (1980) *The Finniston Report*. Cmnd 7794. London, HMSO.

McGill, I. and Weil, S. (1989) 'Continuing the dialogue: new possibilities for experiential learning' in S. Weil and I. McGill, (eds) *Making Sense of Experiential Learning*. Milton Keynes, SRHE and Open University Press.

Marsham, D. (1988) 'Can subject studies and capability co-exist?' in P. Candy and D. Jaques (eds) *Learning for Action: course development for capability in higher education*. Oxford, SCED Occasional Paper, No. 51.

Marton, F., Hounsell, D. and Entwistle, N. (eds) (1984) *The Experience of Learning*. Edinburgh, Scottish Academic Press.

Price, C. (1987) 'Dons as lobbyists'. *Higher Education Quarterly*, 41 (3), 257–67.

Ramsden, P. (ed.) (1988) *Improving Learning: new perspectives*. London, Kogan Page.

Robbins, D. (1988) *The Rise of Independent Study*. Milton Keynes, SRHE and Open University Press.

Robbins, Lord (1963) *Higher Education: report of the Committee under the Chairmanship of Lord Robbins*. Cmnd 2145. London, HMSO.

RSA (1980) Original campaign literature. London, RSA.

Salmon, P. (1989) 'Personal stances in learning' in S. Weil and I. McGill (eds) *Making Sense of Experiential Learning*. Milton Keynes, SRHE and Open University Press.

Stephenson, J. (1990) 'The Student Experience of Independent Study: reaching the parts other programmes appear to miss'. Inaugural Professorial Lecture, Polytechnic of Northeast London, 6 February.

Stephenson, J. and Bromley, T. (1992) 'Capability through Art and Design' in J. Stephenson and S. Weil (eds) *Quality in Learning*. London, Kogan Page.

Stephenson, J. and Weil, S. (eds) (1992a) *Quality in Learning*. London, Kogan Page.

Stephenson, J. and Weil, S. (1992b) 'Obstacles and ways forward' in J. Stephenson and S. Weil (eds) *Quality in Learning*. London, Kogan Page.

Thompson, K. (1984) 'Education for capability: a critique'. *British Journal of Educational Studies*, 32(3), 203–12.

Weil, S. (1986) 'Non-traditional learners within traditional higher education institutions: discovery and disappointment'. *Studies in Higher Education*, 11(3), 219–35.

Weil, S. (1988) 'From a language of observation to a language of experience: studying the perspectives of diverse adults in higher education'. *Journal of Access Studies*, 3 (1), 17–43.

Weil, S. (1989a) *Influences of Lifelong Learning on Adults' Expectations and Experiences of Returning to Formal Learning Contexts*. PhD thesis, University of London.

Weil, S. (1989b) 'Access towards education or miseducation: adults imagine the future' in O. Fulton (ed.) *Access and Institutional Change*. Milton Keynes, SRHE/Open University Press.

Weil, S. (1992) *'Managing Up' in Higher Education: pig in the middle or eye of the storm*. London, Office for Public Management (Management development programme details).

Weil, S. and McGill, I. (1989) *Making Sense of Experiential Learning*. Milton Keynes, SRHE and Open University Press.

Weil, S. and Bridges, D. (1992) 'Capability through teacher education' in J. Stephenson and S. Weil (eds) *Quality in Learning*. London, Kogan Page.

Weil, S. and Frame, P. (1992) 'Capability through business and management' in J. Stephenson and S. Weil (eds) *Quality in Learning*. London, Kogan Page.

Weil, S. and Melling, D. (1992) 'Capability through humanities and social sciences' in J. Stephenson and S. Weil (eds) *Quality in Learning*. London, Kogan Page.

Weil, S., Lines, P. and Williams, J. (1992) 'Capability through engineering' in J. Stephenson and S. Weil (eds) *Quality in Learning*. London, Kogan Page.

Wildemeersch, D. (1989) 'The principal meaning of dialogue for the construction and transformation of reality' in S. Weil and I. McGill (eds) *Making Sense of Experiential Learning*. Milton Keynes, SRHE and Open University Press.

Wright, P. (1990) 'Strategic change in the higher education curriculum: the example of the Enterprise in Higher Education initiative' in C. Loder (ed.) *Quality Assurance and Accountability in Higher Education*. London, Kogan Page and Institute of Education.

13

Learning through Enterprise: The Enterprise in Higher Education Initiative*

Peter Wright

Introduction

This chapter considers the impact of the Enterprise in Higher Education (EHE) initiative on curricula and forms of learning. EHE is nationally the most important, if not the only, instance of planned curricular development in UK higher education.[1] EHE was initiated in December 1987, by the (then) Manpower Services Commission (MSC)[2] with the support of the Department of Education and Science and its Scottish and Welsh counterparts (Jones, 1988; Glover, 1990; Macnair, 1990). It had been born out of discussions early that year between the Secretaries of State for Education and Science, and for Employment, and the Chairs of the (then) Higher Education funding bodies (the National Advisory Body for Local Authority Higher Education (NAB) and the University Grants Committee (UGC)), heads of colleges, polytechnics and universities, and senior officials of the MSC.

The context and origins of EHE are important. They throw light on the form that the initiative took, on the ways that it was perceived within HE institutions and on its subsequent development. There can be no doubt, for example, that the impetus to create it was carried forward, at least in part, by a tide of opinion that had been growing for several years among higher educational policy-makers, viz. that in order both to expand and to respond to demands from the employment market, UK courses would have to be broader, more flexible and give deliberate prominence to what were coming to be called 'transferable and intellectual personal skills' (Bradshaw, 1985). That view began to crystallize in the 1984 joint strategy statement of the National Advisory Body and the University Grants Committee (NAB, 1984,

* The author's views are expressed in a personal capacity only and should not be taken to represent those of the Employment Department.

pp. 4–6), and was to be further elaborated, and linked more explicitly to employment, in NAB's May 1986 statement on 'Transferable Skills' (NAB, 1986) and, in the following spring, by the founding declaration of the Council for Industry and Higher Education (CIHE, 1987) and the newly expansionist tone of the 1987 White Paper on higher education (DES, 1987).

Equally, however, there can also be little doubt that, to some extent, the form that EHE was to take was influenced by, if not framed in terms of, what Raman Selden has described as the 'rhetoric of enterprise' (Selden, 1991, pp. 58–71): what he saw as a self-conscious attempt by Mrs Thatcher and her ministers to create an 'enterprise culture' that would begin to reverse the, supposed, decline of 'the industrial spirit' that had been lamented in Martin Weiner's widely influential book (Weiner, 1981).

As I shall argue in more detail later, the relative influence on the birth of EHE of what one might call the educational policy concerns and the 'rhetoric of enterprise', though interesting, is not a particularly important issue because it throws little, if any, light on the nature and subsequent development of the initiative. All governmental policies are developed and couched within some rhetorical framework or other. Their ultimate impact is likely to be determined primarily by the ways in which they relate to key structural forces of a social or economic nature and by the extent, and manner, to which particular interest groups use them to advance their own particular interests.

The final public shape of EHE was set out in the EHE *Guidelines for Applicants* of December 1987 (MSC, 1987). These stated that higher educational institutions (HEIs) were invited to submit individual enterprise plans that would specify how, over five years, they would provide for all their students to '. . . be able to develop competencies and aptitudes relevant to enterprise', which should be acquired, '. . . at least in part, through project-based work, designed to be undertaken in a real economic setting, . . . jointly assessed by employers and the higher education institutions' (MSC, 1987, para 5).

The maximum sum normally available to institutions from the MSC for a single EHE project was £1 million over five years, which would be conditional upon the institution raising significant support from employers in cash or kind. This had to be the equivalent at least of 25 per cent of the MSC's funds during the first two years and a 'substantial' proportion thereafter. In addition, the proposals would have to meet five other requirements: be closely integrated into the institution's existing educational provision; provide a plan for staff development to support the changes proposed; specify intended outcomes; be monitored and evaluated by the institution itself; and, finally, include a commitment to sustain the programme after MSC funding had come to an end. Submissions were invited by March 1988 for round one, then by April 1989 for round two, and, again, by April 1990 for rounds three and four.[3] In all, 135 applications for funding were received. Those who bid encompassed every polytechnic, the vast majority of universities and Scottish Central Institutions, and a significant proportion of colleges. By the end of the fourth round in 1991, this had resulted in a total of 56 EHE contracts involving 59 whole HEIs and eight part-institutions (some contracts being with consortia). These contracts will terminate progressively from October 1993 until November 1996.

Distinctive features of EHE

EHE possesses several distinctive features that justify it being regarded as a major programme of curricular development. First, it has been deliberately designed to stimulate and enable, rather than to be prescriptive, and, in that respect, among others, has drawn on the MSC's experience with another of its programmes, TVEI (Gleeson, 1987, pp. 4–11).[4] Within the specified criteria – which are themselves both general and legitimately susceptible to differing interpretations – HEIs have been encouraged to make a wide-ranging assessment of their work in order to determine their own definitions of enterprise and to make their own decisions on how best to realize them.

In the early stages of EHE bidding, some institutions were predisposed to see the initiative in narrowly vocational terms and to interpret 'enterprise' as simply a synonym for 'entrepreneurship', or as a not-too-veiled injunction to transform their courses into something little more than direct preparations for predetermined slots in the labour market. By a delicate turn of irony those most inclined to interpret EHE myopically found themselves sharing many common assumptions with some of its most impassioned opponents, such as Peter Groves, who denounced it as an attempt to subordinate:

> . . . *every* degree course, *all* students. Any subject: divinity, philosophy, astronomy, astrophysics, classics, psychiatry, the history of art . . . [to] . . . a national purpose narrowly conceived [which] cannot contemplate values and activities outside of the productive and the commercial.
> (Groves, 1989, p. 13 – italics as in the original)

Some commentators profess to detect a significant shift in the way that the MSC and its successor bodies have interpreted what they mean by 'enterprise' within EHE. Ainley and Corney, for example, write that:

> 'Enterprise' was at first defined in an entrepreneurial sense of business skills but this narrow approach soon broadened into ideas of encouraging work placement and project work in economic environments [and finally] settled upon an emphasis on personal transferable skills . . .
> (Ainley and Corney, 1990, p. 12)

It is hard to find documentary evidence for such claims. From its earliest public statements on EHE, the MSC fought shy of prescribing a definition of 'enterprise' (and was often criticized for so doing), preferring instead to illustrate the concept through what it regarded as existing good practice. In the original 1987 *Guidance*, for instance, having commended many existing 'individual efforts', it then mentioned four central initiatives that it regarded as advancing 'enterprise'. (These were PICKUP, Teaching Companies, the MSC's own Graduate Gateway Programme and the RSA's 'Education for Capability' project)[5] (MSC, 1987, para 1). Together, they embrace examples of each of the three elements that Ainley and Corney regard as successive stages.

The nearest approach to a definition of enterprise was a passage in the press release issued to mark the launching of EHE.

What do we mean by 'enterprise'? We mean:
● generating and taking ideas and putting them to work
● taking decisions and taking responsibility
● taking considered risks
● welcoming change and helping to shape it
● creating wealth

(DoE, 1987, 2)

Again, it is not easy to see why these should have been thought to constitute a 'narrow entrepreneurialism'. One is tempted to wonder whether the supposed 'reinterpretation' was one resulting from a widening of the imaginative horizons of some who read the *Guidance* rather than from the MSC/TA/ED abandoning its original vision.

EHE submissions cast in narrow terms tended to be unsuccessful not because of a shift in emphasis but because they were unrealistic. Some, for example, were inclined to make the untenable assumption that all graduates could, or should, aim at self-employment. Others assumed a very static and mechanistic relationship between higher education and the employment market. That is to say, they acted as if degree courses prepared their graduates for a predictable, narrow range of relatively unchanging jobs whose requirements were easily identifiable and uncontentious. By doing so, they ignored the considerable mass of evidence to the contrary including the findings of Roizen and Jepson and the HELM (Higher Education and the Labour Market) research project (Roizen and Jepson, 1985; Boys *et al.*, 1988; Brennan and McGeevor, 1988).

Such proposals also disregarded the importance that groups of employers such as the Council for Industry and Higher Education (CIHE) were increasingly coming to place on the need for their future employees to be prepared for lifelong learning, flexibility, and multiple change careers and to possess a wide range of personal capabilities. In the Council's inaugural declaration in spring of 1987, for example, it had stated that UK employers needed imaginative young people equipped with a broad general and liberal education in which maths, science and technology played a part as well as the humane values derived from the arts and humanities. That, it was argued, would enable graduates to be versatile and adaptable, and should equip them with a range of personal skills (CIHE, 1987, pp. 11–13).

As EHE has progressed, so entrepreneurialism has typically tended to be perceived as simply one beneficiary of a more generalized set of 'Enterprise' aims. Indeed, I would contend that the flexibility and non-prescriptive openness of the concept of the term 'enterprise' within EHE is, probably, its greatest strength. HEIs that wish to take part in the EHE programme find themselves obliged to ask searching questions about their purposes and how best to achieve them. They find themselves involved, willy-nilly, in the process of strategic curricular development, which I have argued elsewhere (Wright, 1990) has been all-but-unknown in higher education. They have, for example, to begin to make conscious and deliberate decisions about who are the relevant stakeholders and clientele for their institutions; what should be the appropriate outcomes for their graduates; how these should best be achieved and then assessed; and many other things besides. Such a process, I would argue, stands in striking contrast with the usual mechanisms of curricular change in HE, which have been aptly described as 'discipline-led incremental'[ism] (Boys *et al.*, 1988, p. 196). That is to say, with few exceptions (and those more often in new areas of study), degree courses have tended to take their clientele and entry requirements for granted, have left their intended outcomes relatively inexplicit, then have done little to evaluate which are the most effective means of facilitating learning and have concentrated heavily on time-honoured modes of assessment. When change has come, it has typically resulted from the growth of research, shifts in staff interests, the additional requirements of professional bodies or, sometimes, shifts in student demand. Seldom has it come from a root-and-branch attempt to review the purpose and nature of a course, still less one involving dialogue with a variety of stakeholders. This interpretation is supported, I believe, by the revealing fact that some HEIs have found the non-prescriptiveness of EHE a novel and, even sometimes, a disquieting experience[6] (as did schools with TVEI).

Another distinctive aspect of EHE has been the HEIs' planned use of collaboration with employers to improve the design, content and assessment of courses and to provide new occasions for enriching the experience of students. Such involvement was not simply designed to increase the direct vocational relevance of courses, although in the more obviously work-related fields it often did. It was also intended to involve employers more intimately in the world of higher education and academics in that of employment. The implicit assumption was that both could benefit from the experience of the other and that the greater insight into each other's worlds would make it easier for each to play to its strengths and gain more from collaboration. Thus, in seeking to involve employers – as well as increasingly the students themselves[7] – in defining the aims and criteria of higher education, EHE began to make it possible for these previously inconspicuous stakeholders to elaborate their own conceptions of HE alongside those of the producers – the academics.

In another way, too, EHE has contributed to the growth of a more open and externally-accessible debate on the proper aims, the nature of higher education, and the concepts of quality appropriate to them. It has done this by insisting on explicit objectives and specific outcomes. Each EHE proposal, for example, has to demonstrate the institution's own deliberate plan for the attainment of its chosen aims by means that it has – itself – consciously decided upon. When selected for funding, the institution has to translate these into a contract with the MSC/Training Agency/Employment Department which has to embody, on a year-by-year basis, the institution's chosen aims, and the specific targets, or indicators, by which it has decided to monitor their achievement.

The preparation and execution of such plans and contracts naturally tends to increase the visibility of the process of curricular development and change. It renders the implicit assumption of the academic professionals explicit, and thus open to challenge (by, for example, specifying exactly what the graduate of a course may be expected to do and know). It causes aspects of higher education that had seemed natural or predetermined (for instance, the familar mixture of lectures and seminars, or a dependence on assessment by three-hour unseen examinations) appear as issues for choice and action. The drafting of the contract, and its annual review, concentrates attention on the need for self-consciously considered decisions to be made. (What are we to undertake to do next year? And how?) It also makes possible greater insight into the taken-for-granted assumptions of the academic world and lays bare to scrutiny the efficacy of traditional patterns of teaching and course organization.[8] Although some of these characteristics were also encouraged by the course validation and review mechanisms of the Council for National Academic Awards, the crucial distinction is that the EHE contract focuses on *achieved performance* while the CNAA system tended to concentrate, instead, on *intentions* (Adelman and Alexander, 1982, p. 17).

These processes seem, in my view, to establish explicit chains of accountability in higher education, where they have previously been absent or tenuous: they encourage an HEI to be precise about how, and to what extent, it is accountable, and by what criteria, to its students, to employers, and to society more generally. They also promote accountability within the institution by linking the allocation of resources for teaching to the achievement of explicit and pre-defined elements of curricular change.

Finally, EHE is distinctive in that it sets out explicitly to assist institutions in bringing about changes in their structures and cultures that will be both thorough-going and permanent. It does this by requiring that enterprise programmes should be closely integrated into the fabric of courses – not 'bolted-on' – and should be sustained after the cessation of government funding. This is of central importance, as has been shown by the experience of many previous attempts at innovation. If movements for change are to be preserved from the dangers of atrophy and diversion, effective ways must be found to integrate and consolidate them before the disappearance of the stimuli that produced them.

Impact of EHE on the curricula and students' experience of learning

After three years' experience of EHE, it is now possible to draw some general, but tentative, picture of its consequences.[9] Any generalizations, however, need to be tempered by the recognition that HEIs vary greatly (as do, often, the faculties or departments within them) in their history, ethos, organization and market position, and that these factors colour strongly the ways in which the institutions, and their parts, are affected by EHE. One institution, or department, for example, may need several years of EHE-funded effort to introduce a new form of learning, such as the use of self-assessment by students, that is already common in some others even before the start of EHE.

The picture is further complicated by the fact that EHE has been established through a succession of rounds. Not only do HEIs find themselves at different points in a development cycle, but knowledge of the experience and lessons of the early rounds means that the latecomers may not need to traverse exactly the same series of stages as those who went before. It is my personal impression, for example, that HEIs in later rounds have, with the encouragement of TA/ED staff, been quicker to establish local evaluation than those in earlier rounds. It is also the case that there has been a tendency to move from contractual outcomes framed in terms of product targets (e.g. 'X courses will undergo Y by date B') to a succession of self-reflective processual stages (e.g. 'by date a group I will have consulted all courses and encouraged them to reflect on the learning methods that they employ, and will then involve groups K, L and M in deciding which X courses should implement their proposals by date B').

It may be helpful to group the impact of EHE on curricula and learning under five headings:

1. Institutional discourse and rhetoric.
2. Working practices and administration.
3. Changes in particular courses.
4. Legitimacy.
5. Resources.

1. Institutional discourse and rhetoric

At the first level there can be no doubt, as the National Foundation for Educational Research (NFER) found in a specially commissioned study, that EHE has '. . . been instrumental in raising issues concerning teaching, learning and assessment and in focusing debate more directly upon changes in practice'. (NFER, 1991, p. 99). This has, in turn, been associated with a shift from '. . . the traditional, transmissive mode of formal lectures, towards an emphasis on students' responsibility for their own learning'. (NFER, 1991,

p. 93) This has happened for two reasons. The first is that EHE has been the first occasion on which concerted attention and resources have been directed towards the issue of how best to encourage learning in HEIs. The second is that the collection of meanings evoked by the notion of 'enterprise' have tended to emphasize qualities such as activity, responsibility and participation, as opposed to more passive models of learning.

2. Administration and practice

So far, such improvements have generally been piecemeal; and there has been little sign that EHE has yet succeeded in generalizing a full-blown process of curricular development within higher education such as can be found in the best work within schools and FE. That is to say, a process that deliberately sets out to design a programme of learning (involving content, pedagogy and assessment), taking account of the capacities of the students and the resources available, to achieve, in the most effective way, a range of desired outcomes that respond to the identified needs of students and other stakeholders. (I have described this elsewhere as 'strategic curricular development'; see Wright, 1990, p. 63.) To do so would involve not only the growth of new attitudes to the nature of academic programmes but also the establishment of new mechanisms for designing and developing curricula. There is but little sign of this so far in most HEIs. In contrast, as the NFER comment, most academics are disposed to see debates over the curriculum '. . . in terms of course content rather than [as] strategies for delivering the curriculum' (NFER, 1991, p. 99).

It is interesting to compare this view with that of the CNAA/Leverhulme research study on higher education and the labour market (HELM) undertaken between 1984 and 1987. From it the conclusion was drawn that:

> Curriculum development is likely, therefore, to be discipline-led, incremental, strongly influenced by student demand and staff preference and to show no consistent relationship with employment objectives.
>
> (Boys *et al.*, 1988, pp. 196–7)

The impact of EHE, it seems, may have been to have made the process rather more public and self-conscious, rather less incremental and more closely related to employment, especially through the involvement of employers from the private, public and voluntary sectors. How far this will lead to a fundamental transformation may well depend on how far the movements set in train by EHE supplemented by the many other forces affecting the system: new mechanisms for quality assurance and funding, a growing consumerism on the part of students, and so on.

Although few examples can be found of curricular development in the thoroughgoing sense defined above, there are some. They generally seem to concern the creation of new courses, often in close collaboration with employers, and are mostly to be found in polytechnics and colleges where the CNAA-derived system of course development and validation may have been adapted to the design, from scratch, of programmes of study tailored to meet the defined needs of various external stakeholders. In one polytechnic for example, such a course in technical authorship has been designed from scratch under the aegis of EHE. Nonetheless, as EHE has progressed, institutions have become increasingly inclined in their daily practice to accord less emphasis to disciplinary content of courses and more to the cultivation of a wide range of non-subject-specific skills among their students. They have, for instance, tended to give greater prominence to a variety of competencies and qualities that their students may have acquired, and practised, outside the academy: in one college, for instance, History students have been rewarded for the skill with which they have handled the interpersonal aspects of working with elderly local residents in connection with work on Oral History.

3. Courses

Paradoxically, this may first become visible through additions ᵗ ⸍ curricula. Many EHE-funded institutions have laid stress on what have come to be called 'personal transferable skills' and have introduced into their courses elements designed to cultivate such qualities as an awareness of (and competence in) modern information technology, foreign languages, numeracy, an understanding of the commercial applications of their subject, or preparedness for work placement and skill in applying for jobs or undergoing interviews.

Sometimes this new emphasis may take the form of changes in the modes of learning employed in the teaching of established disciplinary topics. (In one EHE university, for example, team skills such as directing a discussion, drawing out diffident members and deciding upon the distribution of tasks have been developed among History students by the use of student-run seminars on conventional disciplinary topics without a member of staff being present.) At other times the development of such capabilities may be concentrated into special units or introductory courses for new students. Although there are few institutions where the assessment of such qualities has been fully integrated and make a significant impact on the level of final class of award there are numerous attempts to move in this direction, many involving the use of Records of Achievement[10] (or profiles) to supplement conventional forms of assessment.

At the level of particular courses there seem, as yet, to be relatively few examples of programmes in which all elements of the students' experience are systematically harnessed to achieving an agreed blend of skills, knowledge and understanding. It seems that three conditions are required for this to happen. First, among all staff teaching on the course, a consensus has to be built that critical self-appraisal and change are needed. More often than not, the greatest barriers to this are not the opposition of particular members of staff, but rather the absence, in some institutions, of the notion of a 'course team' and the difficulties of finding occasions when staff can meet in an unhurried way for wide-ranging discussions of the purposes of their course, the changing forces impinging upon it, and its relationship to employment. Secondly, accepted mechanisms need to exist, or be created, by which the course can be reviewed formally and contributions elicited from academic peers, students and employers. Thirdly, requirements for the accreditation or approval of a course by external bodies (especially the professional associations) must not be such as to exclude the changes that appear to the course team as desirable. Although it is certainly the case that some professional bodies do seem, on occasion, to impede curricular development by their insistence on constant additions to subject content, there are also others, often to be found in the newer professions, who promote it. It needs to be recognized, too, that assertions about the supposed intractability of external accrediting bodies should not always be taken at face value: they may often serve as a debating ploy to trump one's opponents within an HEI (as appeals to lack of time or money, or the prohibitions of God have sometimes been used in other contexts).

In other words, the lesson appears to be – perhaps not unsurprisingly – that the essential condition for thoroughgoing curricular development is staff development in its broadest and most flexible sense. To be effective, it seems, staff development will need to provide a group of academics with opportunities to reflect on their experience, to draft plans for change and, in the light of these, to acquire any skills that they may then find that they need. Experience suggests that this is a more effective form of staff development than one driven by a series of events (perhaps seminars on new teaching techniques or on educational technology) on topics that the institution's managers have judged to be important.

Certain general trends in the use of particular learning approaches in courses do seem to emerge from the experience of EHE. EHE appears to have encouraged a movement from knowledge-based to skills-based conceptions of learning, to have stimulated greater variety in the use forms of learning environments, to have widened the assessment of students' work to include the evaluation of 'process' as well as 'outcomes' and, in general, to have advanced somewhat more 'student-centered' approaches at the expense of the 'content-centered' (NFER, 1991, pp. 108–11). One EHE university, for instance, is seeking to review and re-design its degree in chemical engineering by starting from asking students, staff and employers: what do chemical engineers actually need to be able to do to work effectively in a 'real-world engineering context'? From the answers received they have sought to determine the skills, content, and variety of learning environments (inside and outside the university) that they judge would be most effective in attaining these ends. Those concerned believe that this represents a strikingly different method of course design from that by which their previous degree evolved, which they perceive as involving, essentially, the piecemeal accretion of particular segments of subject knowledge with little attention to their impact on the overall, lived experience of their students or their subsequent induction into employment.

Several EHE institutions have reported that the initiative has led to an increase in group work, some have reported that it has encouraged the use of role play and simulations and have pointed to examples of the creation of self-instructional packs and study skills packages (NFER, 1991, p. 98).

Typically, this has also entailed the greater use of forms of learning based upon collaboration with employers. The evaluation evidence shows that in the 25 first and second round HEIs and one consortium covered by the NFER study, EHE has been primarily responsible for initiating new work placements for students, developing 'live' projects and involving employers in course design (NFER, 1991, pp. 114–21). It has also played a major role in involving employers in the assessment of students, persuading them to provide additional financial or other resources and a significant part in introducing Records of Achievement (loc. cit.).

So far there is little evidence that great progress has been made in introducing forms of assessment that match the changes in emphasis that EHE has encouraged in the aims and content of courses and the methods of learning used in them (i.e. reward the acquisition of a wide range of personal capabilities in the final class of award).[11] Where innovation in assessment has occurred, it has most often been of a formative kind and has tended not to have consequences for the student's final class of award. Unless this problem can be overcome it is likely to act as a major obstacle to thoroughgoing change in curricula. There is much evidence that the demands of final assessment exert a dominant influence over how students see their courses and determine their priorities.

There may be several reasons why assessment has tended to prove resistant to change. First, its forms are usually specified in considerable detail in regulations that can only be changed with difficulty and by the higher committees of an institution. Secondly, assessment often has a disproportionate symbolic importance and is sometimes regarded as the most important safeguard of 'standards' (as controversies over GCSE have shown). Thirdly, the process of assessment places massive demands on staff time and other resources which makes academics particularly wary of moving to unfamiliar methods, especially when at first sight some of these appear to make even greater demands on resources. Finally, because of the importance of the final degree classification to students, the students themselves are naturally hesitant about techniques such as group, peer or self-assessment that they fear could lead to the award of a mark that did not fairly reflect their personal performance.

Evidence on the attitudes of employers to assessment is sometimes unclear. There can be no doubt that many employers lay great stress on the personal and practical qualities of students which they frequently say they give more weight than to the class of degree. On the other hand, there can be little doubt that employers also use the higher educational system as a sifting mechanism and give considerable weight to the imputed status of HEIs and, for some types of job at least, to the class of degree in selecting candidates for employment.

4. Legitimacy

To understand the impact of EHE on ideas of worth and legitimacy within HEIs, it is important to recognize that EHE, though funded by and involving external agencies, is not a force extraneous to higher education, and does not stand in complete contrast with all that had gone before. Its strength has been that, although novel, it is in sympathy with, and has reinforced, currents of long standing within higher education. Rarely has it brought into existence anything totally new or, of itself, undermined an existing orthodoxy. Instead (like TVEI before it), it has triggered a series of seemingly slight and subtle shifts in the balances of power within institutions, has begun to re-interpret or re-shape dominant presuppositions, and, most importantly perhaps, has furnished new sources of support and legitimacy to those who had already been trying to innovate.

The advent of an EHE contract may quite transfigure the enthusiasts for innovative teaching within predominantly research-oriented departments. The institution's EHE-derived requirement that all departments contribute to the programme re-defines the value of the enthusiast for teaching: he or she may be transformed almost overnight from being an impediment to the advancement of the department's research to being the bearer of the department's honour in a new, if unfamiliar, environment. There is now an increasing number of institutions (mainly polytechnics) where involvement in EHE-sponsored curricular and learning development has led to promotions that otherwise seem unlikely to have occurred.

5. Resources

One particularly obvious way in which EHE has affected curricular development and the improvement of learning is through the provision of resources for them. This is of vital importance because, as Adrian Leftwich has argued, at present there are no other significant sources of funding for the improvement in teaching within UK higher education (Leftwich, 1991).

While institutions differ in their methods for distributing EHE funds, all, in some way or other, make substantial amounts available for projects in these two fields and for the staff development necessary to support and enhance them. In some cases, groups of staff, and sometimes students, are invited to bid for funds to improve curricula and learning and decisions are made in the light of criteria that the HEI has established centrally. In other cases, finance may be made available to all departments or courses to undertake such developments at some point during the five-year cycle of funding. Funds are most often used to cover the whole, or partial, release of staff from teaching or other duties, to provide for travel to study practice elsewhere, to buy materials or to attend courses.

Unresolved issues

In its impact on curricula and learning, the Enterprise in Higher Education initiative has highlighted several issues that remain to be fully addressed, let alone solved. The first of these concerns resources, rewards and recognition for good teachers (or, more accurately, good facilitators of learning) in higher education. The prime importance to an individual's career of research and publication is constantly reinforced by the overt values and implicit practice within each discipline and within each HEI as a whole (and not just the universities). These values are further strengthened by the UGC/UFC's research selectivity exercises which are now being extended to institutions previously funded by the PCFC. Certainly, many institutional heads and other senior staff have proclaimed the high importance that they attach to teaching and have made efforts to ensure that teaching excellence can lead to promotion. Nonetheless, there is much anecdotal evidence to show that junior staff do not believe that they can advance their careers by developing teaching excellence at the expense of research. This point was borne out by the NFER evaluation which showed that whereas only 21 per cent of 'senior academics' believed that good teaching was 'recognized through promotion', the proportion of 'lecturers' who held the same view was yet smaller at 4 per cent (NFER, 1991, p. 103).

Another question remaining to be determined is that of how EHE will interact with other factors leading to change in higher education. For example, the pressure exerted through the funding system, and elsewhere, to increase the number of students and, in consequence, raise student:staff ratios does not, in my view, necessarily conflict with the aims of EHE (it could even be argued that a sudden substantial rise in student numbers must serve to direct conscious attention onto curricula and forms of learning). Nonetheless, many HEIs may find it easiest to respond to such expansion simply by making greater use of the most conventional forms of teaching (such as large lectures) and gradually expanding the size of seminar groups to such a point where they become very ineffective in achieving their objectives.

There is also the issue concerning the differential impact of EHE on either side of what used to be called the 'binary line'. There seems little doubt that institutions familiar with the practice of the CNAA, and its related mechanisms for course review and validation, have found it easier than those lacking this experience to undertake thoroughgoing curricular development and enhance the quality of students' learning in a concerted way (Sandberg and Sommerlad (1989, pp. 5–11).

It still remains to be seen whether the coming of the CVCP's Academic Audit Unit has begun to erode this distinction. One can, as yet, no more than guess at the impact of the proposed mechanisms for quality assessment and assurance on the higher educational system that will emerge when, or if, the Further and Higher Education Bill becomes law.

Another question that demands consideration is that of the importance of the subject, or discipline, as a focus for both staff identity and learning development in higher education. Hitherto, EHE has taken its field of action as the whole institution: an approach for which there are powerful supporting arguments. Nonetheless, especially now that there has been a pause in funding further rounds of EHE in its present form, the academic discipline emerges once again as the key theatre for future development. The discipline is not just a channel for crossing the boundaries between EHE-funded and non-EHE-funded institutions; it also provides the most powerful means by which to influence the values of its members and to re-shape their behaviour. One fruitful development might, perhaps, be for a governmental agency to collaborate with relevant professional or disciplinary bodies to stimulate the development of EHE-type projects across all departments teaching in its field.

Finally, further attention needs to be given, within EHE, to the contribution of the students to the processes of their own learning. Higher education, we are sometimes told, is moving into a world where the power of the academic producers will decline and students will increasingly come to see themselves as discriminating consumers. So far, students have played a relatively small part in EHE. There seem to be several reasons for this. The first is that, for undergraduate education at least, higher education is still, in most subjects, a seller's market: the problem is for a potential student to find a place, not for an HEI to find students. Secondly, many students enter HE after having already been inducted into attitudes of passivity by their experiences of A Level, athough this is now beginning to change. Thirdly, the task of ensuring credible student representation in decision-making bodies is a difficult one. Not only are students only present in an institution for a short period, during much of which they are naturally preoccupied with adapting to its new demands or preparing for their final assessment; they also tend to follow their programmes of study in numerous sub-cultures differentiated by discipline, age, place of residence and, even, political views. Fourthly, many students may have a very instrumental attitude to their work and in consequence feel more comfortable with models of learning that are passive and predictable. They may, as staff also do, fight shy of risks to self-image and self-identity that may result from greater involvement and responsibility for their own learning.

As mentioned,[7] some progress has now been made with the appointment of Student Enterprise Officers in several institutions. Nonetheless, many issues relating to the position of students in higher education have scarcely been touched by EHE. For example, little attention has been given to the question of how students come to perceive and understand the courses that they follow nor how they determine what is required of them for success. There are many reasons for supposing that the 'curriculum-in-use' as perceived by students differs in many significant respects from the 'curriculum-as-rubric' as expressed in course documentation and prospectuses and possibly in the minds of many academics. We know that EHE has begun to change several aspects of the formal curricula and to introduce a wider variety of teaching methods; we know very little about its impact on the informal culture of students and their tacit assumptions as to what higher education is 'really about'.

A related point is that we also know remarkably little about what are the actual, as opposed to the idealized, outcomes of higher education. What, for example, does a typical lower second class Honours graduate obtain from his, or her, experience? It could just be that, in a system as dominated by norm referencing as is that in the UK, the only clear result for this student is that he, or she, has failed to achieve what has come to be described as a 'good Honours degree' (a first or upper second class Honours).

Conclusion

Overall, it appears that EHE has exerted significant pressure for change in curricula and forms of learning within UK higher education but that this has, as one might expect, been constrained by several structural factors within the system. The strength of EHE, it appears, has been considerably reinforced by the fact that it draws on existing strands within HE (building on and consolidating, for example, many hitherto isolated instances of good practice), even though it has been funded and administered from outside. That this should be so is not surprising: it is neither plausible, nor desirable, to suppose that the practice of a professional group such as academics, or even medical practitioners, can be reformed by external fiat. To be effective, change in such circles must always occur through shifts in the balance of internal forces, not by wiping the slate clean. EHE, as the origins of its birth suggest, has never been, notwithstanding the hubris of politicians, an attempt to introduce into higher education, and to impose upon it, an alien approach. What it has sought to do is to magnify and strengthen long-standing aspects within the academic tradition. It has, I would contend, given greater force and prestige to two themes: the importance of the experience of learning and self-development that students undergo; and, relatedly, the vision of higher education as a process of liberation and empowerment for those who experience it. These are strands which some would argue are more deeply rooted in the origins of Western higher education than the drive towards research and publication.

It may seem strange to make such claims on behalf of EHE, a programme which is explicitly directed towards improving the quality of highly-skilled labour, which has been funded by the Employment Department and employers and which is widely regarded as vocational. That is only so if one begins from a narrow – and peculiarly insular, English – view of vocationalism. Definitions of vocationalism are highly variable and greatly dependent upon the standpoint of their authors. At times in the past, Western universities were highly vocational in the sense that they were intricately linked with the requirements of the Church and, in some countries, of the law or medicine: but this is not usually regarded as a blemish on their tradition.

Again, even though the ideal of success embodied in many degree courses until recently – perhaps still – has been that of the 'brilliant first class Honours' leading to a career in research, it has not been normal to categorize such courses as vocational. What is more, of course, the notion of 'liberal education' as a foil to set off and contrast with vocationalism, was more or less consciously developed in nineteenth-century universities to sanctify the introduction of new subjects, or to distance them from vulgar associations with trade or production (Bud and Roberts, 1984; Slee, 1986). Indeed, I find it hard to resist the definition of vocationalism, which I recently heard expressed by an anonymous German participant in a conference. Namely, that 'liberal education' was the vocationalism of 'dominant groups' and 'vocationalism' the vocationalism of subordinate groups.[12]

The power of EHE as a force for change in curricula and learning is that it has obliged higher educationalists to ask searching questions about the needs of all major stakeholders in higher education and how these might best be reconciled and attained. It has obliged them, too, to ask what are the special qualities that higher education alone can preserve and foster. The fact that EHE is directed towards the world of work (private, public and voluntary) has been particularly beneficial because it has forced higher educationalists to focus attention upon what their graduates are going to do in their future lives and how, in the widest sense, higher education with its particular values and qualities, may prepare them for it. In the absence of such deliberate reflection and debate until recently, it had been all too common for higher educational institutions to evade issues of purpose and means. One could detect an inclination to slip into one (or, even, both!) of two contradictory, and generally unspoken assumptions about the role of UK higher education. I shall caricature as follows.

The first was a form of debased Newmanism which simply assumed that higher education by its very nature and existence continued to transmit a uniquely valuable pattern of values and moral qualities. Because this was assumed to be an intrinsic characteristic of the system there was thus little, if any, need to take account of myriad changes and expansion that it had undergone in the previous century. The second was a narrow instrumentalism that insisted that higher education should supply exactly what employers were thought to demand, irrespective of wider changes or, indeed, the success of these employers in international competition.

EHE, by encouraging dialogue between academics and employers and by concentrating attention on the question of to what extent, and how, higher education should serve the world of employment has begun to encourage the HE system to develop a new, self-conscious and publicly-accessible vision of its own mission. As is so often the case, one of the surest ways by which to determine and become confident of one's own identity is to discuss it and set it against that of others.

At the cost of mutilating Kipling's well-known lines, one might ask:

And what should they know of Higher Education who only Higher Education know?

Notes

1. Other initiatives, including the Royal Society of Arts' Higher Education for Capability project and the work of the National Council for Vocational Qualifications have had – or will continue to have – a substantial impact on the work of UK higher education; but neither, I would argue, have had the general impact of EHE either because of their slender resources (HE for Capability) or because they affect only some aspects of the work of HE (NVQs).
2. The MSC later became, successively, the Training Commission, then the Training Agency and now forms the Training, Enterprise and Education Directorate of the Employment Department (ED), within the UK Civil Service.
3. In the autumn of 1991, in the context of the Chancellor of the Exchequer's Financial statement, the decision was taken not to provide additional finance for a fourth round of EHE contracts in 1992, although, naturally all existing contracts were to continue to be funded.
4. The Technical and Vocational Education Initiative, orginally a pilot programme but subsequently extended to embrace all 14–19 education.
5. PICKUP is the Department of Education and Science's (DES) Professional, Industrial, Commercial Up-dating Skills Programme (principally concerned with the provision of continuing professional development). The MSC's Graduate Gateway Programme provides experience for graduates of work in small businesses and the RSA's 'Education for Capability' is a movement:

   ... initiated in 1979 to counteract the academic bias of British education and to promote the value of the practical, organizing and co-operative skills too often underrated in our present system. It encourages creativity in its widest sense and believes learners should share responsibility for their own learning (RSA, n.d.).

6. As ever, Laurie Taylor's column in the *Times Higher Education Supplement* neatly captured the flavour of the times. (See his piece portraying academic reactions to the Enterprise in Higher Education initiative (Taylor, 1988).)
7. Students have been involved in EHE projects in various ways. Firstly, there is generally a student representative, or representatives, on the institution's EHE Steering Committee. Secondly, in some HEIs groups of students, or the Students' Union, have planned, and run, EHE-funded activities (such as the production of a desk-top published student news-sheet in one polytechnic with widely dispersed sites). Thirdly, since 1990 many EHE institutions have followed the successful experiment in one college of appointing a Student Manager (typically) a current student or recent graduate to provide a link between students in general and the staff who are involved in promoting EHE. This has led in 1991 to the creation of a National EHE Student network that has organized conferences.
8. It is also worth commenting that the experience of Annual Reviews since 1989 seems to have enabled both the Employment Department and the institutions it has funded to achieve a greater understanding of the processes of institutional change.

9. Many of these can be drawn from the growing literature spawned by EHE. This includes two national evaluations (ED, 1990; NFER, 1991), six working papers arising from the first national evaluation (TIHR and various authors, 1989), three publications describing the key features of successive rounds of EHE (TA, 1989; TA, 1990; ED, 1991) as well as Jones, 1988, 1990; Glover, 1990; Macnair, 1990; Wright, 1990; E & T, 1991; and Gray, 1993, forthcoming.

10. The terms Records of Achievement (RoA) and Profiles may be used in different contexts with a variety of meanings. The underlying principle of both however, is to serve as a means by which an individual may show that s/he possesses, or is progressing towards possessing, a range of skills or competencies defined in terms of certain standards (often called criterion-referencing) rather than – as with traditional examinations until recently – in relation to an individual's perform-ance relative to others (often called norm-referencing). Typically, RoAs only give details of those competencies that an individual has demonstrated – other competencies are regarded as 'not yet demonstrated' rather than absent. Typically, such methods emphasize success rather than failure. (Contrast this with the English Honours degree system where more than 90 per cent of graduates may be regarded as having failed to get first-class Honours!) National Records of Achievement were introduced early in 1991 for general adoption in schools and are also being widely adopted by employers. They are beginning to be taken up in higher education.

11. In March 1991 the Higher Education Branch of the Employment Department set up the Recording Enterprising Achievement in Learning group (REAL group). In essence, its terms of reference are to advise on the need for development work on how best to record 'enterprising' skills in HE, and to link this to other relevant priorities such as the Council for National Academic Awards' (CNAA) general educational aims. It does this, taking account of existing practice and the constraints and possibilities that this offers, together with other relevant develop-ments such, for instance, as the assessment of 'core skills' under the National Council for Vocational Qualifications (NCVQ) and the Schools Examinations and Assessment Council (SEAC).

   The REAL group meets quarterly and is composed of members drawn from all sectors of HE, from the CNAA, the Employment Department, from the Standing Committee on University Entrance (SCUE), employers, NCVQ, the Further Education Unit (FEU).

12. For a discussion of the historical power of vocationalism as a force for change and democratization in English education see Wright (1989).

References

Adelman, C. and Alexander, R.J. (1982) *The Self-Evaluating Institution: practice and principles in the management of educational change*. London, Methuen.

Ainley, P. and Corney, M. (1990) *Training for the Future: the rise and fall of the Manpower Services Commission*. London, Cassell.

Boys, C.J., Brennan, J., Henkel, M., Kirkland, J., Kogan, M. and Youll, P.J. (1988) *Higher Education and the Preparation for Work*. London, Jessica Kingsley. (One prod-uct of the Higher Education and the Labour Market (HELM) research project.)

Bradshaw, D. (1985) 'Transferable personal and intellectual skills'. *Oxford Review of Education*, 11(2), 201–16.

Brennan, J. and McGeevor, P. (1988) *Degree Courses and the Labour Market*. London, Jessica Kingsley. (One product of the Higher Education and the Labour Market (HELM) research project.)

Bud, R. and Roberts, G.K. (1984) *Science versus Practice: chemistry in Victorian England*. Manchester, Manchester University Press.

CIHE (Council for Industry and Higher Education) (1987) *Towards a Partnership*. London, CIHE.

DES (Department of Education and Science) (1987) *Higher Education: meeting the challenge*. London, HMSO.

DoE (Department of Employment) (1987) 'Norman Fowler launches Enterprise in Higher Education'. *Press Notice*, 285/87, 9 December 1987. London, Department of Employment Press Office.

ED (Employment Department) (1990) *The First Year of Enterprise in Higher Education: final report of the case study evaluation* (carried out by the Tavistock Institute for Human Relations). Sheffield, Employment Department.

ED (Employment Department) (1991) *Key Features of the Enterprise in Higher Education Proposals, 1990–91*. Sheffield, Employment Department. (Successor to the booklets previously published by The Training Agency.)

E & T (1991) 'Light the blue touchpaper'. *Education and Training* (special issue devoted to Enterprise in Higher Education), 33(2). Bradford, MCB University Press.

Gleeson, D. (ed.) (1987) *TVEI and Secondary Education: a critical appraisal*. Milton Keynes, Open University Press.

Glover, D. (1990) *Enterprise in Higher Education: a briefing for employers*. Cambridge, CRAC.

Gray, H. (ed.) (1993 forthcoming). *Going with the Grain: the experiences of the EHE initiative as a force for educational change*. Basingstoke, Falmer Press.

Groves, P.R. (1989) 'Enterprise, culture and anarchy'. *Higher Education Review*, 21(3), 7–20.

Jones, A. (1988) 'The Manpower Services Commission's Enterprise in Higher Education initiative'. *Industry and Higher Education*, 2(2), 117–19.

Jones, A. (1990) 'A responsive higher education system' in P.W.G. Wright (ed.) *Industry and Higher Education: collaboration to improve students' learning and training*. Milton Keynes, SRHE/Open University Press.

Leftwich, A. (1991) 'Pedagogy for the depressed: the political economy of teaching development in British universities'. *Studies in Higher Education*, 16(3), 277–90.

Macnair, G. (1990) 'The British Enterprise in Higher Education initiative'. *Higher Education Management*, 2(1), 60–71.

MSC (Manpower Services Commission) (1987) *Enterprise in Higher Education: guidelines for applicants*. Sheffield, MSC.

NAB (National Advisory Body for Public Sector Higher Education) (1984) *A Strategy for the Late 1980s and Beyond*. London, NAB (Section 2 of this document, entitled 'Higher education and the needs of society' was a joint statement between the NAB and the UGC (University Grants Committee)).

NAB (National Advisory Body for Public Sector Higher Education) (1986) *Transferable Personal Skills in Employment: the contribution of higher education*. London, NAB.

NFER (National Foundation for Educational Research) (1991) *Enterprise in Higher Education: second year national evaluation*. Slough, NFER.

Roizen, J. and Jepson, M. (1985) *Degrees for Jobs: employers' expectations of higher education*. Guildford, SRHE-NFER.

RSA (The Royal Society for the Encouragement of Arts, Manufactures and Commerce) (n.d.) *Brochure*. London, RSA.

Sandberg, S. and Sommerlad, E. (1989) *Curriculum Development in EHE* (Working Paper 4 on the Case Study Evaluation of the EHE initiative). London, Tavistock Institute for Human Relations.

Selden, R. (1991) 'The rhetoric of enterprise' in R. Keat and N. Abercrombie (eds) *Enterprise Culture*. London, Routledge.

Slee, P.R.H. (1986) *Learning and a Liberal Education: the study of modern history in the Universities of Oxford, Cambridge and Manchester, 1800–1919*. Manchester, Manchester University Press.

TA (The Training Agency) (1988) *Enterprise in Higher Education: supplementary notes of guidance*. Sheffield, The Training Agency.

Taylor, L. (1988) Laurie Taylor's column, *Times Higher Educational Supplement*, 13 May 1988.

TIHR (Tavistock Institute for Human Relations) (1989) Working Papers produced as part of first-year evaluation of Enterprise in Higher Education (London, TIHR):

WP1 'Background and Origins of EIIE', H. Brown and J. Turbin
WP2 'Organization and Management of EHE', E. Stern
WP3 'Staff Development within the Context of the EHE initiative', S. Sandberg and E. Sommerlad
WP4 'Curriculum Development in EHE', S. Sandberg and E. Sommerlad
WP5 'Students in EHE', H. Brown
WP6 'Employer Involvement in EHE', E. Stern and J. Turbin

Weiner, M.J. (1981) *English Culture and the Decline of the Industrial Spirit 1850–1980*. Cambridge, Cambridge University Press.

Wright, P.W.G. (1989) 'Access or exclusion? Comments on the history and future prospects of continuing education in England'. *Studies in Higher Education*, 14(1), 23–40.

Wright, P.W.G. (1990) 'Strategic change in the higher education curriculum: the example of the Enterprise in Higher Education initiative' in C.P.J. Loder (ed.) *Quality Assurance and Accountability in Higher Education*. London, Kogan Page/ Bedford Way.

Index